To the soldier's
grandson

George Robert Hilton

This book
is
dedicated

Library of Congress Cataloging-in-Publication Data

Johnson, Charles F., 1843-1896.
The long roll.

Reprint. Originally published: Duluth ed. East Aurora, Erie
County, N.Y.: The Roycrofters, 1911.
1. Johnson, Charles F., 1843-1896. 2. United States.
Army. Regiment Infantry, New York Volunteers, 9th (1861-
1863)—Biography. 3. United States—History—Civil War,
1861-1865—Personal narratives. 4. New York (State)—His-
tory—Civil War, 1861-1865—Personal narratives. 5. Soldiers—
New York (State)—Biography. I. Title.
E523.5 9th.J64 1986   973.7'447   86-4153
ISBN O-938634-08-9

Cover Design: Diana Donley Morgan

Carabelle Books, Box 1611, Shepherdstown, W.V. 25443
1986

Charles F. Johnson
From a Portrait Taken at the Close of His Enlistment

PLATE I

THE LONG ROLL:

BY CHARLES F. JOHNSON.

ONE OF THE ···

HAWKINS ZOUAVES.

1861· 1863·

This is the Duluth Edition of "The Long Roll," Being the Civil War Experiences of Charles F. Johnson of Hawkins Zouaves. Of this edition Five Hundred Copies are being printed, by Elbert Hubbard, of The Roycrofters, East Aurora, New York, and of this edition this Volume is Number 340

"Toujours Pret"

Courtesy of David Ericson

ATTENTION!

Acknowledgment is hereby given to Duluth, for making this volume a real memory of a man; to David Ericson, for a page from his scrapbook of sketches; to Fredrick B. Johnson, for his design for the title-page of his father's story; and to Sergeant J. H. E. Whitney of the Ninth New York Volunteers, from whose book entitled, "The Hawkins Zouaves," has been taken material for foot-notes concerning the names of places and men.

And friends, both old and new, with interest in this old-new story, listen for the sound of the Bugle Call "To Arms!" and as, perchance, this interest may be questioned, take heed now, for as from the soldier himself comes the Countersign

"Thanks Be To You!"

PLATE II

The Long Roll

Being a Journal of the Civil War, as set down during the years 1861 - 1863 by Charles F. Johnson, sometime of Hawkins Zouaves. *Illustratea with many Sketches & Photographs*

Duluth Edition

Done into Print and Bound into a Book by The Roycrofters at their Shop, which is in East Aurora, Erie County, State of New York
M   C   M   X   I

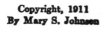

Copyright, 1911
By Mary S. Johnson

CONTENTS

LIST OF ILLUSTRATIONS

FOREWORD

IT may be well to explain somewhat of the manner in which I commenced to read, which involves the result of my experience in the country district schools of the Province of Smaland.

" 'Luther's Little Catechism' is the First Reader of the Swedish child, with this difference, that it must be committed to memory; for as soon as the luckless wight has worried through the Primer, the Smaller and Larger Catechism are put into his hands to be so committed as fast as the mind can be made to bear the strain; and woe betide the unlucky 'lummox' who, on the dread examination-day at the close of every term, fails with the ready answer to any one of the prescribed questions from any quarter of this tear-stained book.

"After this Catechismal purgatory comes the New Testament, which may rank as Fourth Reader in an American Free School; then the Old Testament, as the Fifth or Reader par excellence. The Bible is not actually committed to memory, but it is abbreviated into a sort of a synopsis called Biblical History, which is actually beaten into the head of the child for recitation. With this is blended a course of Arithmetic extending into the principles of Division in simple numbers and a series of chirographical maneuvers, greatly assisted by the lively accompaniment of flexible rattans over the paper; which rattans at times, guided by the unsteady hand of the master, fall upon the knuckles of the child, causing such nervousness that it often becomes quite impossible to write at all.

" This is the actual extent of the education of the Swedish 'Bonde' * boy or girl; and without even the vaguest notions of Geography, of History or of Literature except such as were contained in the books I have mentioned, he or she is pushed out upon the world to serve as food for the mirth and wonder of the educated classes everywhere; mirth caused by their uncouth appearance and the extreme simplicity of their ways, and wonder at the fact, which is a source of surprise to many,

* " Bonde " means Land-Owning Farmer.

FOREWORD

that a people giving such signs of ignorance should one and all
be able to read and write so well, and who, differing so materially in every particular, should, in so short a time and in so
many instances, fall undetected into the American ranks.

" It will thus be readily understood, nor seem strange, that
I, when but six years of age, had been made to read the New
Testament three times through. This I can well remember
was something to boast of at the time, but if I had then been
thrown out of the reach of said Testament, I should now be
able to remember of it never a word, but I presume it must
have made some impression upon my infant mind at the time,
and I feel kindly disposed to give all things their due.

" I was born in Gisnabo in the Province of Smaland, Sweden,
April 18th, 1843. We went to the United States in 1853. On the
way, in Gotheberg, my Mother died. Arrived in Chicago,
Illinois, in 1854, where I served in an American family, learning
the language; during that Winter I attended a city school for
four months. Went to Minnesota with my Father the following
Spring, arriving in St. Paul, May 4th, 1855. I apprenticed
myself to a bookbinder, with whom I remained off and on until
the Fall of 1860. I went to New York and while there the war
broke out, and I enlisted in the ' Hawkins Zouaves,' with whom
I served their term of two years."

Thus far is quoted directly from an Introduction to a
manuscript entitled "My Own Bibliography," written in
1870, and forming in itself a prelude to the story to follow
far better than any one else could write.

The brief sentences of biography, if enlarged upon, would
show a book-hunger in those early years scarcely to be understood, much less appreciated, by the youth of to-day, who throw
away more reading matter than this boy ever dared to dream
of possessing. In later years, when his library represented a life-
time of study, hope, work, sacrifice and the sheer joy of the
learning, he often talked of his boyhood, when every scrap of
printed matter was saved, studied and pondered over; a
process that unconsciously became a habit and trained the
mind, making of it, as the boy grew to manhood, a well-filled

6

FOREWORD

room from which came solace and contentment even unto the Valley of the Shadow.

War-time, and books were more than scarce; paper and pencils, oddities; even the Newspapers were but lists of the wounded and unaccounted for. But time, dulled with the monotony of camp life, had to be filled, and the boy saved any paper he could find to make his Journal notes and sketches, binding them into pamphlets, with Newspapers for covers. And he wrote his hopes, his plans, his ideas—descriptions, anything to occupy the leisure that camp routine gives to one, broken by the awful intensity that battle means, giving a contrast in these pages as the sunshine of life beside the shadow of death.

And now is offered to the world this sample page of the life of one whose simple tastes led him always to seek the less conspicuous place; but his record as a soldier and a man gives him his promotion, and he rises from the ranks, by faithful response to "The Long Roll," to find his place among those who really live, and by their example unconsciously give hope and faith to others.   E. L. J. H.

THE LONG ROLL

CHAPTER I

CASTLE GARDEN AND RIKER'S ISLAND

Castle Garden, N. Y.
May 12th, 1861.

IT is now about two weeks since I joined this, the First Regiment of New York Zouaves,* and I get along remarkably well considering that I never played soldier before. We are at present quartered in Castle Garden, but barracks are being built for us on Riker's Island, some ten miles up the East River, where the Colonel says we are going to-morrow, but "to-morrow" probably means Tuesday.

Yesterday, at drill, the boys of our Company took it into their heads to see how long they could go the "Double-quick." When about half of them had exhausted their strength and fallen out, some one stepped on my foot, wrenching it so that I also was obliged to give up the contest, and I was glad to lie down on the grass in a pleasant spot in the Garden. The rest of the boys immediately after left the parade and broke ranks in the Castle. Having recovered my breath, I went to the gate for oranges and apples, but when about to pay for them, I was surprised by some one I had not noticed, saying, "I will pay for them, please." When I saw it was a lady and a handsome one, I could not refuse.

I am doing guard duty to-day. It does not seem a very hard thing to do, for one is on post only two hours out of six.

Two foreign war-ships are in the harbor, a Brazilian school-ship and a Spanish frigate, which latter arrived this morning, and cast anchor not more than a quarter of a mile from Castle William. At twelve, she saluted our flag with twenty guns. The "Great Eastern" came in a short time after. She is as large as she is represented to be in the many cuts in the illus-

---

* So styled at the time of enlistment; afterwards, the "Ninth New York Volunteers," one of the four Zouave Regiments from the State.

9

trated papers I have seen. Some of our fellows call her the big " Blunderbuss," and she is unquestionably a big thing.

Riker's Island, May 17th.

Evacuated the old Castle day before yesterday, embarking on a barge towed by an old steamer, the " Young America," and about ten o'clock took possession of this Island. It is quite a pretty place inhabited by one family. There is a growth of apple-trees now in full bloom, around the rather time-worn house. I believe this is to serve as the Colonel's quarters.

May 21st.

Received a full-dress uniform last Sunday morning, which is certainly very pretty, if not fine; of a deep blue cloth with scarlet sash, fez and trimmings. It presents a lively appearance in line. This makes us two complete suits, the other a blue sort of flannel Fatigue, very comfortable in warm weather.

Some little excitement last Saturday evening; the question of enlistment for " three years or the war " was being discussed as I came into quarters from a game of ball on the parade-ground. I came in while the excitement was at its height; the Captain of our Company was carried on the shoulders of his men to the Colonel's quarters, where that gentleman was speaking, and great enthusiasm prevailed generally.

May 26th.

Received a letter from my sister last Wednesday, reminding me that I had not been at home since I joined the Regiment; but how to succeed in getting a pass was the question, for hundreds are clamoring for passes every day. I hit upon the plan of volunteering for extra guard duty, which entitles one to some favors. So Thursday night I went on guard and also served as extra police, who are required more or less owing to the stratagems nightly practised by the officers to enforce the strictest discipline among the men, and a troublesome night I had of it.

Lieutenant Leahy was Captain of the guard, and the extra police were called often from one post to another, not only on

10

THE LONG ROLL

account of the practise of discipline which we are now under-going, but more owing to the constant efforts of some of the men to leave camp without passes. A strict watch is needed around our quarters, and that night we were more than once required at some post where some one either had succeeded in getting away or had been caught in trying to do so; to search for or to bring the prisoner to the guard-house, as the case might be. At about two o'clock a call was passed through the chain of posts from No. 11, whither the Captain and two of us repaired in hot haste. The sentinel reported some one having attempted to pass his post, and get into camp without the countersign, but being stopped, had escaped into the field. This field we scoured, but to no purpose, and we returned to the guard-house. Hardly were we there, however, before we were called to the same post again. Leahy now told my com-panion to follow him, and for me to take the other direction around the barracks to head him off in case he should be able to make his escape that way. Making all possible haste, I got to No. 11 just in time to see Lieutenant Leahy struggling with some one who had evidently thrown a blanket over his head. He succeeded in extricating himself, however, and ordered us to charge bayonets. We obeyed as far as to place our bayonets against his breast, demanding the countersign, and I now saw it was Lieutenant Flemming of our Company. Without com-plying, he succeeded in getting my comrade's bayonet in his hand and wrenching it from the gun, but I as soon, with a couple of passes, knocked it out of his hand. I put my foot on it, and thoughtlessly enough stooped to pick it up. He seized my head in an instant, but I recovered myself with a desperate effort and gave him a slight scratch with my bayonet above the ear. Leahy repeated his orders to " Charge," " Run him through," etc., and my comrade, having recovered his bayonet, we forced him against the barrack-wall, where he surrendered, also giving the countersign, " Washington."

I have been thus particular in writing this trivial adventure, for it was the first time I came in contact with Leahy and Flemming, the two friends from first to last, and whose later

11

adventures, taken together, would make more than one yarn for a Charles Lever, and good long ones at that.

May 27th.

And so I succeeded in getting a pass last Friday evening. Waited so long for a steamboat that most of our boys had hired small boats and were rowed over to the nearest point home, while I was compelled to wait. Cause—I had no "rhino," but when I saw Sergeant Jackson and Corporal Davis prepare to go in the same way, Bell (who was in my fix) and I jumped in regardless of consequences. Private Brown paid our way, and we reached Fort Harris by dusk, cut over to Harlem on a Double-quick, and took the cars down town. I left my friends at One Hundred and Eighth Street, skipped upstairs, and in the hall met a number of the lady boarders, whose exclamations of surprise were agreeable enough.

These ladies wished to do me some service, and set to work on a soldier's Companion, which they filled with everything conceivable, things of use and things of no use, I should think, for I have as yet, of course, had no occasion to test their value, though I was, as on duty bound, most thankful. While the ladies were thus agreeably at work, a male friend insisted on shaving my head in the Zouave fashion, and he succeeded to my utter dismay and astonishment. The operation was certainly not as painful as the famous "love-o'-God" shave, but it must have been less skilfully performed, for nothing ever cropped could have presented an appearance anything like my head, unless perhaps a rich meadow mown by some obstinate novice, whose dull scythe he had not sense enough to sharpen. And the mortification had to be borne, for as I have intimated before, I was at the time entirely without money, or the first barber-shop would have repaired the injury. (Ah, Harry, I could forgive you this, did I not know thy soul cramped smaller than the quarter that would have taken me to *that* barber and repaired *this* injury.)

Saturday morning it rained and I spent my time very much to my liking, in spite of my ridiculous head, in the company

12

of the ladies, the kind contributors of soap, towels, pins, needles, thread, pens, pencils, paper, envelopes, etc., etc., etc.

I met a Major Walton in the smoking-room, a diminutive individual about four feet high, and forty years of age, I should judge by the old, wrinkled face. A Mr. Hunter introduced me with due ceremony, but I regretted not being able to stay and cultivate his acquaintance, and was soon on the Hoboken Ferry on my way to my home in Hudson City.

May 31st.

We have now received our full complement of arms and accoutrements, muskets, knapsacks, haversacks and canteens, everything satisfactory enough except the muskets, which seem to be old-fashioned, altered flintlocks, instead of the rifles which were promised us. This notable difference was the cause of considerable excitement at first; in fact, our Company grounded arms once, amidst the most deafening cheers from the other Companies. The Captain looked serious and commanded " Raise Arms." There was a pause, and things looked like a crisis. Fortunately, the Captain had too much sense or experience (he looks every inch a soldier) to put on too much new-fledged authority; so he said, " Do it for my sake, Boys," and I, willing to give the start, or acting from impulse, sung out, " Do it for the Captain," which was immediately echoed by most of them, and all, more or less reluctantly, raised their pieces and marched into their quarters; and so this excitement ceased. But to-day we have had another—and that an election, nothing more nor less.

It seems this Company had a First Lieutenant named Buck who had been transferred to another Regiment, and this caused a vacancy which was filled by the Colonel's appointment of a Mr. Russell, subject to the approval of the Company. I did not favor Mr. Russell myself, thinking that Flemming ought to fill the vacancy and Sergeant Jackson be made Second Lieutenant. Mr. Russell was elected, however, and it may be best for the Company. One consolation is that, if Jackson is not promoted, as I think he ought to be, we thereby escape the

13

tyranny of a certain Sergeant P——, next in rank, a bully certainly and more cowardly than brave, if I mistake not. During the contest, I divined some ambition for preferment in the mind of this Sergeant, and made public what must have been his secret thoughts in a manner calculated to draw on me his ill-will, if not hatred. Later, when it was growing dusk and I did not notice that I was alone in a corner of the barracks, I saw him come at me with a drawn sheath-knife. It did not startle me as much as it might have done, however, under the circumstances; indeed, I felt no cause for alarm, but seized a broomstick that happened to be at hand, and made so lively a pass at him, that he at once put up the knife, and feigned play. He tried to smooth it over, but I am not likely to forget it.

It is now almost certain that we go South next Monday. Our destination seems to be Fortress Monroe, Virginia.

Sunday, June 2d.

We had orders to march, or rather to embark, to-day, but we will not get away until to-morrow. At any rate, this is the last Sunday we will be in this Northern latitude for some time.

I did not want to be put on guard to-day, and to avoid it I volunteered for guard duty yesterday. Meanwhile, General Dix was up here and reviewed the Regiment and promised us a speedy exchange of these old muskets for rifles. The review has occasioned, of course, a puff in the "Herald."

Last night between twelve and one, while I was on post, the camp was aroused by a couple of pistol-shots or something of the kind from the guard. The "Long Roll" beat "To Arms," and for two or three minutes the barracks seemed like a hive of bees about to swarm. The confusion then gave way to the sharp orders of the officers, then to the solid tramp of men, and in six or seven minutes, the Regiment was in line with a couple of Companies thrown out in different directions to find the enemy. These returning with the report that no enemy could be found, the Battalion was dismissed, with thanks for its promptness.

CHAPTER II

EN ROUTE

On board Steamer " Marion," on the Atlantic.

June 6th, 1861.

Took our final leave of Riker's Island yesterday (Wednesday) morning, and are now en route for the seat of war. The steam-tug " Saturn " and another, the name of which I do not know, conveyed the Regiment from the Island to the foot of Thirtieth Street, East River, where we formed, proceeding up Thirty-fourth Street to Fifth Avenue, and down that Avenue to the residence of Mrs. A. W. Griswold. From her, with most appropriate ceremonies, we received a very handsome National flag. We then went to the home of Mrs. W. D. Moffatt, where a Regimental flag awaited us. This last was in design extremely simple, though of material as fine as the other, of red silk upon which was inscribed :—

" Ninth Regiment New York Volunteers "
" Toujours Pret "

The motto, " Always Ready," seems appropriate to the kind of warfare for which a Zouave Regiment is intended. From Mrs. Moffatt's we marched down the Avenue into Broadway to Pier Four, North River, amidst dense crowds of people and conscious that we created favorable comment from all— if not for soldierly appearance, at least for a smart look and proficiency in drill. But for encomium on our appearance and march, with all the minute particulars of the incidents attached thereto, into which I care not to enter, the " Herald " of this date is referred to as furnishing an account both flaming and sufficiently explicit. One thing I must say, however, in justice to our Company, which I have been in the habit of running down as the worst in discipline and the least proficient in drill of any in the Regiment, that no Company in this Regiment marched better, conducted itself in a more soldierly manner or gained more applause from the reviewing crowds, than ours, this same despised Company I, which was made up,

15

THE LONG ROLL

it is said, of what was left out of the others. This is true enough, except in regard to Company K. Still, this Company, though the last, which usually contains the scum, so to speak, of a Regiment, seems to have formed itself with some motive of mutual attraction influencing it, thus leaving our Company the mongrel of the Regiment.

Reaching the pier where the " Marion " lay waiting to receive us, the gates were closed on us before we broke ranks, and we were guarded on one side by our soldiers and on the other by the police, in anticipation of the rush that would be made for one more moment of liberty. Friends and dearer ones crowding around the gates for a last word or a glimpse even of some one beloved, would have entered by force, so great seemed the pressure, but this only compelled a half a score or more policemen to exercise (more gently than usual, I think) their necessary duty. It was only after the " Marion " had run out from the pier and dropped anchor in the bay, that I heard of a gentleman and two ladies who had been anxiously looking for me, but who had been prevented even from seeing me through the gate. One of the ladies was probably my sister. They were undoubtedly crowded out by others more clamorous than they, or by the stern orders of the police.

The steamer first cast anchor between Bedloe's Island and Castle William, where the Colonel, finding the " Marion " too small for our accommodation, left us to secure another boat for our transportation, and also, I suspect, to scare up a number of absentees who had not yet been able to " tear themselves away." Here we passed the night as best we could. I slept on a pile of anchor-chains in the bow. Here, too, transpired the first casualty to the Regiment. George Warren of our Company fell overboard and was drowned. " Tobe," for so he was commonly called, was a splendid fellow. He was my file-leader during our farewell march through the city, and it seemed that while I was without a single face in the vast crowds to recognize me, we could not go a block without some one calling to him by a familiar name. But these very friends with their signs of regard, of which I (I almost blush to say) had

16

Frigate " Minnesota," Flagship North Atlantic Squadron

Casemated Gun at Rip Raps

PLATE III

Sawyer Gun at Newport News

The Schooner " Enterprise "

PLATE IV

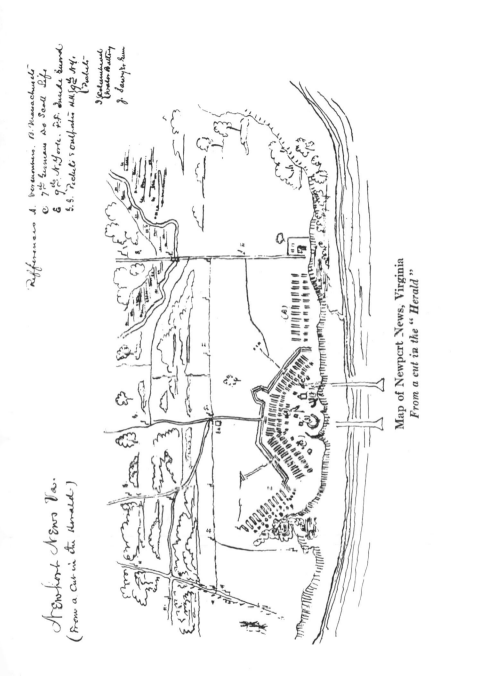

Map of Newport News, Virginia

From a cut in the "Herald"

PLATE V

Old Gun, Rip Raps
Hatteras Light

Albemarle Sound

Dismal Swamp

PLATE VI

none, were probably the cause of his much regretted and untimely end.

It is not with the least degree of satisfaction that I cast these reflections on " Tobe " Warren's end, for of envy I am certainly at this time innocent. But his many friends hailing him from every corner made my feeling of utter loneliness the more intense by contrast, and his tragic death these same friends unwittingly caused, God knows, could not but call up strange reflections, the tendency of which must be obvious to every one.

This morning, the Sixth, we weighed anchor and moved slowly down the stream, but anchored again off Staten Island, where we lay for a time waiting for the additional transportation. The " George Peabody " finally arrived and relieved the " Marion " of about four hundred men, and we then weighed anchor and steamed out of the harbor for good. We are now plowing the Atlantic, the " Peabody " keeping continually in sight and sometimes within hailing distance on our coast side.

CHAPTER III

Camp Butler, Newport News, Va.

June 8th, 1861.

WE are at last in the enemy's country. I can hardly realize it as yet, for Camp Hawkins on Riker's Island seemed to breathe more war than this, but we are told that the enemy prowls about at night in yonder woods picking off our pickets, so I dare say I shall realize the fact soon enough.

We arrived at Fortress Monroe about eight o'clock yesterday morning, passing a thirty-two-gun frigate, the "Cumberland," as we came in, the crew manning the yards and rigging and cheering right gallantly. Anchoring off the Fortress, Colonel Hawkins went ashore to report to General Butler for orders. They were, to proceed to this post, and we at once steamed up the James. Some batteries of the Secessionists were pointed out to us on the other side of the river, and it seemed to me that we went out of our course to see them or for them to see us. However, we were not disturbed and in about an hour were disembarking at Newport News. There we found a Regiment of Vermonters, the Seventh New York (Germans), and the Scott Life Guard entrenched behind an earthwork a mile or so in extent covering the wharves and buildings, and facing or commanding an open piece of country about a mile in width, skirted by a line of woods running parallel with the James River.

The camping-ground first assigned to us directly in front of the works, and between these and the woods above mentioned, seemed a very disadvantageous one, and was given us by some officer of the day in the absence of the General Commanding. But that gentleman, General Phelps, has assigned us a pleasanter and a better location to which our camp was moved to-day, a position North of the breastworks, with the rear against the James.

The cut accompanying this has been reduced from one in the "Herald" published some time later, or just as we were

18

anticipating an attack. It is interesting because it caused no little indignation at the time, as being calculated to furnish valuable information to the enemy relative to pickets and outposts, with which the artist seems to have been designedly particular.

Sunday, June 7th.

Have just come off picket and am happy to state that the difficulty of being able to realize that we are in an enemy's country is fast wearing away. The first night here (Friday) I was on guard and slept but little, and the next day (yesterday) with the moving of camp there could of course be but little rest, and last night, volunteers were called to form a picket commanding an important road Northwest of the works. I volunteered, wishing to participate in the first real soldiering, and my wish was gratified. I think now that I shall be satisfied to let my time come for duty, for it does seem as if the more a man is willing to do the more is put upon him.

Our pickets were established along the line of a fence across the open space between the James and the woods, then following a road into these woods to the first cross-road where our advance picket was placed. It so happened that I was posted next to this advance picket, though the darkness was too intense to enable me to see him.

All was quiet until about eleven o'clock, I should think, when my companion hailed me in a whisper and informed me that he heard voices in the woods, and immediately disappeared in the darkness. I myself could hear nothing, and was getting used to the stillness again, when he challenged and fired. This, of course, being the signal, we rallied on the main guard, and while the " Long Roll " beat in camp, our hearts beat high, expecting an enemy, which, however, did not appear. Another relief was sent out and posted, while we were drawn up in line ready for any business at hand. This fresh relief had not been on their posts more than a few minutes before we all heard distinctly commands of " File Right and Left " issuing from the woods. Our sentinel's challenge followed immediately,

19

one or more shots were fired and the pickets came in on us pell-mell.

The officer of the guard (Lieutenant Leahy, I think) now called upon the sentinel who had fired, to report. He said that as soon as he had been on his post a short time, he could hear not only voices, as we did, but the tramping of feet, and only when he saw a figure approach him, he challenged, and not being answered, he fired. He waited for some effect of the shot and heard curses from some one for not doing so and so. By this time two Companies arrived from the Regiment, scouts were sent out to reconnoiter, but as nothing could be found, seen or heard, they soon came back and returned to camp. After this our fellows became so possessed by excitement that it seemed as if every rustling leaf provoked a challenge and a shot; so that in an hour's time over a dozen shots were fired, I really believe, at nothing; for, with the one exception, I had certainly seen or heard nothing to fire at. And this voice giving the command that we heard, may have proceeded from some party of our own, some neighboring picket perhaps, or party returning from forage. If this was the case, it seems strange that they could not answer when challenged, and prevent alarm to the camp, if nothing more. I am, more by this fact than anything else, forced to the opinion that it was some small detachment of the enemy that thus stumbled onto us unawares, and were very glad to beat a hasty retreat.

This first night's picket service was never afterwards referred to without provoking the ruling opinion that the voices we heard were imaginary and the men we saw were stumps, and I gradually fell into the same belief.

Owing to the hubbub, the men were all kept awake till two o'clock, when it was time for me to go on again and the rest went to sleep, officers and all, and slept so soundly, too, that it was an impossibility to waken any of them; consequently, I was kept on the whole night without one wink of sleep. But when I was released at daybreak, I made up for lost time, and did not awaken before midday and after the old guard had been relieved. The officer of the new guard told me he had been given instructions to let me sleep it out, after trying in vain to waken me, as I had been accidentally kept on post all night. I have been thus particular in noting down the incidents of my first actual service, thinking that, if Fate spares me, it may be pleasant to remember in after years.

CHAPTER IV

THE FIGHT AT BETHEL

Tuesday, June 11th.

YESTERDAY a battle was fought between our forces and General McGruder's, at Little Bethel, some eight or nine miles from here in the direction of Yorktown, of which this Bethel seems to be a fortified outpost.

Our forces were repulsed with considerable loss, which is most severely felt in the death of the gallant Greble, a regular army Lieutenant who superintended the construction of our works here and seemed to have possessed to a notable degree the two qualities most needed at this time, namely, military skill and presence of mind in face of the enemy.

Our Regiment did not participate in the action, though three Companies (A, B and G), engaged in bringing up supplies, had reached the scene of action in plain sight of the fortifications, when they were ordered to cover the rear of our retiring forces. About noon, the balance of the Regiment received orders to march in all haste to their re-enforcement, and we started on Double-quick time, which we were soon glad to exchange for the ordinary step, for the day was very warm and sultry.

This seemed a genuine taste of war, for we had heard cannonading in this direction during the morning, and the extra supply of cartridges distributed indicated that something more than play was looked for. But after a march of some three miles, our advance met the forces from the post in full retreat, and all we now could do was to fall in with our other Companies in their rear, for all was over.

We stopped to refresh ourselves at a farmhouse, where the body of the lamented Greble passed us on an artillery-wagon, and here our men seemed to take a morbid pleasure in acquainting themselves with the details of the fight.

The expedition, it seems, was planned by General Butler, and its execution entrusted to General Pierce, and it was the intention to surprise the enemy; but this part of the plan was frustrated through a misunderstanding of the countersign between the German Seventh from this post and Colonel Townsend's Regiment from Hampton, which proved as disastrous as it was aggravating. The Regiments met during the night at the rendezvous; but, either on account of having different countersigns or not understanding them to be the same, actually fired into each other, thus giving the enemy ample cause for alarm and time for preparation. Nevertheless, the attack was made at daybreak, and though our forces are said not to have wanted bravery, the fortifications were defended so well that nothing could be accomplished. Duryea's Zouaves, the Fifth New York, from all accounts fought well, even desperately, making three or four charges, and at one time actually had possession of a portion of the works, which they undoubtedly would have carried had they been properly supported. I heard an account of one of these Zouaves, who jumped inside the breastworks, capturing a musket, with which he succeeded in getting back unharmed, but a comrade who followed, was instantly shot down. Numerous instances are related of individual bravery, but the fact can not be concealed that our forces were entirely defeated, that our first battle is a decided repulse of the Union arms.

And another fact can not be concealed, and that is that the troops from this post are certainly lacking in discipline, if not in valor, for on our return march there was not the least attempt at order among them, and had the enemy pursued us, our Regiment would have been the only one in condition to oppose them. The rest—Vermonters, Massachusetts men and Germans—presented nothing but an indiscriminate horde of stragglers. This fact seemed to worry our Major Kimball most, who being the only one with any military experience among us seemed to think we might be pursued; and no one felt worse than he at this contemptible affair, and no one regretted more being cheated out of a fight.

Wednesday, June 12th.

With a scouting party under Lieutenant Leahy of Company H, when not far from camp we espied a boat with two persons in it coming down the James. The Lieutenant fired a pistol-shot over them, which brought them to—a negro and his wife escaping from the Secessionists. The negro showed us the marks of a pistol-ball on his back that he had received from a former master from whom he had tried to run away. He was sent to camp under guard, with instructions to report to General Phelps. Farther on we met one of our boys returning to camp with a mule. We wanted it for foraging purposes, but the fellow refused, and said it was his, for he had bought it. How much had he paid? "Fifty cents." He was finally induced to part with it, and farther on we got a cart. We returned to camp that night with a cart-load of slaughtered sheep, of which our Company got one, and our men a good share.

Sunday, June 16th.

Service by the Chaplain, the Reverend Mr. Conway, from the piazza of a house a short distance from camp, the Regiment disposed comfortably in the shade of the orchard.

Tuesday, June 18th.

Am not doing duty to-day. Am both bilious and feverish, feel cold and hot by turns, with other strange sensations, the result of not having our food properly cooked and from sleeping on the damp ground.

Saturday, June 22d.

I have reported myself well to-day, although I do not feel strong enough to do much. I have had chills and fever, or the ague, and have actually eaten nothing for the last three or four days, and I do not remember anything much that has transpired during that time, except that Beith would occasionally put blankets over me when I was shaking.

Sunday, June 23d.

Turned out with the Regiment for the first time since I was taken sick, and attended service at the same place as last Sunday.

24

THE LONG ROLL

Wednesday, June 26th.

Our Company was one of five of our Regiment under Captain Jardine sent out by orders of General Butler, last Monday, to reconnoiter the vicinity of Bethel. Encamped during the night some six miles from here in an orchard. Resumed our advance the next morning, joined by three Companies from other Regiments of this post. Chased one of the enemy's troopers across a field and drove in one or two pickets from their outposts, and while our advance was in hearing of their drums beating the Long Roll, we lay some fifteen minutes waiting for their movements. Our orders were positive not to bring on an engagement, so we turned back. This is the farthest advance yet made, I am told, by any of our forces since the fight on the Tenth instant.

There was considerable plundering on our return march, and for the first time have I witnessed the pure wantonness of destruction. In one instance, a carpenter-shop, just because it was full of shavings, I believe, was set on fire, and everything that could not be appropriated was destroyed. Somewhat sickened at this heartless propensity, of which I could never be guilty, I obtained permission for my chum (Thain*) and myself to go on ahead, which we were glad to do. We entertained ourselves here and there with the hoecake and the conversation of the slaves, who are now the only inhabitants of these plundered homes in this region of the Old Dominion. Thus we strayed on quite a distance in advance of our force and concluded to stop at a farmhouse and wait for our comrades to come up. While here, we saw two horsemen dressed in light Summer suits come out from a piece of timber toward the farm, and the old negress with whom we were talking saw them, too, and became greatly alarmed for our safety. We were both slightly built and young-looking, and she probably thought us unable to cope with any very furious riders of the Chivalry. She begged us to go, " for God's sake," or we would surely be killed. Neither Thain nor I had a mind to get killed, but we would not have thought much about it if the old woman had

---

* Hamilton H. Thain, Company I.

not shown such alarm. We concluded to slip into the orchard behind a fence, where we would be equal in advantage to the horsemen; and with pieces cocked, and somewhat shaky as to the outcome, we awaited their approach. They proved to be our surgeon and some other officer, taking a cross-cut to camp; so our valor was not put to the test this time.

This poor country presents a most melancholy appearance. Not a white soul to be found in all the homes I have seen. None but negroes for caretakers, and they, in the absence of their masters, do nothing but eat and sleep, and in fact have nothing more to do, for their masters, I ween, would hardly thank them were they to store the abundant crops now so nearly ripe, for the benefit of their enemies.

Who can blame the Southern citizens for not staying here to witness the destruction of their property and the desecration of their homes? Their cause as men and freemen is just. We are the invaders, and it were right for them to drive us from their soil. It is on the instigators of the rebellion that the crime of this heartrending calamity rests. On the return march through this rich if not altogether beautiful region, I had both time and inclination to reflect on the scenes of desolation about me; and while my comrades were thoughtlessly making it greater, I often said to myself, " God help this poor, distracted country ! "

Friday, June 28th.

Was detailed this morning for picket duty, which I prefer to the camp guard, as one is more free and the extra vigilance required helps to wear away the dulness of the two hours on post. Some firing from the batteries opposite, at the mouth of the Nansemond, this morning, told us the enemy were evidently trying their guns. About noon, Company K of our Regiment and a Company of the Rifles came in through our line from a scout, our men carrying a Rebel flag, stars down, which they had captured somewhere, but under what circumstances I have not yet been able to learn.

THE LONG ROLL

Saturday, June 29th.

Rained very hard during the night and soaked us to the skin. At one time it was so dark, while on my post in the woods, that I had to feel for the roadway while walking my beat. It commenced to rain again after daylight, just after my relief had been put on, and as I undertook to "secure" my piece, about a pint of water poured from the muzzle, as I had left it standing, muzzle up, against a tree while trying to get a little sleep, and it must have been filled by the water trickling down in the grooves of the bark. I lost no time in swabbing it out and reloading, which operation I had just performed when my next man came down with word from the officer of the guard, to use extra vigilance, as we might expect the enemy on us at any moment in full force for attack. I was further informed that two Rebel soldiers had run onto our picket-line above and delivered themselves prisoners of war, having lost themselves during the night and stumbled upon us. They belonged to a Louisiana Zouave Regiment, and reported a force of five thousand Secessionists only six miles from us.

But it is now afternoon, and nothing definite is heard from them. No apprehension whatever seems to be felt here on account of their proximity, though, to be sure, a private soldier would not be apt to know much of events in expectancy. Still, there is always something in the air that he can feel when danger threatens, and our camp to-day droons away under the hot sun in its usual manner, and more indifferent to the terrible five thousand than if they were quietly in camp, like ourselves, at Yorktown. And as to that, five thousand might disturb our usual routine, but nothing more, for it would take more than twice that force to endanger the post of Newport News by any daytime attack; and as for a surprise, with our present General, I do not think it possible.

Sunday, June 30th.

Company A was sent out in the afternoon yesterday—to see what had become of the Rebel force, I presume. They returned last night with two more of this same Louisiana

27

Regiment. One of the fellows captured was formerly a New Yorker, and did not seem to regret very much the calamity of falling into the hands of the enemy.

We had, yesterday, an opportunity to witness the extraordinary power of the new Sawyer gun recently put in position in our water-battery. Our General, I presume, concluding to try his guns as the enemy had theirs, the day before, fired five shots at their battery on Pigs Point opposite, which can not be less than five miles distant. I fancy it must have astonished the Southerners to see a ball plow the water in front of their works, almost before the report of the concussion could reach them, and from so great a distance. The first was a fine shot; the second and third were a little out of range; the fourth I did not see strike, and it may have reached the other shore, as some of the spectators would have it, though this seems almost impossible; but the fifth and last was well aimed and with a little more elevation might have reached the battery. We could see it strike close by the fort, with the naked eye, and those who had glasses said it struck close to shore in shallow water, driving a column of sand and water before it. It took the projectile about twenty seconds, as nearly as I could judge, to travel perhaps four and a half miles ; and the gun is not extraordinary to look at—about the weight of the thirty-two-pound Columbiads near by.

Tuesday, July 2d.

Have been reviewed by General Butler to-day. We formed in line of battle and marched by the General and staff in review. Made quite an imposing appearance, though there are but four Regiments of us now—the Vermonters, Scott Life Guards, the Germans and ourselves. The Massachusetts men have been withdrawn from here, and are now stationed at Fortress Monroe.

Have just been finishing a little sketch from here, a quiet, shady nook, and—there !—the drums again beating some confounded call or other. I must go and see what it is. Pay-day is coming soon, I am told, and though I had intended spending

28

a half-hour more here, reading or writing, I must go and see if I am summoned to undergo the ordeal of receiving money, or a poor dinner.

Thursday, July 4th.

We celebrated here at Newport News by a grand parade of all the Regiments, the playing of the national airs by the Regimental band, and by a salute of thirty-four guns for the Union by our battery of Columbiads. In the afternoon we were given general liberty, which I have employed in sketching the curious old windmill not far from here, just beyond the picket-line.

Saturday, July 6th.

Company F, Captain Hammill, returned from a scout yesterday, having had a brush with a superior force of the enemy, somewhere up the James. They came upon them unexpectedly, and opened fire, compelling them to retreat in evident confusion. Hammill kept after them until they were re-enforced with cavalry, when he retreated through the woods as fast as possible until secure from pursuit. His force numbered but twenty-five men.

Upon reporting the facts to General Phelps, that gentleman ordered out five Companies of our Regiment, " Ours " among the number, and three Companies of Vermonters under Major Worthing, all under the command of Lieutenant-Colonel Betts. We at once proceeded to the scene of the encounter and cruised about the vicinity for some time, advancing quite a distance beyond where Hammill had met their force, hoping to have the good fortune to meet them again. With the exception of a large tree felled across the road as if to impede the passage of artillery, no sign of an enemy was to be found.

On our return, we gathered from some negroes that Hammill's fire had proved fatal to some of the enemy, killing and wounding quite a number. Among the killed were two officers, we were told, one of them of high rank, for " they were mighty keerful " or " skeert of him," they said. However, it was impossible to make out from this description just what was his rank.

THE LONG ROLL

Wednesday, July 10th.

Another scouting party came in this morning, reporting that they ran upon a body of the enemy's cavalry estimated at two hundred fifty, and were glad to beat a retreat, which they accomplished without loss by keeping in the woods.

Friday, July 12th.

Had a good opportunity to witness a Brigade Drill of all the Regiments here. "Ours" appeared unusually well, none the less so on account of the havelocks with which their heads were uniformed, and for which we have undoubtedly to thank our New York ladies.

One of Colonel Bendix's scouting parties has returned, minus twelve of its men, killed or missing, and a half-regiment was immediately sent out, but could find no enemy.

Sunday, July 14th.

General Butler has been here to-day inspecting the Post. We fired four shots at the Pigs Point Battery from our long-range gun.

We are told that to-morrow will be pay-day, and it is to be hoped it may prove true, but I have learned that so little dependence is to be placed on such rumors that I shall believe it when I see the money.

I learn that we have had a distinguished visitor to-day, none other than Mr. Russell, the correspondent of the London " Times."

Wednesday, July 17th.

Have just gotten two letters with more than ordinary pleasure: one from my Father in Minnesota and the other from my Sister in Hudson City, the first news I have had from either of these homes since I left New York. All well so far.

Thursday, July 18th.

Have written long answers to the letters received yesterday. Last night was a most beautiful night. The moon shone so brightly as to almost blot out the stars; a gentle breeze from the James fanned one's features with just enough motion to

30

produce a feeling akin to inspiration, and I made my bed out-side, as the thought of a crowded tent on a night like this seemed unbearable. And there I lay dreaming day-dreams far into the night. I watched the comet, wondering if that mysterious little visitor was not perhaps at the same time watched by eyes that would beam gladly into mine: and I composed quite a number of beginnings to addresses to the curious thing, whatever it may be. But the comet is now tired of his visit to these regions of space, or disgusted it may be with the appearance of things on this side of our planet, for he is now leaving in seemingly greater haste than he came, with his tail between his legs, for the unknown regions out yonder. Well, good-by and fare thee well, Stranger And I fervently hope that thou mayst see the face of the Earth beaming with smiles where now her frowns are lowering, on thy next visit, if that should be while this little world is still in existence. And to sleep at last, to dream again not more strangely than if awake, and only disturbed by a little cannonading up the river. The "Monticello" chasing something up there, I believe.

Monday, July 22d.

Quite a chapter of incidents and accidents to relate to-day. Early yesterday morning, a private from the Vermont Regiment and one from the German were fired upon from an ambush. The Vermonter was killed and the other escaped to camp with the news. A party was at once sent out to bring in the body of the unfortunate soldier, and they returned with it, and two Southerners, supposed to be the murderers, because they had been found in a neighboring field, with their hands bloody. They are now in the Vermont guard-house.

In the afternoon quite a brisk breeze set in from the South-east, of which a Rebel schooner coming down the Nansemond endeavored to take advantage and make off up the James. A shot from the "Daylight" (six guns of small calibre) called our attention to the fact, and very soon after, the bluffs over-looking the beach and river were lined with spectators. The "Daylight" fired five or six shots at her, which fell short some-

31

thing over a mile. These were followed by a shot from our Rifle, which seemed to strike as much beyond her as the "Daylight's" gun had struck below. At this, she turned about and took to her heels. Ran so well that we had not time to fire more than three or four more shots at her before she was out of range and she soon disappeared up the River Nansemond from where she had made her appearance.

The breeze brought on a furious rainstorm in the night, from which the whole camp suffered more or less. Our tent had rotted and we were compelled to hold it up or it would have come down on our heads. Weathered it out, however, but at the expense of a good drenching.

The Scott Life Guards have captured four Secessionists to-day. It seems that after they had taken them they made them tell where their arms had been left, which they thus succeeded in getting, also three horses. Their arms consisted of two rifles and one double-barreled shotgun.

There are some queer rumors about the camp that our arms have met with a severe reverse at Manassas Junction—that the Eighth and the Sixty-ninth have been badly cut up. If this is true or merely a hoax, the mail to-night will tell us. The Orderly is just "Falling-in" the Company, and I must lay down the pen.

Tuesday, July 23d.

I have seen the "Tribune" of the Twentieth, according to which our troops lost some thousand men in an attempt to take the batteries at Bull Run; but rumor says there is a later paper contradicting this statement, but I have not seen it. While going through the evolution of the brigade drill under Colonel Phelps yesterday, we heard some sharp firing, which could have been only four or five miles from here. Alternating between "Company fire" and "Fire by file," from the rapid volleys it seemed as if sharp work was going on somewhere, There was also an occasional report of artillery. Our officers are determined to be ready for anything, for at Retreat, cartridges were distributed among the men, and our Company

Wreck of the " Neptune's Car "

Company I Quarters, Camp Wool

PLATE VII

At Camp Wool

PLATE VIII

The Hut Picket

In the Hut

PLATE XII

The Windmill Picket at Hatteras

PLATE XIII

went through some bayonet exercises with more earnestness than is usual (such as "Charge" and "Guard against cavalry," etc.), and when dismissed were cautioned to be ready for the "Long Roll." Inside of the breastworks the troops were equally determined to be ready; for as late as eleven o'clock the First Regiment was at work on the walls of the fortification, filling the crevices made by the last storm.

I had just about dropped to sleep, about twelve o'clock, when the earth gave that peculiar quiver occasioned by the firing of heavy artillery, immediately followed by the report. I counted, after that, eleven guns fired at intervals of about two minutes, but could hear nothing of any smaller arms; then the firing ceased, all was quiet, and giving up the idea of an attack, I went to sleep.

Ten A. M.

Have just heard another volley of musketry somewhere. What does it mean?

Wednesday, July 24th.

Bah! The firing we heard was only Duryea's Regiment practising with blank cartridges; he must have plenty of powder, it seems to me.

July 25th.

Have seen the "Herald" and the "Tribune" of the Twenty-second, and they both agree that instead of the reported defeat at Bull Run, it was a victory after a severe fight of twelve hours. But now, rumor says that the papers of the Twenty-third contradict this again, telling of a panic and the retreat of our forces. To-morrow will probably give us the truth, whatever that is. I presume I might know it now, but I am on the outer picket and have not heard from camp since the mail-boat came in.

Friday, July 26th.

I saw a paper of the Twenty-third last night, and it corroborates the worst. Our forces were defeated and made a shameful stampede, it seems, without the least attempt at order. It has made us all feel badly, but I can not but think that the

33

people at home must feel worse about it than we do. I am sure that I feel the disaster less keenly than if I were a civilian.

One of our Buglers is dead, and as I write, Colonel Allen's band is escorting the body to its last resting-place.

CHAPTER V

An Interpolation

THE leaves in my Journal Number Two, between last date and August Thirtieth, were torn out, after my return home, because of the mistaken notion that the incidents therein dwelt upon might reflect upon my honor as a soldier. I now regret this exceedingly, as it obliges me to write from memory the account of an unpleasant episode, which in my present character of exact historian I dislike to do.* However, the reader may rest assured that the account now given is substantially the same as was written at the time.

A disaffection among the officers which had been smouldering for some time manifested itself at this period in quite a blaze. The Colonel had encountered the opposition of some of his staff and line officers, who had ventured to question his fitness for command, and now, in fact, covertly hinted at the expediency of his resignation. This, of course, created two parties in the camp, of which the Colonel headed one, with Captain Jardine as chief supporter; and Lieutenant-Colonel Betts, I think, though that gentleman was too high-minded to mix in any broils of the kind himself, was the soul of the opposition. Colonel Betts' resignation after the affair at Roanoke was owing to the perpetual disagreements between himself and Colonel Hawkins resulting from this feud. He would have resigned before, but did not wish to risk any imputation that might be raised against him as man or soldier. The Colonel's party proved the stronger, and, by hook or crook (said to have been by ballot), Captain Jardine gained the seniority of the Captain in line, to the great disgust of the other officers, who were certainly the more numerous, and who did not omit to hint at foul play. Captain Graham's Company (I), which was thus displaced, showed open indication of opposition and was, I believe, put under arrest for a time.

The disaffection soon spread through the other Companies,

---

* It is quite evident that this chapter was written soon after the return to Minnesota, not long after the original was destroyed.

where it took another form. Report was now circulated that we were not enlisted for any specified time, having sworn to serve "two years *or the war*," which was indefinite now that the war promised to continue longer than we at that time anticipated. Also, that we were not regularly mustered into the United States service; that the Government did not recognize us, of which last the paymaster's non-appearance made the belief more plausible. Then, as the noise grew in volume, many other little items of discontent were brought in. The food was thought to be unfit for beasts, and indeed the crackers served out to us at this time were most vile, said to have been a condemned lot from the Crimea. Everything was brought to bear that could intensify the excitement. Some one had drawn up a paper, a respectful letter of inquiry. I understood that it asked information concerning the points in doubt; viz., the term of enlistment, etc., and to this paper I, thoughtlessly enough, in fact not dreaming that any harm could come from it, signed my name, and went about my business, which happened to be washing, down in the hollow in the rear of the camp. But the Colonel, on the presentation of this paper, put it in his pocket and took the first boat for Fortress Monroe and returned with the Commanding General. So that, when I got back to camp I was surprised to find the Regiment drawn up in hollow square on the parade-ground, with General Butler speaking to them, and a Corporal's guard waiting to take charge of me; and here, for the first time in my life, I found myself a criminal and a prisoner.

I was immediately conducted to the steamer, plying between Newport News and Fortress Monroe, and found about a dozen other " Signers " on board before me, appearing rather uneasy, though striving to hide their concern; and though I could not feel guilty of any crime, I must confess I felt oppressed by the seriousness of the aspect affairs had assumed. I could now reflect, and it was not without concern, that I found one certain circumstance outside the signing of the paper tending to testify against me in the Court-Martial which I could see was impending, and that was, my failure to turn out with the Regiment.

36

THE LONG ROLL

To be sure, it was an accident, owing to the fact that I had been on guard the night before and was excused from morning drill, but who of the members of the Court would or could believe my absence under the circumstances, to be anything but a design on my part to stay away?

This gave me some uneasiness, for in my innocence I supposed a Court-Martial would inquire into details as minutely as a Civil Court; but at any rate, I thought best to keep the matter to myself. Meanwhile, we were making fast time for Old Point Comfort, with Dave, a fine singer, trying to cheer us with one of his most stirring songs, " The Old Musketeer."

Our destination proved to be the " Rip Raps," the partially finished Fort Calhoun, where we were put in charge of a Sergeant Hodgekins of a Massachusetts Regiment, and received by him and his comrades, more like honored guests than prisoners with grave charges preferred against them.

As we were given to understand that this would be our home until a Court-Martial could be convened, which would not be sooner than convenient, at any rate, there was nothing for us to do but to make ourselves comfortable, and in this respect, we found our situation preferable to that at Newport News. I must here take space to testify my appreciation of that excellent man, Sergeant Hodgekins, and his subordinates, one and all, who for their kindness and considerate conduct toward us while in their charge, making our prison life a pleasure, more than deserve our heartfelt thanks. To be sure, we were not criminals in the true sense of the word, but as insubordinates, we might have experienced much less courtesy without surprise. We were given free use of the best they had, their own quarters, their not inconsiderable library and the liberty of the Island. The library I took advantage of to read something of Fredrica Bremer's, but first—that is, after the first night's sleep—I prepared to satisfy my curiosity concerning this island fortress, named Fort Calhoun, but for some reason, as yet unknown to me, commonly called the " Rip Raps."

The Island is entirely artificial, having been brought from a distance by shiploads and deposited here upon a shallow

37

place or reef in the Roads, and the granite, of which the walls of the fortification were in course of construction, was from New Hampshire. The solidity and massiveness of these walls were something to admire, and I made a sketch of a casemated gun, a thirty-two pounder, mounted and facing the enemy's battery on Sewall's Point, to show the nature of the work.

The fort I thought would be invulnerable when completed, but it was destined with thousands of its fellows to be rendered comparatively useless about a year later, by an event which took place under its very walls; for the New Era of Iron, superseding that of Stone and Wood, was brought in when Ericsson's little " Monitor " proved herself capable of saving the " Minnesota " from sharing the sad fate of the " Cumberland." And in that same instant the walls and defences of every monarch on the face of the globe fell with a great crash, shattered as completely as castles of granite dissolved by enchantment, and rendered as useless as this heap of stones, the Rip Raps, appears to be from the distance; with every capital in the world exposed and open to sack and pillage; with every tyrant trembling like a fox hunting his hole, for fifty Monitors could have mastered all Europe.

The twin to the Sawyer gun at Newport News is here mounted on a dock or pier facing Sewall's Point. A few shots were fired at the enemy's entrenchments there on the occasion of the visit of General Wool on a tour of inspection to the Island, without eliciting any reply. General Wool was then about to supersede General Butler in command of this Department.

There was no attempt made to keep a garrison on the Island at all adequate for its defence in case of attack, the only troops being this Massachusetts Company, scarce a Corporal's guard, under Sergeant Hodgekins; though of course no attack was to be apprehended with Fortress Monroe situated as it was and the Roads blocked by the fleet. But that not even a positive assurance of security can be trusted in war time is proven by *the* great event of Hampton Roads, the attack of the " Merrimac." And had it not been for the

38

"Monitor," that alone of all the fleet had the hardihood to face the vertical plates of the Rebel monster, what would have become of this Key to the Roads then locking the door to the Rebel Capital? Fortress Monroe could hardly cover it, with the "Merrimac" itself secure from harm, tearing it to pieces under its very walls.

I sketched an old-fashioned iron gun or that part of it protruding from a vast pile of granite blocks in which it had been by accident or design embedded, a curious relic of a former age: rust-eaten, battered and cracked, an old Revolutionary warrior perhaps—at any rate, torn by hard service, and now useless and shelved in solemn mockery of former use.

A few workmen in the employ of the Government were noticed here and there on the works evidently doing something, though exactly what I could not discover, for that work, to any extent in the fortifications, had ceased was entirely evident.

A singular adventure happened to me here while I was bathing from the dock. Not so terrible as an affair with a shark or a battle with a cuttlefish, but nevertheless an adventure, if you please—an attack of Sea Nettles. Caleph, Medusa, and many other names are given them, but of them all, for reasons to be made obvious, I prefer the first. Those beautiful creatures we had watched with great pleasure as, with their slow and methodical motions, they propelled themselves about the Island, which seemed to them a favorite resort, for nowhere else have I seen them in such beautiful variety and so numerous. Out of water they become an indistinguishable shapeless mass of pulp, but in their element, they have a bell or cup shaped head of a variety of colors, to which is appended, from the inside, a body terminating in loose streamers. They elongate themselves as much as possible, seeming to inhale the water as air is inhaled by the lungs; then by bringing the rim forward until flattened into the shape of a saucer, they are able to push themselves along quite rapidly, though with nothing like the speed of fish or other active marine animals. They seem to be a family of living leeches of the sea, clinging to decaying substances; but whether the fact of fresh water here mingling

THE LONG ROLL

with the salt has any influence in keeping them in this vicinity, I can not tell.

It happened thus: In taking our usual evening's swim off the dock, I found myself farther from shore than I intended, and made for a buoy a short distance out, to rest on it before returning. I hardly had touched it, however, before it seemed as if I were seized by a legion of little devils with pins in them. I knew at once that I had struck a colony of Sea Nettles and that until I could get out of the water, it would be useless to try to rid myself of them, as they are worse than leeches in their power of holding fast. They seem to glue themselves to the object of attack and then to fall to with all their power of suction, which, by my experience, I found to be tremendous. I made for shore as fast as possible, with every pin doing its worst. On every part of my body under water, they clung, pricking, biting, sucking and stinging, from which occupations, my plunging in the water did not in the least disturb them. One can easily imagine what I had to endure before gaining the dock. The moment I dragged myself out of the water, my persecutors let go, and though my body smarted for some time after, I could not but laugh at the ludicrousness of the adventure.

The Frigate, "Minnesota," Flagship of the North Atlantic Squadron, was at one time anchored between the Rip Raps and Fortress Monroe, and the accompanying sketch was made, though with the worst of materials, only such as I could secure by chance at the time. It may not be as correct as a photograph—a remark, by the way, which may apply to all the sketches here referred to—but as I shall *publish* none except such as are drawn from nature or life, I hope they may not be wanting in interest as much as in matters of detail and artistic merit.

The sketches bring to my mind many a delightful day spent among the Rip Rap rocks, writing, reading and drawing; the ever-varying and shifting scenes of an important naval and military station in time of war, continually furnishing new objects of interest to a mind somewhat alive to the beauties

40

of nature, and I enjoyed everything to the utmost. But there was an end to these days of pleasant captivity, and our stay at the Rip Raps was over far too soon.

The paymaster came and left some gold among us. This was the first and last payment in coin, I believe, from the beginning of the war. After a sojourn of about two weeks on the Island, we were summoned to appear before a Court-Martial at the Fortress. We were taken over in squads as fast as wanted, accompanied by an Orderly. This young man, one of the regular garrison, conducted us to the building where the court was marshalled, informing us about the time he thought we would be wanted, and in the interval, left us at perfect liberty to dispose of ourselves in or about the Fortress as we saw fit. This liberty I availed myself of to see everything worth seeing within and without the walls.

When my turn came for examination, I was called before several stout officers in uniform, among whom was our Major Kimball, and as nearly as I can remember, questions were asked and answered as follows:

QUESTION (the common formula of name, Company, Regiment being disposed of much as in civil courts). "Did you sign a certain paper on —— day at Camp Butler?"

ANSWER. "Yes, Sir."

Q. "What was your object in so doing?"

A. "To find out if there was any truth in certain rumors about the camp."

Q. "What were these rumors?"

A. "That we were not regularly mustered into the United States service, or for an indefinite time, and consequently would not receive any pay if not paid by the State of New York."

Q. "Did you not know such rumors to be false?"

A. "No, Sir. I think the indefinite term of enlistment, 'two years or the war,' tended to confirm some of them."

Q. "Did you not know that it was an act of insubordination to sign this paper?"

A. "No, Sir. I thought no more of it than of asking a question of a superior officer."

THE LONG ROLL

COURT. " But you not only asked questions, but *demanded* answers to them, coupled with assertions mutinous in their tenor."

SELF. " If I did, Sir, I was not aware of it at the time. I supposed I was simply asking for information."

C. " You did not know, then, the nature of what you signed ? "

S. " The paper was brought and read to me during some excitement in camp. I did not read it myself and the demands you mention may have escaped me. I certainly thought no harm could possibly come from it. On the contrary, I supposed I was doing the right thing, as an answer to the questions would restore quiet in the camp. I am not by nature or disposition a wrongdoer, unless it is a wrong to serve a country willingly. I supposed there would be no objection to giving information which it seemed to me we all should have. I certainly felt an interest in the money question. It may be, Gentlemen, that I have those depending on my pay, that makes it important to me."

As this was said with some earnestness not unmixed with indignation, my feelings just then rushed into a heap and conquered me —— (Age Eighteen). A slight sensation — unmistakable sympathy of Major Kimball. His valiant but tender soul felt worse for me than I did for myself, in spite of my outburst. I was dismissed without further questions. After a few days, immediately following the adjournment of the Court, we received orders to report to our Regiment.

The whole thing, from beginning to end, was well-nigh forgotten in the excitement attending our departure for Hatteras. Nearly a month later we were again reminded of the occurrence by an order read at Dress Parade, drumming us all out of the Regiment; *but*, in consideration, etc., etc., etc., grace and peace, etc., etc., etc. Well, this was perhaps not an inappropriate finale to an episode which was looked upon from the first as a simple farce. But the farce, if such it was, might have been curtailed with advantage. In consideration of the fact that our imprisonment and trial were but the means by

42

which our young Colonel regained authority over his officers, more than over his men, which I have reason for believing he had lost through his method of advancing his favorites, I think this last order, though tending to cast only the shadow of a stain upon our records as soldiers, *but still casting that shadow*, might just as well have been dispensed with.

CHAPTER VI

Newport News, Va.
Sunday, August 31st.

AN exciting little affair occurred to-day between a Rebel gunboat and the sloop-of-war, " Savannah," opposite this point. About noon, a little steam-tug managed to crawl along the other shore from under the batteries on Crany Island, to within two and a half or three miles of this post, without exciting notice or suspicion, which, indeed, its diminutive size was well calculated to elude; and before any one had really thought of questioning her—before, perhaps, any one had seen her—she stated her errand herself with a dull boom over the water and a projectile plump under the " Savannah's " stern. That the " Savannah " was taken unawares is not strange, and that there was a lively time clearing for action on board of her may be believed, for the little tug kept advancing and improving in her range at every shot, one or two of which had done some damage. She had time to send in her fourth query before our sloop-of-war was ready with an answer, which, when said and done, fell a half-mile short of the purpose. This, with the cool, sharp rejoinder whistling overhead, seemed to make her perfectly furious, and she shook out whole broadsides in reply, fearful in energy but misspent and lost upon a rival so distant and so small. She had no guns of sufficient range, and had to confess her inability to cope with her long-armed antagonist, by sending a boat ashore to request the aid of our water-battery.

General Phelps was making a tour of the pickets and outposts at the time, but came in just as a Lieutenant of Artillery was taking range at the little fellow with the Sawyer gun. Some kegs of powder were exposed at the time outside of the magazine, which he at once espied, and he was mightily incensed at the Lieutenant for attempting to fire with ammunition so uncovered, and he would not allow a shot to be fired before the powder was stored. This was soon done, and having cautioned the

44

Lieutenant not to fire before he had perfect aim, he himself took charge of the Columbiads. The first shot from the Sawyer gun went over in range. It was followed by the General's Columbiad, which seemed to send a column of water over the deck, and was hailed with enthusiasm by the spectators. But still undaunted, the tug replied, nearly striking our sloop-of-war. The sloop had by this time gotten a greater elevation for her guns by knocking out the ends of the carriages, allowing the breech of each to rest on deck, and she shook out another broadside which was so much better than her former attempts that our surprise was excited. Having accomplished, probably, all she desired, at any rate having stirred up a hornets' nest, the little tug now turned about and slowly steamed down the River in the direction from which she had come, and was followed by our shot and shell until out of range.

Some firing shortly after from the direction of the Fortress indicated that the plucky little devil was saluted for her gallantry by the mate to the Sawyer gun on the Rip Raps.

The whole affair lasted about an hour and a half, the most exciting thing of the kind it has been my fortune to witness.

Sunday, September 1st.

Charles W. Haltzman was accidentally shot while on his post on guard this morning. A member of our own Company was the unfortunate cause of the accident, he being in the act of taking the cap from his piece *for greater safety* when it was discharged into poor Haltzman's head. I heard the report shortly after I got up, and seeing people run in that direction I hastened out to see what had happened, and was in time to see the poor boy where he had fallen, with his head in a dark pool of blood, presenting a ghastly picture. The poor fellow who shot him has been running about all day in a distracted manner that is really pitiful. Haltzman asked me to sketch his face the other day, and I am very sorry I did not do so then, as it might have been of some comfort to his poor Mother.

Another shooting accident after guard mount; a fellow on the beach, where the old guard have an hour or so for firing

45

off their pieces, putting a pistol bullet through one of his thighs; he bawled so fearfully and cut up so many antics, rolling around on the sand, that I thought the man must be killed, but he was only badly frightened, the fatal accident of this morning undoubtedly adding much to his terror.

September 8th.

News received from the Naval expedition which left here about two weeks ago under sealed orders. The object of the expedition has been accomplished; namely, the capture of the forts commanding Hatteras Inlet on the North Carolina coast, with seven hundred fifty-five prisoners, five stands of colors, one thousand stands of arms, thirty cannon, several schooners and clothing, etc., etc., all without losing a man. Our Colonel is now in command of one of the forts, and it is rumored that the balance of the Regiment is to proceed at once to the Inlet to form the garrison. This last part of the intelligence ought to be the least welcome, I presume, because of the well-known unhealthiness of the place. As for me, it will be a change anyway, something new, for though I am well aware that it may be long before we will find another station as pleasant and healthy as this, the life we have here is getting to be rather humdrum, and as for war, we have certainly seen nothing of that.

Hatteras Inlet, N. C.

September 12th.

We trod North Carolina soil, or rather, I should say, sand, for the first time yesterday. I am not in the least disappointed at the dreary prospect, as it is just about the kind of a place I expected to find; that is, a long, low strip of sand between two oceans, the actual coast of North Carolina not being in sight, producing just that impression. Some distance up there are evidences of trees or shrubbery, though what they can be from soil like this, is hard to imagine.

We embarked on the United States Transport, "S. R. Spaulding," night before last. My first care was to find a place in which to bunk. Selected a spot under the Major's buggy, and

46

as I was fatigued from packing and lugging camp equipage on board the steamer, as well as from being on guard the night before, I was soon in a sound sleep, from which I awoke next morning on the Atlantic Ocean, the coast in sight, however. About ten o'clock we came in sight of Cape Hatteras Light-House, which I tried to sketch from under the buggy. We soon after sighted the "Susquehanna" and "Pawnee" guarding the Inlet; also, our flags flying over the forts, and then the forts themselves. We took aboard two pilots before entering the channel, which, judging from the way the breakers roared all around us as the steamer carefully picked her way between them, seemed to be very necessary. Having gotten through, however, we anchored alongside an old time-worn light-ship lettered "Brandts Island Land Shoal"—wherever that might be. Coming in we met two outward-bound schooners captured while trying to make the Inlet, being, of course, unaware of the events that had transpired here since they sailed. One of these vessels was captured by stratagem, which if true is worth relating; at any rate, I will give it for what it is worth, while here with the ship at anchor.

About two days after our forces had come into possession of the forts, a schooner hove in sight, but on being brought to by a shot from the "Cumberland," hoisted the English flag; as nothing actually wrong was found about her she was allowed to depart, but not without strong suspicion that she was a blockade-runner. Accordingly, the following plan was hastily resolved upon. A Rebel flag was hoisted on Fort Clark and with the tugboat "Fanny" under the same emblem, Colonel Hawkins and Lieutenant Crosby of the Naval Brigade ran out, hugging the shore as much as possible to give the impression of slipping by the "Cumberland." The schooner, as soon as she deemed herself out of the frigate's sight, changed her colors from British to Secesh. Our officers, pleased with the marked success of their ruse, boarded the vessel without delay, but still, it seems, without creating any suspicion in the mind of the Captain, for they had hardly reached her deck before the skipper commenced to congratulate himself upon how nicely he had fooled the " Cumberland." " But," said he, a doubt evidently striking his mind, " is that our vessel?" pointing to the "Pawnee" now coming in sight. " That vessel," said the Lieutenant, " is a United States vessel, I am a United States officer and you are a United States prisoner."

They tell me the skipper only looked his astonishment, and did not seem to realize the fact fully until he saw the "Fanny" change flags and uncover two neat little brass pieces, then he suddenly made a dive for the cabin, and when wanted, he was found—dead drunk.

Our camp has been pitched outside of Fort Clark, and we have not had much time to look around. From all appearances, everything will be both new and strange, if not interesting, and I intend to take the earliest opportunity to see what there is to be seen.

Fort Clark,
September 14th.

Worked hard yesterday rafting lumber from the lower fort for barracks, and had to get into the water in shallow places to shove the rafts. In the meantime, I have had an opportunity to look around somewhat and am becoming acquainted with our new situation.

Forts Hatteras and Clark are situated on the Northeast side of the Inlet on this narrow belt of sand which skirts the coast from the Chesapeake to Florida, more or less close to the mainland, and right here in front of North Carolina, making a considerable Eastern detour, with Cape Hatteras, twelve miles above, at its greatest angle. This belt divides the waters of the Atlantic at this point from three important inland seas or sounds, called Pamlico, Albemarle and Currituck Sounds, respectively. These are connected with the ocean by three inlets, the Topsail, Ocracoke and Hatteras. Two of these are nearly if not quite impassable, and we, thanks to General Wool, masters of the third, hold the key to these important and considerable waters.

The forts are constructed of swamp-turf or sod (peat), brought from some distance above, and no better material

48

can be found to resist either ball or bombshell, it being spongy yet strong and as solid as baled cotton or India rubber. The severity of the hammering that these forts, particularly Fort Hatteras, received from our fleets is evidenced by the great quantity of fragments as well as of the unexpected shells strewn about them; for these lay so thick that it seemed to have literally rained shells, as I presume it did. And yet the forts were hardly marred: scarce a dent can be discovered in their outlines from this terrific storm of iron. Commodore Barron, when told that we had not lost a man in the engagement, could hardly credit the statement, having thought that the taking of these forts would cost us thousands of lives, and it would have if the turf could have prevented shells from dropping inside the walls. I thought it worth while to make a trifling sketch of this plantation where the crop was most flourishing under the walls of Fort Hatteras, as in a year there will not be one specimen left: all that will not be carried away as relics will sink and disappear in the sand. They are thinning out day by day. Around Fort Clark they are not so plenty; still quite a number are strewn about, of which a large proportion are not exploded. One of these, a nine-inch shell, I happened to find in a pool of water back of the Fort, and upon removing the fuse-screw, the powder was found to be perfectly dry so that it might have been used again.

Fort Clark is the Headquarters at present of the forces here, which consist of eight Companies of our Regiment (two remaining at Newport News) and a Company of Regulars, the latter doing garrison duty in Fort Hatteras. Our Regiment is equally divided between this post and Camp Wool, two miles up the Sound, Lieutenant-Colonel Betts, commanding.

September 15th.

Fort Clark is not so considerable a fort as Hatteras, but in some ways more interesting. One of the Columbiads in it is dismounted, the trunnions knocked off and the carriage shattered beautifully, an evidence of rough handling Fort Hatteras can not show, though it sustained the heavier fire, as is proven by the greater number of shells around it. But the chief thing of interest to me is an old French cannon, a brass field-piece cast in Strasburg, 1761, and it is consequently just one hundred years old. An old Revolutionary hero evidently and one that must have played his part to our advantage more or less, or he would not be here now to change hands again on this his centennial year. The piece has the old-fashioned handles, of course, and is lettered and otherwise ornamented with scrolls and designs. The crown of fleur-de-lis on the base is excellent, and would not be uninteresting to art students. Altogether, it has a very quaint and ancient appearance beside the two Dahlgren guns in the fort, which, though similarly mounted, are devoid of ornament, and which are now thought to be, as this centenarian was when cast, I have no doubt, all that is excellent in artillery.

September 20th.

Yesterday was a right joyful day for our boys, for early in the morning we caught sight of the well-known proportions of the " S. R. Spaulding " rounding the Cape, and as we had not heard a word from the North since we arrived here more than a week ago, one may be right sure we were glad at the prospect of letters and papers. The expectation was that the " Spaulding " would bring the two companies B and K of our Regiment from Newport News, but in this we were disappointed, for it seems that, by special request of General Phelps, they were retained as necessary for the safety of the Post. We hear that General Phelps wants General Wool to send the whole Regiment back, as McGruder is still threatening. But with our Regiment, he deems himself capable of resisting any force that McGruder can bring against him. Quite a change in the General's mind since we first landed at the Post, when he called us a set of ——— ————— boys.

I received five letters and a copy of the St. Paul " Daily Press," which last, with one of the letters, was from a Minnesotian at Fortress Monroe, now Sergeant in Company B, U. S. Artillery, and a friend of the Zimmermans in St. Paul, on whose behalf he was to have hunted me up while at the

50

THE LONG ROLL

News, which purpose he regrets that our sudden removal has prevented. One letter was from Sergeant Hodgekins at the Rip Raps; one from Harry Palmer in New York; one from Hudson City, and one from Sister Eva in Mansfield, Ohio. So that I have heard from several different quarters of the globe.

September 28th.

Came off guard this morning, which is a more tedious duty here than at Newport News, simply a camp guard, there being no enemy within sixty or seventy miles probably, and from these, Camp Wool, two miles above, is an effectual shield, from surprise at least. Having then actually nothing of interest to occupy my mind during the long twenty-four hours off and on post, except the novelty of the situation, I turned my attention to the natural formation of the sand bank across which our chain of posts easily stretches. Above Fort Clark this beach or bank is so low as to allow the waves, when they are at all high, to wash over it into the Sound, if they have not time to disappear in the sand, and this sand seems to be composed of nothing but shells and shell particles of marine animals, thrown there by the waves, and by time and the elements ground to powder; and in this, the body of the beach, there are perfect specimens of shells of all sizes, shapes and varieties of color; some of them exceedingly beautiful and curious enough to interest any one however ignorant or indifferent to such things. I have gathered quantities of them and then thrown them away, for though I would like to keep some, I know of no one to whom I could send them. I have seen a drinking-cup here covered by a variety of these smaller shells, and it can be said to be ornamented by Nature's self. But if not more beautiful, perhaps more interesting, are the living inhabitants of the sand.

The sand-crabs or spiders, I know of no other name, differ in size from the largest spider to the ordinary lobster, and while on my post yesterday, one farthest oceanward, I had a good opportunity to watch their movements and noted some of their maneuvers.

They live in holes or burrows in the sand, which it is no

51

trouble for them to dig with their great claws, and to these they hie themselves on the approach of the slightest danger. They run fast and are very hard to catch, as I found out in trying to capture one. I took an opportunity to get between him and his burrow and then made for him, but to my surprise, he put for the beach, and before I could reach him had flung himself into the curling breaker of a great wave. I was surprised at this, of course, but more so when on my post again after sundown, to find the beach lined with them, all enjoying the civilizing luxury of a bath. They sat in rows on the beach waiting for the next wave to come up and break over them, which submergence, it seems, they enjoy with a peculiar pleasure. This, then, is the summering place of the crabs, and they were only enjoying a customary luxury. The moon rose beautifully over the waves later on, and from the way the crabs raced around, one would think they were indulging in a social " hop."

The " Susquehanna " has captured another prize to-day, the second I have seen hauled in while here. The poor craft ran for it, but no go, and she is now at anchor in the Inlet with a prize crew aboard.

The little schooner " Enterprise," at anchor between Forts Clark and Hatteras, is interesting as the prize of our Regiment. This is the vessel Colonel Hawkins captured, as before related.

Monday, September 29th.

Have just weathered a severe storm, one of frequent occurrence, I presume, on this coast. It commenced to blow heavily last Thursday, and with increased vigor Friday; Saturday there was a lull, and now all is quiet again.

We had in our barracks, last night, three shipwrecked sailors who had been caught in the gale in the schooner " Neptune's Car " (from Carthage, Cuba, with a cargo of sugar for Philadelphia). They were driven on the breakers about twelve miles above this point. They struck about seven o'clock, Friday evening, remained fast till one the next morning, with the seas washing over them, tearing through the cabin windows and washing out the lights and playing smash generally. About

52

this time, John Maine jumped overboard with a line and gained the shore, and by means of the line, all hands, seven men, were rescued from their unpleasant if not perilous position. They groped around for some time and finally stumbled on to our camp, surprised enough, too, at the new state of affairs here. Maine was quartered in our bunk last night. He is an intelligent man and a fine specimen of the American sailor, very quiet and unassuming, and, it seems to me, with more earnestness of character than we usually associate with men of his class. The " Neptune's Car " has only shared the fate of hundreds that have gone before her on this treacherous coast. There are some thirty wrecks visible from this point to Cape Henry, not quite destroyed by the elements or buried in the sand.

Tuesday, October 1st.

Secured a pass yesterday, and in company of messmate Kirwin visited Camp Wool and such other places of interest as we managed to find on the part of the island we surveyed. Came back under arrest, as it seems we had unwittingly strayed outside of the outer line of pickets.

Brought back seven sketches with me, chiefly little rural scenes which surprised me here and there during our ramble, with a strange musty sort of beauty, nestling under the low range of verdure barely visible from our camp.

The trees skirting the ocean beach are of a stunted growth usually with wide bushy tops; the advance line taking the brunt of all the old ocean's gales and protecting a more valuable crop of pines and other species on the inner side. In some instances, this guard has been overpowered by the storms and swept away; the stems broken off; the tops buried under an avalanche of sand, through which they now present the pitiful figure of blackened stumps protruding, perishable monuments, as it were, of their former selves, when they flourished and made things green around them.

Everything on the Island seems to be devoid of paint— dwellings, barns and windmills, of which latter there are a greater number than I supposed were in existence in the whole country; so that the houses are all dismal enough and are only saved from complete lack of interest by a certain mossy coat which forms on everything except the uncompromising sand, and lends a gray green tinge, which puts all things here from the hand of man, in harmony with Nature in a very short time.

Wild grapes, larger and richer than many tame varieties in the North, are here in great abundance, nourished as much, it would seem, by the salt sea breeze as by the juices pumped out of the sandy soil by the roots. Figs also grow here, but are not yet ripe. I sketched a green fig with its surroundings of leaves, the first I have seen in its natural state. It was our intention to go as far as the wreck of the " Neptune's Car " and then visit friends Hughson and Vanderburg (Company D), but this part of our program was spoiled by our arrest and peremptory return to Fort Clark.

Wednesday, October 2d.

Our camp has just been startled by the intelligence that the tug " Fanny " has been captured by the enemy while under way with quartermaster's and commissary stores for the Twentieth Indiana Regiment at Chicomocomico. Well, we have been quiet so long, what if we should have a little excitement, say I.

The accounts of the capture of the " Fanny " seem to be confused, but all agree that her crew, consisting of nine or ten men of our Regiment, with a larger number of the Twentieth, were taken prisoners. She was surrounded by two or three of the enemy's schooners, so reads one version; was shamefully deserted by her sailing master, was run aground and so compelled to surrender, but not without first putting seven balls into one of the schooners, out of the nine she fired, and then throwing as many stores overboard as possible before being taken. The other story runs: the " Fanny " was taken with all on board, by three small gunboats, while on a shoal unloading in boats, opposite Colonel Brown's camp at Chicomocomico and without making any attempt at resistance.

One of our men captured was a messmate of mine, Beith

54

by name, a good enough fellow, but lazy. He could never be made to drill as an infantry soldier, and actually compelled his superior to detail him for artillery duty whenever it was required, it being impossible to do anything else with him—hence his position as gunner on board the " Fanny " when captured.

While at Newport News, I had once carefully washed a vest, a portion of our full-dress uniform, and hung it on some bushes back of the tent to dry. Meanwhile I was detailed for some kind of duty, and when I came back the vest was gone, and not a person in our mess seemed to know where it had gone to. Now, as it was impossible to appear on dress-parade without a vest, I naturally became somewhat anxious to know what had become of it, and failed not to stew and brew about the missing article of clothing and inquire of every one thereabout for it, and to search high and low, all in vain, *until*, it being nearly time to fall in for Parade, it occurred to Beith, that he had taken some one's vest from behind the tent with which to *patch his pantaloons*—Je-ru-sa-lem! Well—although Beith was heavy, in fact built like an ox, and he could have made nothing of me with one sweep of his huge fist as easily as an elephant with one step of his foot, supreme passion will sometimes, for just one sublime moment, usurp the place of strength. I struck Beith and knocked him over. That is, I suppose, I made him lose his equilibrium and he tumbled over, very nearly, by the way, taking the tent with him as he fell, with all the appurtenances thereunto belonging. What would have become of me had Beith been made angry by his fall, I shall never know, for it happened that Lieutenant Russell passed just then, and had us both put in the guard-house for fighting. But Beith, with that presence of mind which I guarantee stood him in good stead on the " Fanny," restraining any hasty action calculated to roil the temper of the enemy, did not neglect on this occasion to put a pack of cards in his pocket, which, as soon as we were safe in the guard-house, we proceeded to discuss, continuing with great animosity, until we were released the next morning.

THE LONG ROLL

Sunday, October 5th.

As I write, our Regiment and the Twentieth Indiana are on Dress Parade in front of Fort Clark. I have been excused from attendance on account of a forced march from here last Friday night to the relief of the Twentieth, which was then supposed to be hemmed in and fighting its way through a force of the enemy landed below it, to cut off its retreat to this point. About four o'clock Friday afternoon, Captain Jardine came in hot haste from Chicomocomico with the intelligence that the Twentieth was attacked and surrounded at that place and its retreat cut off. By five o'clock our detachment marched off up the beach, the "Monticello" at the same time steaming with us on the ocean side. The "Coses" and the "Putnam," two vessels of light draught, were to have gone up the Sound, and why they did not I can not comprehend. These vessels were made ready for action, and considerable indignation was felt by the men on board, as well as by us on shore, at their inactivity. At Camp Wool we were joined by Colonel Betts' command, and with the exhilarating idea of going to the rescue, all went merrily till about midnight, when the rapid march in the sand, which sank under us at every step to a depth of three or four inches, began to tell on us.

It was a very romantic march to me. After passing the long open beach above Camp Wool, we entered woods more solid than any on the lower part of the Island, and the night being extremely dark, I could at times scarcely distinguish two file-leaders ahead. But the weariness soon became oppressive, and when the canteen gave out, the men began to drop. I asked my companion for a drink once, for my tongue seemed to be parched; it was refused and I did not ask again, but contented myself with chewing the leaves of the overhanging trees, which were covered with a heavy dew. When we had made thirteen miles, the column halted and we turned in as best we could under the trees. As I was, by this time, suffering from an unusual degree of thirst, I could not think of sleep, but with cup and canteen, sallied out in search of water, hoping my good fortune would lead me to some habitation with a well,

56

Fort Clark (Hatteras)

Forts Hatteras and Clark

PLATE IX

Rebel Tugboat " Teazon " Attacking

PLATE X

vannah " off Newport News, Virginia

Old French Cannon at Fort Clark

Dismounted Gun at Fort Clark

PLATE XI

but there was no such luck for me. It is true I fell into a sort of a marsh, after a half-hour's groping in the intense darkness, but as the water was not only lukewarm but brackish, I did not feel much relieved. I returned to our bivouac much disgusted, wrapped my overcoat about me, and slept soundly until morning.

I awakened, stiff from the fatigue of the night previous and with a teeth-chattering chill caused by the sand, which, however dry and hot in the sun, is cold and damp at night. A little "Double-quick" set this matter right and after a march of three or four miles, we met the Indiana Company, or rather came upon them by Cape Hatteras Light House. To this point they had retreated from Chicomocomico, fearing a force would land below them and cut them off, and as they had not a single piece of artillery with which to reply to the Rebel gunboats (seven in all), I think they did wisely in not attempting a stand. They lost some seventy-five men, with, of course, everything in the shape of camp equipage. It seems that, while endeavoring to save as much as possible of their property, they were surprised by a land force from above, and in their disorganized state could offer no resistance. Their Sergeant-Major is reported to have killed a Captain, and their Major to have shot one or two of the men. The Sutler was ordered to stop by a squad, but he took to his heels and ran the gauntlet of seven bullets.

We have since been informed by some of the inhabitants of Chicomocomico that the enemy pursued the Twentieth until told that a force was on the way to re-enforce it, and by this means picked up stragglers and all those who were unable to keep up during the march of unusual severity. Colonel Brown was downhearted at his ill luck and felt sore at Colonel Hawkins for having exposed him to disaster without sufficient protection. His first words to our Colonel on meeting him, were, "You sent me up there with my hands tied!" And well he might complain, in my opinion, for the policy of having an outpost some forty miles from its base of supplies, without a cannon or the protection of a gunboat, and within hailing distance of the enemy, is certainly questionable. It is true, New-port News was occupied and held by a Regiment, but that Regiment was never for a moment left from under the guns of the " Monticello," and here were two light-draught gunboats equal to cope with anything the enemy has in these waters, and with nothing else to do. These vessels were so unaccount-ably inactive on this occasion, however, that perhaps they were kept at the Inlet for some reason that I am not able to fathom.

There was certainly every reason in the world to suppose they would co-operate with us; had they done so, we would probably have re-occupied Chicomocomico—if not permanently, at least long enough to teach the Rebels a lesson; but as they did not, there was nothing for us to do but to turn about, and cover the retreat in the same way we did at Big Bethel.

The " Monticello " was not to be cheated out of her share anyway. Steaming up the Atlantic to a position opposite the Rebel fleet, she shelled the camp and vicinity in a right lively manner. One of her shells, as I watched, either struck one of the gunboats or so near it as to perceptibly swing the vessel to and fro for a moment.

The " Monticello " blazed away all the afternoon and then landed a force that stayed on shore all night. This I was told by one of the Indiana men who escaped by swimming to her, after dodging the enemy through the woods. She returned to her station opposite here, this morning.

We stopped long enough at the Light House to rest our men and for me to get my fill of grapes, which were splendid. I got a sketch of the Light House, but I did not feel able to travel an extra mile or two to ascend, though I very much wanted to. The only thing I have in my sketch-book beside the Light, is a vine-covered cluster of trees grown in the shape of a little Gothic church.

I can not be blamed for thinking it pretty, for in the deep twilight as I saw it, so perfect was it in outline, I could easily imagine a little ivy-covered English church, such as is often seen in pictures.

58

THE LONG ROLL

October 9th.

Information just received that an Indianian is at the house of one of the inhabitants, sick from exposure, having passed some days in the swamps without food while getting away from the Rebs.

Camp Wool,
Sunday, October 13th.

Since my last, the "Spaulding" has made her weekly visit, bringing this time, General Mansfield, who is now in command here. The first fruit of this change is that our whole Regiment is now at Camp Wool, and the Indiamans in occupation of our old quarters at Fort Clark. Our Company has been assigned a very pretty spot for camping-ground, whereon we pitched last Friday evening, on a little dry hill just large enough for the Company, covered with trees and surrounded by a marsh or bog. In this respect it is a small fortress by itself, being surrounded by water on all sides but the rear, where we have a narrow dry passage to the beach—and even this is amply protected by the Company cook-house.

My messmate and I have pitched our tent on a spot under some trees in front of a clear stream of water in the marsh, which is very pretty, though I presume not the healthiest in the world; but then, if one is after health, I think it best to get off the Island of Hatteras as speedily as possible. There are a couple of young wild ducks swimming in the pond as I write : they have been coming and going ever since we came, evidently much annoyed at our proceedings. I would advise these young ducks to fly, if I could quack as they do.

Wednesday, October 16th.

General Mansfield has returned to Fortress Monroe, evidently in pure disgust at the situation, and a Brigadier-General (Williams) is in command. This Brigadier does not deem it beneath his dignity to make the most of the situation at Hatteras, or of his authority as Commander of a Regiment and a half, for of all the disciplinarians in the world, he is the most

THE LONG ROLL

" disciplinious." The following routine of exercises was read on Dress Parade last night, and has been to-day entered upon:

Reveille	-	-	-	-	4	A.M.
Constant exercise under arms until Fatigue						
Call	-	-	-	.	4 : 30	"
Breakfast Call	-	-	-	-	5	"
Dress Parade	-	-	-	,	6	"
Guard Mount	-	-	-	-	7	"
Morning Drill	-	-	-		9–11	"
Dinner	-	-	-		12–1	P.M.
Drill	-	-	-		1–2	"
Drill	-	-	-		4–4 : 30	"
Dress Parade	-	-	-		5	"
Supper	-	-	-	-	6	"
Inspection of Arms	-	-			7 : 30	"
Tattoo	-	-	-	-	8	"
Taps	-	-	-		8 : 30	"

This is indeed a bill of fare for every day in the week, including, I presume, Sundays. Still there may be a grain of wisdom in it all, for this constant activity, although harassing, must be healthy, and as long as we must occupy this sand-bank, health is the main thing.

Five sails, said to be Rebel gunboats from up the Sound, were in sight yesterday, and it may be that to guard against surprise is one motive that prompted Williams in this severe order of exercise. Aside from this, we are better quartered now than ever, and are pretty well fed. We have just been furnished with new tents, which are generally pitched end to end back of the old ones, thus furnishing quarters doubly as commodious as usual.

Fort Clark,
Sunday, October 20th.

The fact is, Camp Wool was more pretty than healthy. One hundred and twenty-five sick at the hospital, of whom three died while there. Had to retreat. Struck tents yesterday morning and arrived at Fort Clark in a heavy rainstorm. Most of our men got soaking wet. I got in with some Indianians and had a most excellent cup of coffee. Got our tent pitched yesterday afternoon, and also a floor put in it, so that we enjoyed a splendid night's rest.

Our Child of the Regiment is not the graceful and bewitching Vivandiere we see in pictures, is not a girl at all in fact, but a boy—and an Irish boy at that, if one can trust the name, which is John Murphy. He is nine years old and believes he has a mother somewhere, and that he had a father once, though of this fact John Murphy is not certain.

Our Charley, while in New York recruiting, enlisted one Thompson from Corporal Thompson of our Company, formerly of the Twelfth New York Militia, then just from the seat of war, and to him he found Johnny clinging, and with Thompson and the Sergeant, Johnny came to Newport News, after having shared the fortunes of the Twelfth during their three or four months' service. Thompson found the boy in Washington originally, growing wild, at any rate, not being able to give any account of himself, and since then has ever cared for him kindly. He keeps him as clean as a pin, and does not allow him to swear. A good ending may be a questionable prophecy from this doubtful beginning, but stranger things have happened. If he is a diamond from the rubbish heap, he is a tough one, that is certain. On the late march to the Light House, he kept up with the Regiment every step of the way, carrying two haversacks and a canteen, and sleeping at night under cover of Thompson's blanket, enduring everything with greater cheerfulness than did many of his grown-up comrades.

Monday, October 21st.

Fort Clark is not now what it was when here last, for the restless energy of General Williams has been more conspicuous than at Camp Wool, for while we have been drilled in and out of season, the Indianians have been kept equally busy at a breastwork of sand in barrels, and turf, which now extends across the whole Island, and rumor has it that this indomitable,

61

unconquerable, infernal Brigadier intends to cut a canal outside of this work from the Atlantic to the Pamlico. Then let the ten thousand North Carolinians come on—if a storm, that is, should not in the meantime, both batter down his works and fill up his canal!

October 26th.

Among the letters received by last mail was one from Sergeant Hodgekins at the Rip Raps. The Sergeant mentions among other matters the fact of one ————, a deserter from McGruder's forces, having been released by the General's orders and allowed to go North. It was through this man, I learned, that McGruder had really been in earnest about attacking us on the night of the Seventh of August last. That, with that intention, he had marched from Yorktown with all his available forces, some seven thousand men fully equipped for an attack on our works, carrying, among other things, one hundred scaling-ladders; but that, when within some five miles of our post, he had called a council of war, which determined the taking of it impracticable, or if not, at least so to hold; so he marched by us and burned the village of Hampton, hoping thereby to draw out either Phelps or Butler.

That Phelps was prepared and ready to receive his old classmate warmly, I have some personal knowledge, having been on the inner guard during the night, and posted where I could overlook the General's headquarters. About dark, the " Savannah " moved up the stream and took up a position opposite the water-battery. At eleven o'clock, two brass cannon came up from the Fort by express, and during the night the General was about alone, moving quietly as a shadow from place to place. He was leaning over the breastworks when the flames from Hampton lighted up the sky, and he turned to a soldier on post and said, " Some one must be very drunk to do that," after which, I am told, he went to his quarters and to bed.

Phelps had expected an attack this time. The day before he had taken an unusual interest in drilling the artillery squads, and had the infantry exercised in all the probable movements

62

THE LONG ROLL

of repelling the enemy, and besides the usual twenty-four hours' notice to quit, which McGruder invariably sends, "there are," Beith had heard the General say, "more signs of an attack now than ever before." It was while McGruder was burning Hampton that the man deserted, managing to steal away toward Fortress Monroe, giving Butler information of forces, movements, etc.

Monday, October 28th.

Our Company seems to be not only unfortunate in the choice of officers, but in the officers chosen for us as well. Captain Coppault, certainly a splendid drillmaster and with every outward appearance of a soldier, turns out a failure in the field, and has resigned. Lieutenant Russell is not much better, and perhaps ought to resign. Flemming is the best of men, but too good a fellow for a disciplinarian, and our First Sergeant is so ridiculously boyish that all his discipline loses its effect. Second Sergeant Peret, the slave of a clique which runs the Company, dares not say his soul is his own, and not an intelligent officer in our tribe, except it be Corporal Davis of the Color Guard, and he, being an artist who cares nothing for this military business except for the subjects it furnishes his pencil, is neither appreciated nor understood. And now we are to have one Barnard for our Captain. This man, for shooting a subordinate in the First New York Volunteers, had to fly for his life, but instead of resigning, he was transferred to this Regiment. Colonel Hawkins refused to recognize him, however, and he is, in consequence thereof, under arrest. Lieutenant-Colonel Betts has assigned Barnard to our Company to fill the vacancy caused by the resignation of Captain Coppault.

It does not suit the temper of our fellows to be commanded much, anyway; and for one of our own Regiment even, unless he carried a pretty strong hand, it might be an unpleasant task to take hold of Company I, and that being the case, the feeling of the Company as a whole can easily be imagined. The idea of being controlled by a man for whom most of us felt an abhorrence, seemed entirely intolerable. This feeling, sharpened

63

THE LONG ROLL

by the notion that we would be submitting to another indignity put upon us, assisted by the contemptuous opinion we held of Barnard as to his bravery, combined to give the Captain a reception such as perhaps no other officer had ever before had from his subordinates. A variety of insults were heaped upon him openly, the moment he entered our quarters, and last Thursday, when he came out to take command, the Company refused to a man to obey his orders. And this, too, after he had made a speech to the effect that the insulting remarks he had heard must be stopped, and that he would shoot another man under the same circumstances, etc.; but all in vain—our boys insisted that they did not know him and would not obey, and he was obliged to retire, leaving the command to Lieutenant Russell.

During that day he was burned in effigy, a caricature was made on his tent, and a variety of greater indignities suggested, should he ever attempt to take command. On Dress Parade, a general order was read assigning him to our Company with every circumstance of name and rank, which only served to exasperate our men the more. Russell did all he could in a few remarks, laying down the law, but his little speech was instantly followed by three cheers for Russell and three groans for Barnard, and that night the Company's quarters seemed a perfect bedlam, so that the poor man dared not step out of his tent. This was the last of Captain Barnard. In the morning, the Major sent in a request that the Company cease their demonstrations, as Captain Barnard had already sent in his resignation.

A rumor to the effect that we are to proceed to Chicomocomico at once is strengthened by the fact that the cooks are preparing two days' rations, by order of General Williams.

Camp Wool,
Friday, November 8th.

We are again at Camp Wool in our old Company Quarters, but expect to be back at Fort Clark to-morrow. Comments on these tedious and objectless counter-marchings between the two places, I do not care to indulge in, for fear it might work me

64

THE LONG ROLL

up to too great an indignation. Suffice it to say, that our General does not seem to be of one mind two minutes at a time. He is apparently at child's play with a lot of wooden soldiers, no sooner having them arranged in one way, than he wishes to see how they will look in another, and so he keeps them constantly on the move.

Day before yesterday, I was detailed for the Hut Picket with some twelve more of our Company, under Sergeant Hill. The hut now used as the advance picket station on the Island is an old wrecking-house built of poles and reeds, and it is an indifferent protection from frost, wind or rain, as I have to some extent discovered. During the day, one man on post, is sufficient, as he can sweep the open sand-bank for a distance of six or eight miles, but at night, it is necessary to have a string of guards across the Island.

The day passed very comfortably around the fire, which, tradition says, has never been out since the hut has been in use as a picket-house. There we sat and slept and smoked and chatted away the hours, until it was time to place the posts for the night.

The wind set in strong from the Northeast that night, and it was not only very cold, but in sweeping down the open sand-bank it carried with it a constant storm of fine sand, which pelted away unmercifully all night long. The sand was carried along with such force that whenever it struck an exposed part of face or hands, it tingled or stung like Virginia mosquitoes, or the bite of horse-flies in cloudy weather, so that I found it necessary to draw my cap down over my eyes to protect them from the continual danger of having them put out. I found my time on post that night more tedious and unpleasant than that duty has ever been before, and that I was not an exceptional case may be inferred from the fact that one of the men on post after me, called for a relief after an hour's time, declaring himself incapable or unwilling to stand it. A soldier has the absolute right to call for relief if he finds it impossible to keep awake, or from any other cause feels himself unable to guard his post. To add to my misery, I

was plagued with a parching thirst which it seemed impossible
to satisfy, and when I was relieved, I found not a drop of water
in the hut in either jug or canteen; and as the idea of going
to sleep without something to drink was simply unbearable,
I took the jug and sallied forth for a fresh supply, although
it meant a distance of a mile or more. Dark as mud. Lost
my way. Think I was half-asleep. The creek was swollen to
treble its usual proportion by the waves of the Atlantic washing
over the beach and pouring into it. I went up and down the
stream to find a crossing. I staggered from the want of sleep
and suffered with the intense thirst. Finally found a four-inch
scantling, lost my balance of course, and was in to my waist.
Waded over and " found myself where I did not know I was."
I am persuaded I must have been asleep. After groping around
for about a half an hour longer, I ran against a house. It looked
as old unpainted houses always look in the dead of night, as if
it might contain either sleep or death. I found a well, from
which I filled myself and my jug. Tried the scantling again,
but with worse luck this time, for I went in to the armpits.
Did I know of having tasted anything stronger than water
for at least eight months, I would say I was drunk. I reached
the hut wet through and pierced to pieces with the Northeast
wind, but I had the jug, and I drank again and again as fondly
as any old toper might a pet beverage of his, and spent the
rest of the night drying my clothes and looking out for daylight.

About the time we were relieved from the hut, the " Spaulding " came in from Fortress Monroe, it was thought to take
us away from this place, but as it has turned out, to take instead
the Indiana Company. I expect to be at Fort Clark again
to-morrow. Would be there now, in fact, were it not that
I am placed here as camp guard, for three Companies of our
Regiment are ordered down there to take the place of the
Indiana garrison.

Meanwhile, I am my own lord and master, and have been killing time by such employments as reading, writing and drawing;
washing, mending and eating; smoking, lounging and sleeping
till all these are equally played out, and I can do nothing at all.

66

THE LONG ROLL

November 9th.

I am here yet and probably will be until to-morrow. I would not feel so badly if I only knew how to employ my time. The most intensely interesting subject under discussion just now with us is the question of being kept all Winter on this unchristian sand-bank. I think, perhaps, if we could unanimously decide in the negative, the Government might take us away. What to do with this place is evidently a puzzle to those who ought to know. It must be held, of course, but it strikes me there are more ways of holding and blockading this inlet than the one now pursued. And as I am at least General of these pages, and do likewise command my own thoughts, I hope I am not presuming too much by venturing to give my opinion.

I would strengthen Fort Hatteras if need be, and blow up Fort Clark. It might have been important to the Rebels, who had a navy to contend with, but it can be of no earthly use to us; besides, it is liable to be washed away at any time, as the last storm fully proved, which not only swept away the camp of the Indianians, but so completely demolished the works they had made that hardly a sign of them is to be seen, so I am told. This being the case, of what use is it? Blow her up, I say, and leave the Inlet to Fort Hatteras and a couple of gunboats. It won't run away, unless washed away by the Atlantic. Then let us go, for God's sake, where we can be of some service to our country. If we are to be, as it is said, an advance guard, it is likely that the expedition just going down the coast will give us places enough to hold, more important than this, and fighting enough too, if that is wanted, and I, for my part, certainly want to see some more active service than we get here.

Fort Clark,
Tuesday, November 12th.

I finally got away from Camp Wool last Sunday night where I had so much time to myself that, when I came down here, I must needs be immediately put on guard duty, from which I have just been relieved.

The General's works here across the Island have been carried by storm, erased, leveled and scattered to the winds! So that the everlasting plowshare, if there were the slightest use for such an implement here, might pass over the sand without knowing from any evidence except it be intuitive, and quite poetical, that it was turning over classic ground. And now, the terrible work of demolishment over, the enemy has retired to his own country, calmed in a measure and satisfied, at any rate, for a while. It must be some satisfaction, however, that it is the Atlantic Ocean, and no human power, that has beaten General Williams.

To my notion the same enemy may come again with redoubled fury, and it is to be feared more, if the safety of these forts is essential to the safety of the country, than the terrible ten thousand now mustering on the other side of the Pamlico determined to retake Hatteras or die.

The "Spaulding" is again in sight, and her decks are evidently crowded with troops, whether for this post or not we can but guess, but should they be, I presume *we will have to go back to Camp Wool.* If the "Spaulding" only brings good news with her troops, I am willing she should bring as many as she likes. We have had good news from the South, now let us have equally good tidings from the North, and we will all "arise and sing."

The "Monticello," on her way North to-day, just stopped long enough to tell us that the result of the naval expedition which passed down the coast some time ago has been the capture of two forts at Port Royal and the occupation of the City of Beaufort, Georgia, which, I presume, is but a prologue to the main play destined to be at Charleston.

Camp Wool (Again),
November 12th.

Came off guard this morning at Fort Clark, struck tents and marched up here and pitched in our old quarters. Have a long letter ready for the returning "Spaulding" to my sister Eva in Mansfield, Ohio, who is now on her way to our old home in Minnesota to visit Father, whose health is not as good as usual. The "Spaulding" brought the Forty-eighth Pennsylvania, who are to take the place of the Indianians, but no news of any consequence from the North. No news is better than bad news, I suppose, but it seems awfully dull that way—along the lines, I mean.

Thursday, November 14th.

Have not been stationed at Fort Clark since the date of my last writing. Have seen the New York "Tribune" of the Eighth. It contains a letter from their correspondent at Hatteras concerning our troubles in the affair with Captain Barnard, and the version given is the popular one with us, and our boys are much rejoiced thereat. I saw the correspondent and talked with him while he was there, and I particularly liked his quiet and pleasant manner. He justifies our Company for refusing to obey Captain Barnard and the feeling of the Regiment in general, and he does full justice to Colonel Hawkins, who is yet under arrest, it is presumed, for insubordination. Our Colonel has, by his spirited action in this matter, regained much of his one-time lost popularity.

Captain Barnard has nominal command, but leaves the active duties of his position to his subordinates, being, in fact, rarely seen in our Company quarters. The feeling is so strong against him, that should he ever go into action with us, I would fear for his life.

Afternoon.

Our gunboats are all outside on some business or other, and, as usual, when such is the case, the enemy is "snooking" around. As I write, a gunboat of theirs is disappearing on the horizon, evidently reconnoitering. She came within five miles of us and sent one of her compliments at Hatteras in general, for it seemed to be designed for no place in particular. Tom Corbin "of Ours" replied with a couple of shots, but they were as compliments returned. It was amusing to see a couple of fishing-boats at our little wharf run up their canvas and make for other waters. They evidently did not want to be in the way in case of a "little affair."

69

THE LONG ROLL

We have heard distant firing all day from up the Sound, probably from Roanoke Island or vicinity, where the enemy is said to be in force.

Sunday, November 17th.

On the Hut Picket again. We came down this morning via Pamlico Sound, before as fine a breeze as ever drove a "Cooner," and in a sailboat which was yesterday at Roanoke Island in the service of the Confederate States of America.

About daybreak, the Windmill Picket below us discovered a sail evidently from some point on the mainland, and when within hailing distance the strange craft was easily persuaded to come ashore. The single mariner proved to be a negro, Ben, from Roanoke Island, who started the night before and succeeded in getting out to sea without being observed, and sailing all night, had, as he calculated, reached Hatteras this morning.

Fortunately for the success of his adventure, the weather was very heavy during the night. His boat had taken in so much water that he had to bail out four times, and he was wet to the skin and very cold. This was why the Windmill Picket brought him down to us, for they being housed, have no fire. It proved quite a treat for us during the slow morning hours, for we did not fail to get from him all he knew, and this was not a little, for he proved himself a person of more than ordinary intelligence, and he answered our questions in a way that convinced us that he was reliable.

According to Ben, there are on Roanoke Island three Regiments, two from this State and one from Georgia, and among these men are many who serve unwillingly, if not under compulsion. There was an order for an advance on us last week, but so many "skulked" to get rid of the expedition that it was given up. The enemy is fortifying the Island, erecting batteries and mounting guns. They have five gunboats, among which the "Fanny" is one of their best. The little brass piece she carried while "one of ours" has been replaced by a heavier gun. One of the Regiments wear overcoats like ours, thanks to the Indianians. They are supplied with Indian meal, bread and coffee, and are paid in Confederate State scrip, of which

70

THE LONG ROLL

Ben gave a specimen to Corporal Downy. It is printed on a sort of brown manilla paper and very poorly executed. Ben was owned by a man in North Carolina who has two sons in the army at Roanoke, one of whom Ben was serving while there.

We anxiously questioned him as to any one being found answering to the description of our Sergeant John McGlinchy. Friends had hoped that he might have been picked up by some one on the Island. The last we saw of him, he was in a small boat on the Sound, and Ben having heard nothing, we are forced to believe that he was driven out in the gale and swamped.

When the new guard came on, we took passage in Ben's "Cooner" and sailed with a "spanking breeze" to camp, which is decidedly more pleasant than the heavy walk through the eternal sand.

The "Spaulding" is in with another mail. Three letters for me and some papers. Good news from both North and South. We have now the complete details of the taking of Port Royal, also accounts of a victory in Kentucky at Pikesville, where four hundred Confederates are said to have been killed and two thousand prisoners taken, among whom were two Generals, Williams and Haws. The Privateer "Sumter" is captured, and Mason and Slidell taken in the "Nashville." "So much for Buckingham."

Thursday, November 21st.

Four of our Companies, commanded by Lieutenant-Colonel Betts, yesterday engaged a like force under Major Kimball, and got "licked like the Devil," all owing to the incompetency of the Second Lieutenant of Company A commanding the Reserve. We advanced within a quarter of a mile of Kimball's force. A company of skirmishers, to reconnoiter, advances, deploys and opens fire on Kimball. He returns the fire. We advance to the skirmish line, who then close intervals. Forward in column sustaining a heavy fire from the enemy. At a distance of an eighth of a mile, he charges on us with a yell. Colonel Betts promptly commands, "About face! Double-quick!" and

71

gallops back to take charge of the Reserve, whose volley is to drive the enemy and behind which we are to re-form. But the Reserve, where, oh where was it? Why, bless us, when the order "About face" was given, they turned also and ran so much faster than any of us that there was no stop to them, and so our retreat was a total rout. Thus endeth the first lesson.

Another exchange of compliments yesterday between a Rebel Gunboat and one of our tugs. As they both seemed anxious to keep out of range, it is presumed that no one was hurt.

Monday, November 25th.

Have just come in from another twenty-four-hour picket duty, this time on what is called the "Church Picket," which is accounted one of the best to be on in cold weather, and yet I feel the effects of what little sleep I got. There seems to be something about this infernal sand-bank calculated for "chills and fever," for even in hot weather the sand is damp and cold and will chill through any frame that must recline on it.

Brought three sketches back from this siege: one of the picket station, one of the church with the graves of the members of our Regiment buried here, and one of the little schoolhouse.

About eight o'clock last night, it fell to my lot to escort two of our men, found outside the lines without the countersign, to Camp Wool, a distance of a good mile. Coming back it was so dark in some parts of the woods that I could hardly see my hands before me. And as a sentinel was fired upon a day or two ago under circumstances which would seem to prove spies about, if not in our very camp, I hope I will not be blamed if I kept my musket at an easy "ready" with a sharp look-out even on the pigs and cows that happened along the lonely way.

Old Stein lives close by the Church Picket, a grizzly, bearded, salt-sea fossil, about sixty years of age, and still following actively his calling, that of a fisherman, as indeed is every one else on the Island. He comes out to smoke and chat with us occasionally, and the following information I have gathered from his conversation.

He was born on the Island, and lived where Fort Hatteras

72

A Hattcras Landscape

The Church Picket

PLATE XIV

Camp Wool Hatteras from the Windmill Picket

PLATE XV

The Breastwork at Trent

Church Picket at Trent

PLATE XVI

Moonlight Scene at Trent
By John Davis

On Duncan Creek

PLATE XVII

is now, until he married. Before the "great flood of '46," the open beach between Camp Wool and Fort Hatteras, also that between Trent and Duncan Creek (the one I fell into twice in one night), was as flourishing with vegetation as any other part of the Island. A stray Northeast wind prevailed for two weeks without cessation, and swelled the breakers to such a size that they finally washed over these parts, carrying with every one, immense volumes of water into the Sound, and tearing up great trees and every other vestige of vegetation. Finally, the waters of the Sound raised to such a height that a great part of the Island was submerged and the inhabitants were compelled to take to the sand-hills that had been thrown up by the winds along the Atlantic side. And when the waters subsided, Hatteras Inlet was cut out and the fairest portion of the Island laid under a desert of sand in which vegetation has not yet been able to show any signs of revival. From whence, Mr. Stein comes to the remarkable conclusion that the Island of Hatteras is fated; "for," said he, "this Island came out of the sea, and it will go back to the sea; in another age, it will be only a reef like those on the coast of Florida."

Some time ago, I found an old Geography, published, I think, in 1833, which was incomprehensible to me then, but which I now find explained by Mr. Stein. That work described these Islands on the coast of North Carolina, but no Hatteras Inlet. Ocracoke was then the only Inlet navigable for vessels. Now this is made plain, and the reputation of the old work re-established. "And so much learned in one day," I remarked as the old man put a fresh coal on his pipe and went to see to his nets in the Sound.

Wednesday, November 27th.

One of Sergeant McGlinchy's party (of three, sometime since drowned), Thomas M. Golding, was a few days ago found washed ashore opposite Fort Clark, and he was buried in a little sand-hill back of our quarters. The members of his Company (F) have taken great pains to fence in and decorate his grave, with such materials as Nature has at hand, in a very beautiful and artistic manner—a touching tribute to his memory, as well as evidence that his comrades feel his loss and knew his worth as a man. I knew Golding well. He was one of the twenty-four " of Ours " at the Rip Raps, where I learned to respect him and became acquainted with some points in his history. A carpenter as well as an engineer by trade, he had once been in the employ of the Chicago and Milwaukee Railroad Company, and for a time had run an engine on that road. If my memory serves me, he had known Squire Hoisington in Chicago. He was one of the best of men, strictly temperate, and moral in all his ways. Never noisy or offensive, but an earnest soldier as well as man. And—here he is buried on Hatteras Bank. In the world, of course, but still it does seem a strange fate to be buried here.

Trent, November 28th.
Thanksgiving Day, 1861.

Having had it in my mind for some time to visit a detachment of our men at Trent, I applied to Captain Barnard for a pass. Now, it seems, two men had just come in from Trent under arrest, whom it was necessary to replace, and so I was ordered to report there for duty instead of pleasure, and here I am.

Our men, about one hundred, are encamped around a church which they have fortified by throwing up a small breastwork so as to enclose the front or entrance to the building, and so make of it a sort of barrack for the garrison, and also command the road. Meanwhile, the church is used only as a guard-house. The men are camped around in huts constructed of pine logs simply thrown into a letter A and covered with pine fir, which furnishes a very rude comfort indeed, but more warmth, I am told, than the church building.

This serves at once as our advance post on the Island, it being only about five miles from Camp Wool, and as a protecting post for the inhabitants in case of raids of the enemy.

November 29th.

I am to-day on picket about a mile from Camp, and my post is on the road that is the most advanced on the Island.

74

THE LONG ROLL

Picket duty is not very strict here, it being only necessary to look out for the enemy. Sketched a little scene on the Pamlico on the inside of an envelope back. It might be made into a moonlight scene and a pretty one.

Camp Wool,
Saturday, November 30th.

Back again. I was taken sick on post at Trent, between twelve and two this morning, and was relieved from duty. The fact is, I had indulged in too many baked sweet potatoes. I offered to stay and make up my time this morning, but the Corporal of the guard would not let me. When I arrived at Camp, I found the two men from below, reported for duty, so, I was ordered back to my Company. I did not come away, however, without a sketch of the breastwork and also of the Trent Mill. Have been excused from duty to-day, and have spent the time in quarters as it hath seemed good unto me.

Sunday Evening, December 1st.

Thain and I have spent a pleasant evening with Corporal Davis and Sergeant Jackson in their tent. Davis is our artist, and possesses extraordinary genius for one so young. He was in the employ of the American Banknote Company when the war broke out, and it opened such a field for adventure and study that he could not resist. I took great pleasure in looking over his sketches from the recent trip to Cord'oke, which by the way was not only romantic, but adventuresome. Davis accompanied the expedition as artist, and relates that they were chased in a sailboat by two Confederate steamers, but by skill of the pilot and his intimate acquaintance with the waters, they succeeded in getting behind a reef and out of range. Davis might have given more information quite as interesting, as to the whereabouts of the enemy, their number, strength and doings, but he had been instructed not to do so.

He visited the camping-ground of the Twentieth Indiana at Chicomocomico, and explained the situation with the help of an excellent sketch. He thinks Colonel Brown, with more presence of mind, might have stood his ground.

75

THE LONG ROLL

Davis gave me some instruction in my favorite pastime. I need to show more decisive shading in my pencilings, make my objects stronger and in sharper relief. He was pleased with my moonlight scene from Trent, touched it up some and then made a small drawing for me from the idea it had furnished.

Wednesday, December 4th.

Yesterday I was on guard at the lower windmill near Company E's quarters back of our camp. The weather was extremely cold, damp and disagreeable during the day and night. This morning, when the sun came out over the Atlantic warm and strong, the vapory masses were soon rolled away in pleasant shapes, clouds which in the distance took on warm and brilliant hues. I sketched the scene of our camp a little after sunrise, from a small square window near the roof of the mill, from which one has a bird's-eye view of several miles of Hatteras Bank, and out over the Atlantic with Camp Wool in the foreground. At this time in the morning, the scene is an animated one. The wharf is thronged with the fishermen selling fish to the soldiers. Breakfast fires are smoking. Soldiers are at early drill, if they can't get out of it; bugles and drums sound this call and that; everywhere activity and life, which produces a very pleasant impression after a cold night on guard, with only shivery snatches of sleep in a rickety old windmill on Hatteras Bank.

These windmills, by the way, are about the only things picturesque on the Island, and as objects of study for an amateur artist they are admirable. I have sketches of them all, I believe, from here to Chicomocomico, taken from all possible points of view, for they are all built after one plan.

The "Spaulding" arrived to-day, bringing the ever-welcome mail and the paymaster. News from home is discouraging. My Father is still down and giving no signs of improvement. I have hopes of seeing him, in spite of the crooked channels this life of mine has run into; but his last words when we parted that we would "not meet again in this world" come to my mind with a heavy weight of foreboding. I have thought at

76

THE LONG ROLL

times that my life, if either, was the one doomed in his mind, but he may have known more of himself than he wished to tell.

Thursday, December 5th.

Quite a skirmish between Confederate gunboats and our own, on the Sound this morning. As many as fifty shots were exchanged and the enemy came nearer than ever before, without being able to induce ours to move from under the guns of the forts. It may be obeying orders, but it looks to me as if orders were *too strictly* obeyed on board these vessels of ours. One of the Rebel boats was the "Fanny."

Saturday, December 7th.

Lieutenant Cooper, formerly Quartermaster's Sergeant, delivered to me a package of drawing-paper and pencils, a very acceptable gift from Frank Hughson of Fortress Monroe.

Sunday, December 8th.

On the last trip of the "Spaulding," came a lady, Mrs. Cameron, Mother of Corporal Robert Cameron of Company A. She came to nurse him, having heard of his severe and dangerous illness, but she was too late. He was buried last Sunday beside my friend Golding. All we could do was to give our most heartfelt sympathy.

Camp Winfield,
Wednesday, December 11th.

Companies A, B, C, H and " Ours " struck tents at Camp Wool this morning and we are now about a mile farther up the Island, on a high sand knoll near Duncan Creek. The new camp is to be called " Winfield," and will be commanded by Major Kimball.

Friday, December 12th.

General Williams, having failed in his breastwork under- taking at Fort Clark, the Atlantic Ocean proving too much for his military activity, is still bent on having a fort of some kind, and he is now engaged in constructing one of no contemp-

77

tible dimensions either, as the reader of these interesting memoirs in the days to come may well rest assured. It is of turf and sand, and situated on the highest sand knoll near the hut on the open beach, where it will serve as an excellent eddying point for all the sand in this region to whirl around in a storm, which will eventually fill it, and cover it and finally pile itself up on it in an immense heap and there be an everlasting monument to the great glory of our General. And it seems that we, with the Forty-eighth Pennsylvanians, were brought up here to work on this fort and not for the sanitary reasons, as we had flattered ourselves. We have done our first work to-day. As far as the work is concerned, perhaps we had better be doing this than nothing; it is only the infernal foolishness of the thing that makes it irksome.

Friday, December 20th.

The work on the fort goes bravely on, and General Williams is every day adding some new laurel to his wreath of glory, some new freak of annoyance for us to swear or laugh at, according to the mood we happen to be in when it strikes us.

Half the force is employed on the fort, constantly wheeling sand and turf, and the other half is as constantly in motion under the order of exercises given out at Camp Wool.

When our turn comes for the work, no one need fear that it is progressing too fast. Our boys will generally get a shovelful in the barrow, and then take a rest until the others have all done the same; then move along at a snail's pace in single file along the string of planks, managing on the way to spill nearly all of what little the barrow contained at the start, and so on, accordingly varied to meet the lively changes of freaks and humors in the men.

The General, having either surmised or been informed that we did not work faithfully, sent our Lieutenant Flemming out to us the other morning with some terrible orders. The bland Lieutenant took his station smiling in his most good-natured way, and as he let it be understood that he did not wish to stay any longer than need be, we performed prodigies

78

of labor for the half-hour that he was with us. He then went to the General's quarters with the report that we could not possibly do more or work harder.

But that officer was scarcely out of sight when a number of the men were detailed to construct a few pitfalls near the walls, arranging boards and brush over them not strong enough to bear one's weight, yet sufficient for a cover of sand so as not to be perceptible. We hoped the General would fall into one of them while we were at dinner, for it was his custom to go out at that time, for the purpose of inspecting the work done, accompanied by his Staff and Orderly, the latter at precisely twelve paces behind him, which distance he is required to keep under all circumstances. It is a comical sight to see, and more so because the Orderly is a good fellow with an appreciation of the ludicrousness of his position, which he adds to by a well-guarded mimicry of the General's carriage and motions. Our plan worked better than we had hoped. It seems the General stumbled into one pitfall the very first thing, and had hardly been helped out of that before he fell into another. This was such a mortal affront to his state and dignity that he has hardly shown himself out of his quarters since. There is a report around that he was shot at the other evening through a window, but this is hardly probable, for General Williams is rather a vexatious than a cruel tyrant.

Saturday, December 21st.

From the Reverend Mr. Passavant in Pittsburgh, a friend and benefactor of our family, I have received a letter of introduction to the Reverend Mr. Holman, Chaplain of the Forty-eighth Regiment, now camped below us on the creek. Thain and I called on him this evening, and spent an hour very pleasantly in his quarters.

John Davis has just returned from another reconnoitering trip to the vicinity of Roanoke, and his account thereof is far from being devoid of interest. The party was headed by Lieutenant Leahy, our Provost Marshal, and consisted of six, all told, including an officer of the Regulars. The information for their guidance was received from the negro Ben, and Davis affirms they reached a point much nearer the enemy than on their former trip. They were disguised as fishermen and were in dangerous quarters, sailing only by night. At one time, however, they ran right under the stern of the "Fanny" in broad daylight. She seemed to be on picket duty at an unlooked-for distance from their headquarters. Our men's position was a perilous one, but their disguise saved them from even ordinary questions. The crew was lazily lounging about the deck, evidently finding it hard work to kill time, and yet under the stern floated a peaceful little fisherman with six muskets and as many revolvers carefully loaded, and with three sabers ready at hand, which, had they been more curious, might have been the cause of killing more than time in one way or another.

They learned from the inhabitants that the enemy had received prompt information of their former trip, as the very morning they left, there was a small force after them, and our party actually chased three men who were left by this force to keep a look-out for them, or stragglers of the same kind. The party were all elated over the success of their trip, which would seem to indicate that they had more important information to communicate to headquarters, though I imagine I have noted the most interesting.

Sunday, December 22d.

Colonel Hawkins has returned from Fortress Monroe on the "Spaulding," where he is said to have done his utmost for the Regiment. He was promptly relieved from arrest on account of the Barnard affair, and has brought with him a battery of three small rifled cannons, a present to the Regiment from either the corporation or the citizens of New York. But lo and behold! No sooner did General Williams find this out than he demanded the use of them for the post as he might see fit. Colonel Hawkins refused to let them land, and now I presume he will be again under arrest. He goes back, at any rate, to Fortress Monroe with the steamer. He was cheered

Sundown at Hatteras

Burnside's Fleet at Anchor, February 6, 1862

Bombardment of Roanoke Island

Bivouac of Burnside's Army, Roanoke Island

Jarvis Farm Hospital

PLATE XX

Roanoke Island Battleground

Fort Defiance, Roanoke Island

PLATE XXI

THE LONG ROLL

enthusiastically by the boys, for "we have all grown to like him better than we once did."

Christmas Eve, December 24th.

Little did I dream last year at this time that I would be sitting here now, writing up my Journal on this, above all others, the most desolate part of creation. I can hardly realize the real, so strangely does it seem interwoven with romance. But then, here I am, there is no mistaking that fact, nor that it is Christmas Eve of the year of our Lord, Eighteen Hundred and Sixty-one. It may not be as pleasant as it is strange, for we are still subjected to the petty tyranny of Williams, who seems to be a monomaniac on fortifications and discipline. But even this is *doing something*, and I am far happier than I was at Mrs. Simpson's one year ago, brooding over the blank prospect then ahead, which has revealed itself so strangely since.

But "Roll" calls and I must stop writing.

Eve of Christmas Day.

It was my intention to spend the day collecting shells and war relics for a museum of Mr. Passevant's in Pittsburgh, but I failed to get to Fort Hatteras, where I expected to get the relics, on account of a channel cut across the bank between the two forts by the storm now raging. This channel was quite deep and the current so swift that if a person lost his foothold, he would certainly be carried out to sea. After getting quite wet in attempting to cross it, I gave it up. The channel must have been from ten to twenty feet deep, though narrow, for we could find no bottom with the longest poles.

Coming home, Thain and I stopped at the home of Mr. Oland, and had as good a Christmas dinner as can be gotten on the Island.

During a similar storm, a tremendous stream of small fish either strayed up on the banks or were driven into the shoals by sharks, for whom they evidently furnished food. These fish were of the size of small herring, and their quantity

81

can be estimated by the fact that every wave washing on the beach would leave hundreds of them high and dry on the sand. So all we had to do was to provide ourselves with buckets and pick them up as fast as we desired. The breakers were soon full of sharks, who were evidently leading a life of plenty at the expense of this small fry, and several of them were caught by a mode of fishing as simple as it was novel and exciting. The fishermen provide themselves with lines quite as strong if not as heavy as an ordinary clothesline, and to these fasten hooks made out of heavy bucket-handles sharpened to receive the bait of fist-sized chunks of " salt horse." This simple apparatus is then thrown into the sea coil-wise, as a sailor throws a line. The sportsman would easily be aware of a bite, as it would be apt to throw him off his feet. He must then promptly throw the line over his shoulder, and walking, haul in as if pulling a canal-boat; in this way the game is landed, snorting and gurgling on the bank, to be dispatched by the ready axe. I saw our Lieutenant Flemming bring in one weighing from one hundred and fifty to two hundred pounds. Only for sport, however, as sharks, I don't know why, are not eaten or put to any useful purpose whatever.

Thursday, December 26th.

There is a rumor, generally credited, I find, around camp, that we are on the eve of an attack. Whether this is more than an ordinary camp rumor, I am unable to say. It is claimed to come by authority and from Fortress Monroe. " An expedition consisting of ten thousand men on flatboats has left Norfolk for Hatteras Inlet." So says this rumor, of which to-morrow will tell the truth.

Friday Evening, December 27th.

Childlike I say, " It is to-morrow," and yet we are not attacked, but the rumor noted last night has grown into " an established certainty." The ten thousand have become twenty thousand, and troops are now landing at Chicomocomico.

Major Kimball and Captain Barnett have been dispatched in that direction to gather reliable information. More excite-

THE LONG ROLL

ment prevails about it than ever was manifested before, and to-night all will be ready for the "Long Roll." Still it is not my intention to lose any sleep.

Wednesday, January 1st, 1862.

The most eventful year of my existence closed last night. I feel like a lost sheep at times, but if one sheep has strayed, another has returned to the fold, and that is a comfort. My sister Eva is now at home in Minnesota with Father and Uncle, and her letters which I receive regularly are extremely interesting to me.*

To my new situation I have taken as well as may be, though more strange than any I ever dreamed of in my most eventful anticipations on leaving home for New York. I get along as well as can be expected with my associates, who are in many cases rude and sometimes contemptible. As I take no thought for the morrow, I am able to give myself up fully to the pleasures of seeing, feeling and thinking whenever the routine of duty ceases, and it seems as if what we experience is just enough to stimulate this kind of mental activity to the quick. If I could neither see, feel nor think (the sense of hearing one might dispense with to advantage in many cases), as too many actually seem unable to do in these camps, I think the life on these sands would drive me mad.

Sketching, though I am aware of the primitiveness of my efforts, furnishes me nevertheless with an endless source of enjoyment. I have read but little during the year, for I have had too much to write about. The "Weekly Herald," my friend Jack McKensie sends me, and this gives me all I want to know of contemporary events, which, it is needless to say, are now only war and rumors of war until one is heartily sick of the word. We gobbled a few books while at Newport News, among which are Scott's "Ivanhoe" and "Kenilworth," two of Fredrica Bremer's stories and a volume of Washington Irving's Sketches (an old edition), and these comprise about

---

* The Father died on this day at the old home in Minnesota, though the news did not reach the boy until the thirty-first of the month.

83

all my reading worthy of mention. To sum up, as I have been in the habit of doing at this time of the year, I have become at least a wiser, if not a better man in a year's time.

Sunday, January 5th.

This has been a cold, drizzly, rainy, disagreeable Sunday. In the afternoon the weather drove me out of camp. Went down to George Stein's home, which was full of soldiers and asses from both Regiments. Angelina Stein is the attraction. She is the only beautiful woman we have seen in this part of the country.

In the evening I paid a visit to Chaplain Holman of the Forty-eighth. Thain went with me and we spent a very pleasant evening. Mr. Holman gave me a late copy of the " Lutheran," Reverend Mr. Passevant's paper published in Pittsburgh, which contains a letter from me to him, printed, with a few words altered, almost entire. This is the first time my pen has appeared in print, and it was quite a pleasant surprise. No name is given, but it is stated the letter is from a Swedish soldier with our Regiment at Hatteras, which leaves a certain result for any curious one, for, as far as I know, I am the only Swede in the Regiment.

Wednesday, January 8th.

Curious as the fact is, it is nevertheless true that a certain kind of Fatigue duty is the only respite we have from work nowadays. After twenty-four hours of guard duty, one has twenty-four hours of Fatigue, and this, which is usually considered work, such as camp chores, etc., is now considered rest. I have been on Fatigue to-day and have had nothing to do but what is pleasant to me, washing and cleaning up, drawing, reading and writing.

A lot of contrabands came into camp this afternoon, having escaped from the main, and were turned over to Lieutenant Leahy, the Provost-Marshal. The raggedness of their apparel beggars description. Patched until their patches themselves were rags, they presented a very grotesque and sorry appearance. They came from the mouth of the Roanoke River,

THE LONG ROLL

the head of Albemarle Sound, from the town of Plymouth, about one hundred fifty miles from Hatteras Inlet, where they were owned by one Jerry Simons. How they succeeded in getting here from this distance is a wonder to us all. They seem to have run right under the batteries of Roanoke Island, as there is no other way they could get here, without even knowing of their existence until they were fired on by both musketry and cannon. Fortune in this favor, however, blew so strong a gale that, though they were in an open boat, a so-called "Cooner," they were not chased, and reached here unharmed.

Monday, January 12th.

General Burnside has come and with him the first instalment of his expedition, a score or more of vessels with the ever welcome and familiar "Spaulding" among them. Major Kimball is mad with joy, for this season of drill and camp routine has been sore against his tastes. While we were out on Battalion Drill this morning, in the rear of Camp Winfield, he brought us into line facing the beach in full view of the heaving armada, and asked *if we would wade out to them or wait till they could come in.* His joy is almost childish, but we all participate in it.

This afternoon I have been out again on the sand-hills to refresh my eyesight with the imposing view of the seemingly endless procession of vessels heaving and pitching in the heavy sea. There are to be about ninety in all composing the fleet. I counted about thirty, and "the cry is still, 'they come'" They are large and small, of all sizes, shapes and conditions from the one-masted sloop to the massive sidewheeler.

Where we are going, the Lord only knows, but that we *are going* is enough for the present.

Wednesday, January 15th.

The fleet seems to have had a fearful time getting in the Inlet, on account of the severe storm raging for the past two days. Day before yesterday, the Sound was so rough that no small boat could come ashore with our mail, which we did

85

not receive until yesterday. Some of the vessels were roughly handled by the gale, but I believe none of them were lost, and now the storm is abating. We did not realize the full force of the storm at Camp Winfield, being some four miles from the Inlet, and sheltered by the belt of woods extending three miles below. I know that Duncan Creek overflowed its banks by the breakers washing into it, but it was not for some time that I learned that the whole fleet had been threatened with destruction, and that an officer and two men were drowned in a desperate attempt to reach the shore in a small boat. A large sidewheel steamer, I think the "New York," was thrown up high and dry on the South bank of the Inlet.

No Date.

We have been in a continual state of excitement since the arrival of the fleet and the expectation of orders, and then have had to bear the long and tedious delay of the vessels in getting over the "Swash," a shoal of only nine feet of water, and into the Inlet. It took some of the larger vessels one, two and even three days to work over, and all this expectancy or uncertainty has destroyed in me all inclination to write.

General Burnside came ashore this morning, and terminated the petty tyranny of General Williams by assuming command. With him came Colonel Hawkins, who had deemed it prudent to stay aboard the "Spaulding" as long as General Williams ruled the Island. Indeed, that extraordinary man had ordered the Colonel's arrest the moment of his reaching shore, but he is here now and grinning at his triumph, evidently safe under the wing of the superior General.

Camp Wool,
January 31st.

Among my letters this morning was one from my Sister, Eva, in a black-bordered envelope. The foreboding was soon realized. My Father is dead. He died on the eve of New Year's Day, just one month ago, nine years after the death of his wife, our Mother. And so I am not only Motherless, but Fatherless, and it was he, and not I, who was to pass

86

away first. I paid him a farewell visit on my way from St. Paul to New York. When it was time to leave, he walked with me to the station and seemed loth to turn back. Finally we parted, and, " My Son," he said, " if you go now we will never meet again in this world." And now these words come back to me with more than ordinary force, as if from a voice not yet quite dead.

Note—No date.

I did not write again on Hatteras Island. Day after day we watched the vessels working over the " Swash " as anxiously as though they were giants straining at our deliverance. Slowly but surely, they took their positions in deep water. A comrade and I paid a visit to a few of them, some four miles distant, in a small boat, with much satisfaction. In fact, so irksome had become our imprisonment on this Island that we loved the whole fleet as our deliverers from bondage.

The Sketch of Hatteras at sundown, from Camp Wool, is about the essence of the last days of restrained impatience. The " Cooner " scudding homeward lightly on the waves, before a darkening sky; the sun sinking large and glorious in its splendor, dyeing the waves in wonderful hues; the huge gun booming over the brilliant waters, and while the white cloud yet curls upward, we say—" Farewell Hatteras !"

CHAPTER VII

On the U. S. Transport "Union,"
Pamlico Sound, February 3d, 1862.

THE " Union " is an exceedingly rickety sternwheeler river steamer, but of very light draught, not drawing more than eighteen inches of water, which enables her to go into very shallow places, which is, of course, her business. Our boys, to whom such boats are not familiar, have so thoroughly rechristened her that she is now known through the whole fleet as the " Wheelbarrow."

We struck tents at Camp Wool this morning, and the Company is now quartered with Company E on the steam gunboat "Virginia," it being the Flagship, I believe, of the Third Brigade, Third Division. Having been on Fatigue to-day, I will sleep aboard the Wheelbarrow to-night.

U. S. Gunboat "Virginia."
February 4th.

Came aboard to-day and reported to my Company.

February 5th.

About nine o'clock this morning the sailing signal was displayed from the Flagship, and it seemed but an instant when the whole fleet was in motion. We went in single file, the sailing vessels mostly in the rear and in tow of steamers. The sight is an imposing and inspiring one. It is probably the greatest display of shipping these out-of-the-way waters have ever seen or will see again for a long time to come.

Thursday, February 6th.

We are off Roanoke Island at anchor. It is raining gently. Do not expect any fighting to-day.

The night was a beautiful one, and the scene one I shall never forget. The moon, in the full, came out and illuminated

88

the thin mists, making a silver transparency of them all, through which the vessels of the fleet could be readily made out, but only as an inextricable mass of hulls and spars.

After " Taps," a perfect mania for frolic seemed to take possession of our Company. It was on this night that the famous " Plum Battery " was inaugurated and executed to such perfect satisfaction.

Our quarters were on the first gun-deck, our Company on the left and E on the right, but in such small space that it was necessary to sleep packed in a somewhat fishy fashion, head and feet alternating, and when thus arranged, we covered the deck so completely that it was impossible for any one to go either foreward or aft, without treading on a very carpet of men. Of course, this attempt was not made unless unavoidable. At first, it would call down a shower of oaths, and when the step was too heavy or would wake a soldier up, the curses were accompanied by kicks. These culminated finally in the regular system of " Plum Battery." The moment any one would try to go through or cross this field of men, all would be quiet until some rascal had his feet planted firmly in the rearmost part of the victim; then a shout of " Plum Battery " and a shove that would send him only on to other pairs of pedal extremities raised everywhere to receive him at the magic words of command; and thus he would go spinning backward and forward from one to the other like a shuttle-cock. He must run the gauntlet of the Company or submit as best he might till he could get down between some two, or capture a kicking leg, or receive mercy. Of course, the sport was not only exciting but laughable in the extreme, and whenever a new victim was caught in the network of kicking legs, it called forth such noise of shouts and furious hilarity that the officers came down several times to put a stop to it, but usually they went back with their errand uncompleted for laughter.

Friday, February 7th.

The ball is opened. Our gunboats hove anchor and moved across the marsh this morning and are now at it hot and heavy.

THE LONG ROLL

We are now, at twelve noon, moving up ourselves and can plainly see the bombardment from our vessel. Have just sketched the scene hastily, as the steamer ahead was aground just inside the marsh, and we had to wait a few minutes for her to get off; but as we are steaming ahead again, I think it is time to put by my Journal and sketches for the present.

February 13th.

To commence where I left off about noon of Friday the Seventh. The bombardment was kept up with spirit on both sides during the afternoon. The " Hunchback," an old ferry-boat with one heavy gun in each end, made herself conspicuous by deliberately placing herself between the Rebel Batteries and their fleet, working one gun on each, keeping the position till dark. A little sloop with one heavy, hundred-pound gun placed herself inside of the line of the fleet and under full sail made her tally of one every time she tacked. A huge column of smoke curled up about two or three in the afternoon, from the rear of the batteries and from where our heaviest fire was concentrated. We were conjecturing what this might be, when the American Flag on the Flagship ran up to the maintop, which was the signal for the troops to land.

The " Wheelbarrow " was again brought into requisition, and by eight o'clock in the evening our Regiment was at the selected landing-place, a very swampy point of land, some two miles below the batteries.

In landing I was separated from my Company and had to make my way through the marsh alone. A flimsy, corduroy road of fence-rails had been improvised, but in the darkness I could not see, and as the rails were half-covered with mud and mire, at every other step the foot went down between, adding the danger of breaking one's legs to the general discomfort. I finally got through this and found the bivouac of the troops. They occupied a field of some twenty acres around a farmhouse, which served as General Burnside's headquarters.

Ten thousand men were bivouacked on this field, ranged

THE LONG ROLL

in huddling groups around hundreds of camp-fires, and a cold drizzling rain fell almost incessantly during the night, keeping the mass of men in constant motion. A few men, more enterprising than the rest, gathered evergreen branches enough from the neighboring woods, to raise the body above the mud and water, an experiment which I also tried with some result in sleep. The most of the men stood talking around the fires all night. Now and then as they moved to replenish the flames or stir the smouldering embers, long gleams of light would flash from out the darkness, reflected from endless rows of gun-barrels and bayonets, sharp, distinct and zig-zag, like a display of lightning when unusual efforts were made at some of the fires, or faint and flickering as the rain poured harder and the flames burned lurid and low.

Everything took on an extremely weird and unusual shape as, now and then, I peered from under the lids of my blanket which the rain was eternally pelting outside, and reflections came both " thick and thin " as I watched or dozed away the long night.

If one cares to contrast this night with the previous one on the fleet, it will furnish quite a lively idea of the extremes to which a soldier is subjected.

Day dawned at last, but it brought no respite from the rain. In fact, rain has followed Burnside more or less from the time he struck Hatteras, and it does not seem ready to suspend operations yet.

A short time after daylight, a false alarm came near creating a serious panic among the troops. Of a sudden, there was a spontaneous movement toward the stacks, and it seemed as if we were to " have it " there and then, but the excitement quieted down as suddenly as it came up, without, I think, any of us finding out the cause of the alarm.

A short time after this, a rumor went the rounds that a couple of Regiments had been sent out to cut off a small force of the enemy and gain a position in the rear of their works. This was the advance of a portion of Foster's Brigade, and the commencement of operations. We soon heard from them.

91

THE LONG ROLL

Quick successive reports of cannon were heard issuing from the woods not over a half a mile away, and these reports were quickly followed by volleys of musketry. There was no longer room for doubt; the ball was open in earnest.

Regiment and Regiment now formed in rapid succession and filed away into the woods in the direction of the fight, and as we waited our turn (we were of the Third Division and held in reserve) the excitement became almost unbearable. We heard a cheer once ringing clear and distinct through the woods, and without knowing whether it boded us good or ill we took it up and returned it with a will. Our good, whole-souled Lieutenant (Flemming) bestirred himself to have coffee for us before we started, which every one needed without being aware of it, and besides it helped to take up the time. At last came the welcome word of command, "Attention Battalion," and without more ado than to stop at the edge of the woods and dispense with our blankets and extra accoutrements, we filed rapidly away in the direction taken by the other Regiments.

As soon as we struck the road, a narrow one, we had to form in ranks of two from four, in order to let the string of wounded men pass on their way to the rear. They came thick and fast, and this was indeed a ghastly spectacle for us to face on the way to our maiden fight.

The poor fellows were in every imaginable condition of bodily suffering; some of them walking bravely or indifferently by themselves, with only slight wounds; others supported by comrades, pale as death from loss of blood; still others carried on stretchers, evidently in their last struggle; and some quite still—*were they already dead?*

Most of these wounded soldiers were cheerful themselves or tried to cheer us by reports from the field of how the fight was going, or such observations as they could think of that would sound well. "We advanced on them twice," a robust fellow said, and he looked as though he might advance on them again. "We are driving them back," from a young, pale-faced boy with clothes too big for his body. "You are wanted up

92

there," feebly uttered another whose life-blood was oozing from him. "Two of their guns are taken," exclaimed one. "We are giving them Hell," shouted another. "They gave me a sore jaw," one huge fellow remarked as he passed. But the most horrible sight of all was one poor soldier on a stretcher with his right arm taken off close to the shoulder, leaving the bloody stump, which, consciously or not, he was working in spasmodic jerks and from which the red blood was streaming. Many others passed us in ghastly array: a Captain, assisted by a couple of men, had apparently an eye torn out; another, in a sitting position, was spewing pure blood; but none seemed to freeze my very life as that terrible spectacle of the spasmodic stump with its severed arteries squirting blood.

I remember after that a sort of sickening sensation as if I was going to a slaughter-house to be butchered, and as we neared the field and saw ominous shapes here and there, bodies wrapped in blankets, too deathly still for sleep, a cold shudder as of the grave passed over me. I can not believe that this was cowardly, for I know that no such idea as escape entered my mind. I was simply walking into the jaws of death for the first time, made more horrible by the sights and sounds around me, and I felt I must be deathly pale. This feeling made me nervous, too, for even then pride struggled to conceal my weakness; but as I looked around me to see if it was noticed by my companions, I was surprised to see the same feelings working more or less transparently through all the faces I could see back in the line. I realized the truth then, that every individual was, like myself, undergoing the same experience, and that I was not alone in looking into the awful abyss of non-existence, or trying as best I could to shake hands with Death. Strange to say, the realization of this truth gave me what I needed and that not so much courage, as sympathy for my comrades, and this took my thoughts from myself and my single individuality. It put an end to the struggle as far as I was concerned, so that when we arrived upon the field all dread or fear seemed to have passed away, and I have often thought since that I went through in that short march to the battlefield, on Roanoke, all that

93

THE LONG ROLL

mortal can, but Death; that I had, in fact, looked him square in the face, and placed myself within his reach, and though I have been nearer him since, I have never felt that feeling, nor do I think I ever will.

As we entered the opening (filled with timber to allow full play for their guns), a bullet whistled over us, the first one that ever went over me from an enemy. I could not but laugh at my file-leader, who dodged down half his length, long after the bullet had passed him, not that I would not have dodged too, but that I knew it was too late. A minute after, a couple of our men fell, but from wounds or not, I can not say, only that I had to jump over them. I was surprised and greatly confused; this was to me anything but a field of battle, for I could see no enemy, and our men were lying around in the swamp on either side of the road behind trees and stumps, firing at what I could not make out, for everything was in a whirl of confusion.

It was impossible to form in battalion line, and it was not attempted, for the trees felled in every direction would have prevented, even if the nature of the ground (a swamp) had not most effectually done so. We advanced up to a bend in the road, where a squad of the marine artillery were working one of their howitzers, when we were told to drop on account of a special volley that it seems was expected would be fired for our benefit. We disposed of ourselves without any attempt at order, on either side of the road among the other troops. All the men were crouching low behind objects of shelter and firing as fast as they could load. I took the right side of the road, looking ahead very naturally, to see what was the aim of all the shooting.

I saw a body of men moving slowly along the other end of the opening, and seeing most of the guns around me leveled in that direction, I also took aim to fire, but luckily snapped my piece. I say "luckily," because as I was in the act of repriming, the officer commanding the gun cried out to stop, "For God's sake!"—we were shooting our own men! I had been aiming like many others at a body of our men who were

94

endeavoring to flank the enemy. Wishing, simply enough, to know "what in thunder to shoot at then," a low, broken line was pointed out to me in the edge of the wood, which I was informed was a battery behind which the enemy was posted. As I was looking, I saw some one, evidently an officer, very probably Captain Wise, jump up on the works and stand there quite bravely gesticulating, but how long he was there, I do not know, for I had no time for further observation. Just then our Bugler sounded, "Cease Firing," and then I heard the hoarse voice of our Major give the command, "Charge Bayonets," and all I know is that I was out on the run running and yelling with the rest of the men, and that with a successful leap over a wide ditch full of water, we were all together pouring pell-mell over the breastworks. When I came up and jumped into the works, there was not an enemy in sight. They must have left the moment we charged, but a dead soldier was in standing posture, slightly bent over the muzzle of one of the cannon, shot while in the act of loading. In his hands he yet clutched a charge of grape, and so lifelike did he appear that for a moment I thought he must be yet alive. One of our boys, an Irishman, and one of the first to mount the works, was so strongly under the same impression that he actually clubbed him with his musket before finding out his mistake. A wild cheer arose as our flag was planted on the fort, everybody shook hands in congratulation, all laughed and, I think, some cried, but every one was equally overjoyed at our first victory.

The enemy had left the rammers in their guns, and their knapsacks and muskets were scattered about in such confusion that it was evident they had made a hasty flight after their brave and wonderfully stubborn resistance. During the enthusiasm over our success, all order was forgotten, and I felt some apprehension that the enemy might be re-forming and come on us while we were yet in confusion. Nothing of the kind happened, however, and we were soon re-formed and in pursuit of them.

A detachment of ours captured a boat-load of them as they were endeavoring to escape toward the mainland by way of

Nags Head, and among them were a Major and some line officers. The main force of our Regiment halted in a field near a farmhouse upon which the yellow flag was displayed. This was the Rebel hospital, and we came up just as the gallant Wise was expiring from the effects of four bullet-wounds, the last two of which, if reports be true, our Regiment gave him. He had fought with two until our Regiment came up, when he received two more and was carried from the field. And this virtually ended the battle.

Before night the enemy had surrendered some twenty-seven hundred prisoners, three or four batteries, thirty guns, and we were left masters of the Island. General Wise, the father of the brave Captain who had given his life in its defense, managed to escape with some few troops by way of Nags Head.

General Burnside gave us the lion's share of credit for the victory and subsequent surrender, and it is gratifying to hear warm accounts of our behavior from the whole-souled tars of the Marine Artillery, whose gallantry, at least, none can do otherwise than respect. But my opinion is that, to *our* Major Kimball and a piece of good fortune, more than to any special fighting qualities in ourselves, is due this rather brilliant success.

I have given as good and as perfect an account of the affair, as far as I was personally concerned, as my narrow quarters on a shelf on the "Virginia" will allow. It only remains now for me to give, if I have time and opportunity, a few incidents and observations that came under my notice during our three eventful days on the Island.

Lieutenant Leahy of Company H led our Company into e fight, as we were destitute of all officers except our Second eutenant Flemming. Leahy is a brave, restless, energetic cer and a stern disciplinarian, which makes him somewhat opular in the Regiment.

It will be remembered that while he was Provost-Marshal Iatteras, he undertook several expeditions in this direction arch of information, on some of which our Corporal Davis npanied him. He certainly had very definite knowledge

6

of all the military works here. When we halted at Jarvis Hospital and there seemed no more hope of active operation that day, Leahy knew there was a battery somewhere below us, which, with a squad of men, he hunted up and captured with its force of two men, who were only too glad to surrender. Having no flag with which to signalize his conquest, Leahy elevated his fez on a pole, that the necessary amount of " pomp and circumstance of war " might not be wanting.

Our regiment remained where we had halted on Jarvis Farm during the night, and as the usual rain came up again, making this time for the sake of variety with a little snow, I joined with several others in a search for shelter, which we finally found in a house that is indicated in the light of the sketch. We discovered in the morning that it had been used as a pigsty, though it was then dry and clean. As we had slept well, and on new hay which we had ourselves brought, the pigs were forgiven.

The house of which I have a sketch as faithful as need be, is a more than usually interesting one for the run of houses in this region. It is old and unpainted, of course, and gray, if not green, in spots, with a sort of moss formation upon it, with two immense chimneys at one gable and another at the other. It has a shingled, double-hipped roof, which makes it appear as if the sides, too, were shingled. Low, shed like extensions descending gently from the eaves in front and rear give it a very quaint and comfortable appearance, and it looks very much as if it had grown during the slow process of time, without any special design or effort on the part of the inmates.

Jarvis, the proprietor, seemed to be a part of the house. He is short and thick-set, very, and to all appearances born right here. With the possible exception of a trip to Nags Head in a " Cooner," he looks as though he never had been off the Island. He was greatly bewildered at the extraordinary events transpiring around him, as frightened at our occupation of the Island, and, more than all, distressed at the use of his house in the bloody business of a hospital. He told us there could not be a person living " more tired at the sight of blood."

I believe it was his firm conviction that we would, in the event
of taking the Island, massacre the inhabitants generally, for
even now, as if some display was not altogether unnecessary
to show his entire, though it might be hopeless, subordination
to our wishes, and possibly for some charming virtue of protection in the letters, he carries about an old, rusty die for
stamping the letters, "U. S.," however he had come into
possession of the thing, and this he persistently affirms that
he has "never been ashamed to show." All very much as
if displaying some "skull-and-crossbone" sign to a lot of
pirates.

On the Ninth, I was one of a Detail to return after the
Company's blankets, and I had a good opportunity for reviewing the field, which I also improved by making a couple of
sketches.

The battery for which we paid so dearly is named Fort
Defiance, and mounts three guns, one of which is an old Mexican
brass piece, the one in the right of the sketch.

It is no great affair to my notion, but most excellently placed
so as to sweep the road, which is in part a sort of causeway
through the swamp, and the only passable approach from the
lower to the higher part of the Island. My other sketch shows
where we first arrived upon the scene and where our forces
must have suffered most, judging by the dead, which, on
the day after, were yet unburied. They were just as they
had fallen, and miserably enough for the most part, in knee-deep
mud and mire. I came upon two poor fellows between some
stumps, evidently killed by the same cannon-ball. They were
both shockingly torn, one through the right side and the other
the left, and they must have died instantly. Not far from
these was one of the Fifty-first, with a part of his brain protruding from the side of his head, which had been pierced by
a musket-ball, his hat beside him just as he had placed it,
with holes through it identical with those that killed him.
I also particularly noted a handsome young fellow with coal-
black hair, stretched out with a horrible-looking wound in
the shoulder and neck which must have killed him instantly.

but, by far the most horrifying sight to me on the whole field was a single, human hand, bloodless and shriveled, alone by itself, away from everything else of human shape. I came upon it suddenly, and though I had been accustoming myself to look at death in the various forms here displayed, the sight of this lonely hand was so unexpected and startling, that I felt a cold shiver under the very roots of my hair.

Lieutenant-Colonel Victor de Montueil was killed while acting as a Private in our Regiment, only a few moments before the charge was made which decided the day. He was separated from his Regiment, the D'Epineuil Zouaves, and attached to ourself to ours quite naturally. He died, I am told, with words of encouragement to our Regiment, as we were preparing to charge.

To our Major Kimball more than to any one else, we are indebted for the rather brilliant termination of the fight. He is an old Mexican army officer, and in that war achieved the distinction of being the first to pull down an enemy's flag at Tehuantepec. As soon as we arrived on the field, he saw at once that a bold stroke was all that was needed to win the day, and he proposed to General Foster to make the charge. That General was, I presume, by this time equally convinced that something was needed, and glad to find some one who knew what it was, with experience and boldness enough to carry it through, and in a couple of minutes, the deed was done.

Now, in charging at the head of the Regiment, Kimball of course did not see anything in the heavens above, or on the earth beneath, but the breastworks between; so that when he arrived at the ditch in front of the works, the bottom of things dropped from under him, as it were, and he suddenly found himself floundering in muddy water more like a porpoise than a Major of Infantry. Being rather short and stout did not help the matter, and his head acted as a sort of sinker to a cork, and would, in his frantic efforts to right himself, continually bob out of sight. As he was floundering and spluttering in this way, our Lieutenant Flemming, a six-footer, cleared the ditch with a bound, not hearing or heeding the

Major, who frantically called on him to help him out. He afterward explained in my hearing, " Lord, Major, I would not have helped me own father up then." How he did get out I do not know, but that he lost his saber is certain, for he walked up to one of Porter's Marines, took a cutlass out of his hand, saying simply, " Here, young man, I want this." He had no further use for it that day, however, and his own sword was returned to him, fished up by some one who had witnessed the misadventure.

The night of the Ninth was put in as well as might be near the center of the Island back of Fort Bartow, around which most of the troops were camped. It snowed quite hard at dusk. I fell in with a " regular Southerner," a citizen correspondent of some paper, with whom I had quite a dish of conversation. on one topic of course, the Rebellion. He seemed to think that this Island was not half protected by defensive works or we never could have taken it, and he also predicted that we could never put an end to the Rebellion. My magnanimity was such that I would not gainsay him, but " we have taken the Island anyway, whether we put an end to the Rebellion or not."

On the morning of the Tenth I had an opportunity to see and sketch Fort Bartow, which is the principal work here. The effect of the bombardment is very perceptible in the bomb-proof powder-magazine, but has hardly disturbed the outline of the work itself, which is built of turf or peat. Since our return to our old quarters on the " Virginia," I have sketched the fort from the deck where we were anchored, including the little white Rebel steamer, waiting, under a flag of truce, to convey the body of the brave, young Wise to Norfolk.

Commodore Goldsborough made short work of Lynch's fleet, chasing them as far as Elizabeth City, and either sinking or destroying all, including the " Fanny," and excepting the " Ellis," carrying two guns, which was captured.

Monday, February 17th.

I have mentioned the escape of " Uncle Ben " from Roanoke Island. He was immediately employed by Lieutenant Leahy

100

THE LONG ROLL

as cook, in which capacity he served until our departure for the Island. He is no ordinary man, but far superior to many in both intelligence and modesty. He proved himself not only of great use for the information he possessed, but a man of mettle as well. On the night before the attack, while we were bivouacking as miserably as could be in the rain, he was comfortably closeted with General Burnside in the house that served as headquarters, giving information of the different works on the Island, and it was through him that exact information was received of the battery defending the only pass to the enemy's rear, which he had helped to build. He guided General Foster's force to it in the morning. I am told he was one of, if not the very first, to fire into it, and he used up some forty rounds of cartridges during the day. A few days ago, one of our Lieutenants, either Leahy or Flemming, with a small party, visited the mainland under Ben's guidance, and went to see Ben's former master and associates in slavery. They were greatly surprised to see him, rigged out as he was with red, officer's cap, pistol in belt and musket capped in hand, for he had been reported drowned. It is presumed this was done to prevent the other slaves from making a similar escape.

We are on the eve of another expedition, rumor has it to Elizabeth City or Middletown, to-morrow will tell which, if either, or at all, though it seems to be decided that we are going somewhere.

A curious incident, happening to a member of our Regiment, has just come to my notice. During the recent fight, while charging, he was struck down, and from the sensation he experienced thought he was hit in the abdomen and mortally wounded. After waiting a reasonable time for death to ensue, he began to think that "something was wrong," and upon examination he found that the ball had struck his belt-plate, and glancing, had not even hurt him. But I am tired to-night, best pack myself to sleep, while I may. The Lord only knows where I may be to-morrow night. Let me have strength to meet my fate, wherever it may be and whenever it may overtake me. That is all I can ask at present.

101

CHAPTER VIII

THE BURNING OF WINTON

Old Quarters (on my shelf)
" Virginia " off Roanoke.
February 22d.

W E have just returned from an expedition up the Chowan River, resulting in the destruction of the town of Winton. Our Regiment was the only land force employed. We are now quietly moored at our old station, which seems to be the head for future operations in these extensive inland seas.

About noon last Tuesday, our Regiment was distributed among a fleet of gunboats and vessels consisting of the following : Gunboats, Spar-rigged, four to seven guns, the " Delaware," Flagship, the " Louisiana " and the " Lockwood "; Old ferryboats, two guns each, heavy calibre, the " Hunchback," the " Morse," the " Commodore Perry " and the " Commodore Barney."

Companies E and I were quartered on the " Barney." At a given signal, we hove anchor and steamed rapidly Northward into the Albemarle Sound, soon leaving the Island and neighboring shores, with the pretty Light-House, just above Roanoke, as indistinct lines or specks on the horizon. Our destination was a mystery to all of us, and many were the speculations on the subject, some professing to know all about it with each particular plan and detail. We were not going to Middletown, the course we were taking answering that in the negative. The most prevalent opinion among the sailors of the " Barney " and us soldiers was that the object was the destruction of a certain railroad-bridge over the Chowan River, which I find by my maps, somewhere near the boundary-line between this State and Virginia. And this appeared likely enough, for it would cut off direct communication between this State and Norfolk, a desirable object certainly. About dark, the fleet anchored opposite the city of Plymouth, and at day-light we were again under full steam and away. In about an hour, we came to the mouth of the Roanoke River, up which one of the old ferryboats proceeded to " feel " and for a time disappeared, while the rest of the fleet dropped anchor to wait and see if she came out all right, or to help her if she found trouble.

No solid banks could be made out on either shore of the opening, and the forest, for the most part of pine and kindred fir trees, seemed to grow out of the water. This fact, with the india-ink blackness of the water, and the long tufts of gray moss suspended from the trees in great quantities, all contributed to give the scene a very peculiar and grisly, if not ghostly appearance, entirely new to me. Indeed, as we waited for the gunboat to appear, I thought again and again that it would make a suitable entrance to the great Dismal Swamp itself, with which it is closely connected, if not an actual part.

The tug returned and we took the course of the " Delaware," which was by this time nearly out of sight on its way up the river. The description of the mouth of the Roanoke will also serve for the Chowan for at least twenty miles. It is from one to three miles in width, and more like an arm of the Albemarle than a river. The decidedly yellow tinge of the water proves its origin in genuine Virginia soil.

Our fleet headed by the Flagship made a lively display as we ascended this river, and a novel one for these peaceful-looking waters, I 'll warrant, composed as it was of vessels of the utmost contrast in purpose, build and appearance. The old ferryboats, painted black as the ace of spades, are the most strange to see as gunboats, but as such they are excellent, being strongly built and capable of operating in very shallow waters.

About five o'clock, while we were thinking no more of danger than if upon a pleasure excursion, we were startled by the reports of cannonading ahead, and simultaneously, the engines of the " Barney " ceased working. While Captain Renshaw was making out the signals ahead, the " Delaware " appeared, herself a signal to " put about," and she actually passed us before we had our pilot-houses and rudders changed.

The " Delaware " had been fired into, the pilot-house and one wheel-house being perforated with musket-balls. No harm

103

done, except to cause our Colonel and another officer, who were in the crosstrees on the lookout, to make a hasty and graceful descent. Meanwhile, the orders were to fall back and to prepare for action the next day.

The guns were kept manned during the night, and we, of course, were ready. The wildest kind of conjectures prevailed as to the probable events of the morrow. Some said artillery as well as musketry had been used in the attack on the " Delaware," and that our landing would be desperately resisted; but we had an excellent night's sleep, the better because all unnecessary noise was prohibited.

The morning was spent making the most formidable preparations for an attack. Bullet-proof casemating was put around the gunwales of the " Barney." Huge piles of cutlasses and navy revolvers were brought out from the Lord knows where, and placed ready to hand, in a promiscuous heap on deck, where they certainly looked dangerous. But we dispatched breakfast, that is, those of us who had any, and I was not one, and swiftly, as on the day before, proceeded up the river.

At nine, the advance opened on the village of Winton from where the " Delaware " had been fired into the day before. About twenty shots, mostly heavy shells, were sent into the town by the different vessels, and then we landed, without opposition, and marched up a steep, clay bank, upon which Winton is situated. I am told there were twelve hundred men, with three field-pieces, there the night before, but they beat a hasty retreat at our first shot, accompanied, I should judge, by every living soul of the village who could get away. There had been a " ball " or something in the way of rejoicing the night before on account of our repulse. But it turned out anything but brilliantly, for the village was miserably plundered and burned. Two men confined in the jail under the Court-house would have been burned with the town, had it not been for one of the gallant tars of the " Barney," who chopped them loose. They took to their heels, as might be expected, with the double object perhaps of escaping from justice as well as from the enemy. This same sailor told me he saw one other inhabitant

Lieutenant-Colonel Victor De Monteuil of the D' Epaneuil Zouaves

PLATE XXII

Fort Bartow (Roanoke)

Fort Bartow (Roanoke), Rebel Tug " Sea Bird," under flag of truce, Waiting
for Body of Captain Wise

PLATE XXIII

The Captured Gunboat " Ellis "

Winton Expedition Going up Chowan River

PLATE XXIV

Camp Reno. Roanoke Island

PLATE XXV

beside the criminals, " an old woman, gray and wrinkled all over."

Not having been on hand *in time* for the burning, our Companies were not allowed to break ranks, and this I did not regret, as burning and pillaging is a part of the performance that is not to my taste. This brave deed having been accomplished, either by the orders of the officers commanding, or by the men without any protest, it was deemed prudent to return without attempting the object of the expedition, the destruction of the bridge, as it was found that a much larger force was stationed there than we could expect to cope with successfully, especially as re-enforcements would have time to reach them from Norfolk before we could get there. So, with a miserable village burned, a couple of felons liberated, and no particular harm done to an old lady, the fleet steamed down the Chowan again, quite bravely.

Sunday, February 23d.

The paymaster was a pleasant person to meet on our return from Winton. That beloved official has been waiting for us for two days, and yesterday he disbursed among us the amount which is considered sufficient compensation for what killing and burning we have to do, and for other considerations which need not be mentioned. Of course, so much money was apt to burn severely, and as life was an uncertain thing at best, and we might not long want the little here below, our Mess concluded to spend some of it if possible, and celebrate in a fitting way our late successes, including, of course, our deeds of valor at Winton. We accordingly visited every vessel in the fleet, including the " Barney," but could n't get rid of our money.

The crew of the " Barney," and the officers as well, seemed to be heartily glad to see us, and found fault because we did not bring a boat-load and come in time for " Grog." Even the grim old Captain Renshaw seemed pleased, and returned our salutes with a hearty, " How are you Zou-Zous? " He inquired where we were going next and hoped we could go together.

THE LONG ROLL

We were hardly prepared for, but greatly pleased at receiving so much good-will and courtesy. The fact is, our success in putting a sudden end to the fight on the Island has since grown into a matter of some importance and, whether deservedly or not, it creates a feeling for us in the fleet that is very pleasant to experience.

We expect to go next to Middle Creek, wherever that may be.

Tuesday, March 4th,
Schooner " *Eva Belle.*"

Received a mail yesterday and papers up to the Twenty-fifth, with bushels of the most glorious news from all quarters where our forces are operating, but best is the capture of Fort Donaldson with some fifteen thousand prisoners. This is rather the most decisive thing of the war, and eclipses decidedly our achievements here.

It is singular that we should have the first news of this great triumph through Rebel sources. While at Winton, some of the contents of the post-office was brought aboard the "Barney," and in a Confederate paper, the Petersburg "Express," we read accounts of a terrible conflict raging around Fort Donaldson, and which had at the date of the latest accounts been in progress then three days. Nothing final was known, but certain misgivings expressed as to the result might have created more remark at the time, had we considered the importance of the operations in that quarter.

We have not participated in any new movements or expeditions in any direction since the miserable affair at Winton. Everything is exceedingly quiet and idle in the fleet. Our Company was yesterday transferred to the Schooner " Eva Belle," where we have more room in the hold, but certainly not as pleasant quarters as we had on the " Virginia." I had grown quite attached to my shelf, of which I had the undisputed possession. I had just room enough in this corner, though none to spare, and, being raised some four feet above the level of my comrades, saved me from much unnecessary friction.

106

A boat crew was organized as soon as we got settled in our new quarters, and of this I became a voluntary member. Our life is getting too humdrum, and it is my object to relieve the monotony, and exercise and some experience will not come amiss.

Wednesday, March 5th.

Commenced my new duties as one of the boat crew this morning by getting famously wet in bringing a couple of water-barrels from the "Curlew." Just in from the "Phœnix," where we received from Lieutenant Andrews the rather unwelcome intelligence that we are to be Post Regiment on Roanoke Island. Colonel Hawkins is to be acting Brigadier in command.

CHAPTER IX

March 8th.

THE afternoon of the Fifth, the " Wheelbarrow " took us aboard and conveyed us to Camp Reno, where we have stepped completely into the shoes and barracks of the late Secesh occupants. The barracks are very comfortable, and I doubt if we would ever have been provided with as good, if Fortune had not placed us here. There are in the camp about fifteen houses, each accommodating two Companies, with room to spare, and all arranged similarly to the tents in an encampment, the quarters being divided into compartments for Mess of some twelve or thirteen. Each apartment is provided with a fireplace and chimney, a luxury that we have never had since we entered the service of Uncle Sam. And we are not the only ones thus unprotected, for I hear that the Army of the Potomac dare not think of such a thing as fire. I have been so closely occupied since we came here that I have not had an opportunity even to ask for a pass, much less to go outside the camp; but as it is likely that we will stay here for a couple of months at least, I will have time enough for exploring the Island, and I will give my observations of such things as I deem interesting enough for these pages. Meanwhile, it is enough to say that Camp Reno is situated on the Northern point of the Island, in a fine, dry location sheltered on all sides by woods.

March 14th.

By a new order all sentinels who do their duty faithfully shall receive passes to go all over the Island, with liberty from the time they come off duty until Dress Parade at four o'clock. Yesterday morning I came off guard, and with a couple of my messmates started out to see what was to be seen.

We took, of course, the only road that we had never been on before, which led us in a Southwesterly direction from Camp Reno. This brought us to the sand-hills, which looked so inviting and so bold from the level, woody ground we started

108

from, that we could not resist the desire to scale the bluffs and see what was beyond, and well did the effort repay us for our trouble. The scene was not what we could call beautiful, but it was as new and strange as picturesque and bold. We found ourselves on high, white piles of pure sand, with which the wind and tide, having formed them, had played curious pranks. They sloped now gently, then abruptly, toward the beach of the yellow, shallow waters. The horizon was relieved by the continuation of the banks on which we lived for so long, about seventy-five miles below this point, and from here, they appear like small islands of sugar. Beyond, a faint blue line is visible and that is where the waters of the Atlantic meet the horizon in our line of vision. It might be considered bleak and desolate for being barren of the common covering that Nature provides, but the ever-green cypress trees have taken root frequently on the very summit of these white hills, making a contrast that is far from unpleasant, considering the scenery we have been used to for the last five months.

After loitering around long enough to get accustomed to this new phase of Nature, we continued our march till we unexpectedly came upon Jarvis House, which I have mentioned before as the house in which Wise died. Here we got a drink of water, which refreshed us so much that we concluded to go down to the masked battery. I got a sketch of the fort, and then we marched back to camp at the rate of four miles an hour. We were tired out completely, for we had traveled ten miles, and that after being on guard and consequently awake most of last night.

Camp Reno,
April 3d.

I have neglected my Journal considerably of late, but I have one good excuse and that is nothing of particular interest has transpired. I may except the New-Berne affair, but as we did not participate in its capture, it has nothing to do with my memoirs. We are still at Camp Reno, and are kept in a very strict state of discipline, so much so, in fact, that I am sometimes inclined to think they are trying to make regular Regulars of us, and indeed they have pretty nearly succeeded. There have been a great many changes in the Regiment since the Eighth of March. I have noted that Hawkins was acting Brigadier and Commander of the Island, and it is lately rumored that he has gotten his commission, which has caused a great deal of pleasure, and at the same time a great deal of apprehension. We feel of course pleasure in seeing him promoted, but we dread losing in him our Colonel, for that would place the command on Lieutenant-Colonel (formerly Major) Kimball. I like him very well as a Major or Lieutenant-Colonel, but I would not like to see him Commander of the Regiment, for his changeable moods unfit him entirely for command.

A later rumor has reached us, which, if true, will place our Colonel deeper than ever in the hearts of us all. This is that Colonel Hawkins will not leave the Regiment for the offered commission of Brigadier, that he thinks more of the Eagle that commands the Zouaves than of the Star that would command five times as many men. Our boys need but the confirmation of this to fairly worship the " King of the Hawks."

Immediately after the fight a Roanoke, Lieutenant-Colonel Betts resigned and Major Kimball went to New York and came back to us as Lieutenant-Colonel. Captain Jardine was promoted and is now Major. Lieutenant Leahy, who had command of our Company in the fight, is our Captain; Ensign Flemming is First Lieutenant, and that is all that just now concerns us.

When the news of the victory of Roanoke reached New York, the inhabitants of that goodly city made a great stir about it. Our charge soon got to be famous. It was pictured in a dashing style in the " Frank Leslie," and more modestly (and more truly) in " Harper's Weekly." For a time the young ladies talked about getting up medal for us, but I am inclined to think that movement is dropped, and I am not sorry, for in truth, though of course I would be proud to carry a medal from the war, I do not think we have done enough to deserve it. Well, I don't know—we certainly have the honor of having

110

taken the first battery in this war at the point of the bayonet, but, deserving it or not, I do not think we will get it, so I 'll drop the subject. The Regiment has subscribed about three hundred dollars with which to get a sword for Colonel Hawkins, and we are unanimous in wishing to make this present worthy of the expression of our esteem, and of its intended owner.

But I have forgotten to speak of another honor that has been paid to our boys by the young ladies of New York who seem to take a sincere interest in our welfare. This is a beautiful new flag. It looks very bright beside our two torn and worn old flags, which were just as bright nearly two years ago on Fifth Avenue, but which now look and are really veterans beside the new recruit.

Sunday Evening, April 6th.

To-day has been one of the most pleasant and, I may add, joyful days that I have experienced with the Regiment and I don't believe I am far wrong in saying that it has also been the best Colonel Hawkins has spent with us. Yesterday, we got our much-talked of and really handsome Zouave uniforms, and to-day we have worn them for the first time at Inspection and Dress Parade. Colonel Hawkins was present, and of course everybody from other Regiments, with a large majority of commissioned officers, were there. We did our best to look our best, as of course we did. But the orders that were read were the best of all, as it was unexpected and appropriate for the occasion. Colonel Hawkins took the opportunity to express his thanks to the Regiment and his determination to accept no higher position than that which commands us. He used these words, " I seek no higher position than that which commands this splendid body of young men." He took this occasion to speak of the prevailing habit among the commissioned officers, of drinking and tippling. (The Colonel is a strict temperance man.) He said that he had seen this for a long time, but had said nothing, hoping that the officers would see and remedy the evil of the poor example they showed to those who ought to take pattern from them. He had waited in vain, and now was the time for him to step in and without any partiality arrest the progress of the spreading evil. Now this speech caused not a man in the ranks to blush, for the whole was directed to the officers, and that made us feel particularly good. Colonel Hawkins has never exactly agreed with the officers, but he could not help himself so far, and they had the best of him. But now, when he knows that he has men in the ranks whom he could put in any office, he can well feel independent of them, and so it is that this is King Hawkins' day, for the officers had theirs when the Regiment was in its infancy.

When the parade was over and our ranks broken, some of the Company surprised Hawkins with the wildest cheers, as he was talking with a knot of officers who had congregated around him. He was really so affected that his handkerchief was brought out to dry the big drops from his eyes. As soon as the first lot disappeared, H and G went up and cheered him and went back at a Double-quick, but the best was the last. Company B went up in four ranks at a Double-quick, gave the nine cheers and the " Zou-Zous " as the others had done, and then broke ranks, and with one accord started on a breakneck run for quarters, seemingly afraid the Colonel might be too much affected, and wishing to give him something to laugh at, too.

Well, this day has demonstrated two things: the Colonel thinks too much of us to leave us for the command of a Brigade, and his regard is returned by every man in the Regiment. We knew before, that he liked us, but now, in spite of the offices that are between us, we would die for one another.

Wednesday Evening, April 9th.

Last Monday two Companies, H and I, were detailed to go on a reconnaissance up the Sound with a detachment of six Companies of the Sixth New Hampshire, Major Jardine commanding our detachment, and all under the command of Lieutenant-Colonel Griffin of the Sixth. We went on board the " Virginia," which has been changed into a passable gun-

112

The Charge of Hawkins Zouaves, Camden

COLONEL RUSH C. HAWKINS

"PRIVATE" JOHNSON

AIN LAWRENCE LEAHY

"CIVILIAN" JOHNSON

boat. We were favored with "Burnside" weather when we started, which followed us till we returned, but this did not discourage us, for as long as it rained, we took it for an omen of good luck. Our destination was Elizabeth City and our object was to break up a recruiting-office near the city and bag as many "Wild-Cats" as possible. How we succeeded, I will try to tell.

The fleet consisted of six gunboats: the "Stars and Stripes," "Commodore Perry," "Eagle," "Morse," "Virginia" and one other. We made Elizabeth City Monday evening and anchored in the mouth of the river for the night, but as early in the morning as we could see, the anchors were weighed and our detachment disembarked on the wharf of the city. It did not take us long to form, and before the few negroes who were in the place were out of their beds, we were marching through the desolate streets. I never saw a deserted city before and I never want to again, for it was a sorrowful sight indeed. The streets that should have been teeming with life to give the blocks expression were desolate and oppressive. Hardly a white soul was to be seen. A large district was burned and a blackened mass of ruins was all that was left of many blocks of frame and brick buildings. It was a new experience for me, novel and not pleasant, for I could not but think how many innocent families must now suffer as fugitives before our arms. But we had not much time to indulge in such thoughts, for we were now in the outskirts of the city, and we did not know but that this day might be the last for some of us. We had hardly gotten outside the place when two pickets were taken, and from them the Major got some information of importance, for when we got to a little bridge, he left the prisoners there with a guard, and gave us "Double-quick" for some distance through ankle-deep mud, for the rain still followed us. We came to a halt in front of a large white mansion, and sure enough, this was the recruiting-office, but instead of showing fight, they showed the white feather, and we bagged about twenty-five of them. But Wild-Cats! They were certainly the tamest of any I could imagine, without a show of uniform

113

and mostly without anything like proper arms or equipments, and they presented but a very sorry spectacle to a soldier. And most of them seemed to be glad that they were taken. It was much regretted that we did not get the Captain, who was apparently the only one in the Company who wanted to fight, for he ordered the men to fire on us, and when he could not get them to, he made tracks for the woods and escaped. His name was Banks. As soon as a guard was provided for the prisoners, we resumed our march up the road at a very rapid rate in spite of the rain and mud. But though we came upon a few of their quarters, they had all taken the alarm and fled. But not to escape, mind you, for before they knew anything, they were embraced by the New Hampshire Regiment, which had gone up the Pasquotank River in the " Eagle," to cut off their retreat. By this maneuver they succeeded in taking some sixty prisoners, who ran into them in running away from us. A great many of our boys were in ignorance of this plan, and when we heard the firing ahead and came upon them in a solid body blocking the road, we thought there was a fight in the wind, and skirmishers were deployed. They were soon called in, however, for the supposed enemy showed us the Stars and Stripes.

We had now traveled about five miles, and we did not advance much further, but returned by the same road, stopping at the recruiting-office to refresh ourselves with the bread and coffee we found there.

On the way back, I noticed the " Eagle " with her two white pilot-houses looking for all the world like a Southern summer home through the trees, and I am certain that a great many who saw her thought she was the abode of some Southern planter. We returned to the " Virginia " yesterday afternoon and are back in camp, having succeeded in our object beyond our expectations. The elements did not favor us with anything but frowns of a dismal sort, for as we embarked in a rain, so did we disembark, with the additional pleasure of being nearly swamped by the rough sea, in Colonel Hawkins' launch. I am sorry that I was not able to make a couple of sketches up

114

there, too I saw two or three points of interest. Excepting the city itself, the principal one was the locality of the little naval battle where Lynch's fleet was destroyed, for there, not far from the city, lay the " Fanny " and the " Curlew," their iron skeletons, red with rust, just visible above the water's edge. That is the last of the poor " Fanny."

CHAPTER X

The Battle of Camden

April 14th.

YESTERDAY was Sunday as surely as to-day is Monday, and I was on guard. General Burnside arrived suddenly with a fleet of gunboats from New-Berne, early in the day. He brought a mail for us from Hatteras. In the guard-house, as we prepared to give him the usual review and salute, speculation was rife as to the meaning of his sudden appearance, but we did not come to anything more definite than that it meant something. Burnside usually means something. About four o'clock, the Regiment marched out to the drill grounds and was reviewed by the old, slouchy-looking General. We were all in our new Sunday-go-to-meetings and did our prettiest. Company K saluted with the usual thirteen rounds, and in return he complimented us very warmly.

After the review, the General stationed himself in front of the Colonel's quarters for the Dress Parade, and I had a good view of him. His features are well known to us all, and his clothing is certainly curious, though perhaps characteristic of the man. He was dressed in a suit which reminded me of some old fish-peddler, with a huge sack coat, of a faded brown color, coming down below the knees, meeting his top-boots, and showing his splendid stature to advantage. He was crowned by some kind of a black stove-pipe hat bound with a white band. It was not a military hat, and it was not and never could have been a dress hat, and who it could ever have been built for, is hard to imagine. But as plainly as he was dressed, or rather, as badly as he tried to dress himself, he never could succeed in hiding that magnificent figure. As Company C was escorting colors, he went to see the prisoners we had taken at Elizabeth City, and I now noticed that he wore nothing to mark his rank but the belt and his famous silver-mounted pistol. When he got back, he found the Regiment released from their muskets and ready to cheer him, and heartily did they do so as many as twelve or fifteen times, and they seemed to be delighted to

116

get a peep at the General's bald pate, as he gracefully lifted the wonderful hat and waved it in return, as General Phelps used to do at Newport News.

An order was read out on Dress Parade which throws a little light on the sudden appearance of General Burnside. The whole force of this post is to be held in marching order, and with three days' provisions, be ready to start after six o'clock to-morrow night; and as this will be a dangerous as well as a fatiguing reconnaissance, so the order states, no man but one able to bear any amount of fatigue will be allowed to go. So much we know. We will know more or nothing at all, three or four days from now.

June 30th.

Yes. Not only April, but May as well, has gone, and here I am at the end of June, and I have no doubt that the Journal has entertained doubts as to my existence, for it has been tossed about in my knapsack for two months and a half and never even been looked at. This conduct might well imply some serious doubts, coming as it does after the order noted over two months ago. The interval of space on the page is not long between my note of the evening of April Fourteenth and the lines I am now writing, but the interval of time has been as long as the dates imply, and in that interval events have transpired not only in the country at large which in these records I do not pretend to chronicle, but in the little world composed of our own Regiment. Many a poor fellow, in full life and spirits when I last penned notes in this Journal, is now no more. Cruel War has placed them far beyond our reach, and it is of this that I have something to say, for I came nearer to the brink of death than, so far as I am able to know, I ever was before. I will now commence to trace, as nearly as I can, the events in which I have played my humble part. It must be from memory, for I have not been able to take my notes since the Nineteenth of April.

On the Eighteenth of April—my birthday, by the way—the three Regiments composing Colonel Hawkins' Brigade, the Eighty-ninth New York Volunteers, the Sixth New Hamp-

117

THE LONG ROLL

shire Volunteers and our own, joined the Twenty-first Massachusetts and the Fifty-first Pennsylvanians, which had come
from New-Berne with a portion of the Marine Artillery, the
whole commanded by General Reno. We embarked in a fleet
of half a dozen transports and as many more gunboats, and
started from here toward Elizabeth City. We were on the
" Ocean Wave " and we found ourselves in quarters close
enough; but I have a peculiar knack of getting myself a lone
corner, which I did on this occasion, and settled myself down
and was soon fast asleep. From this I was aroused about
eleven o'clock to " Fall in." We were in the Pasquotank River,
about two miles below Elizabeth City, and here we were to land.
All the small boats were now brought into requisition and
silently they were filled with dusky shadows intermixed with
shining steel, glistening brightly against the large, beautiful
moon. The boats were propelled almost noiselessly toward
the shore, giving place to the other boats, which were likewise
filled to overflowing with human freight and firelocks. But
alas, I can not make it all romance, for the water was so shallow,
as we approached the shore, that we had to leave the boats
and splash ashore as best we could in knee-deep water for about
a mile, so you may come to the conclusion that we got ashore
on rather " wet-bottomstandings." Owing to this method of
landing, which could not be accomplished very well without
some time as well as noise, it was quite a while before the Regiment could get together. It took the Marine Artillery and our
battery longer still to get the cannons ashore, so that it must
have been nearly two o'clock Saturday morning before the
column got orders to go forward. Meanwhile, the advance
guard was thrown out, and I had the honor of being one chosen
from our Company. This advance was, in the present instance,
composed of two privates from each Company, with a Sergeant
and a Captain. Lieutenant Klingsoehr, * a brother-in-law of
General Siegel, had the latter honorable position, and com-

* First Lieutenant Victor Klingsoehr, Company A. There is some doubt as to this name on
account of the peculiar spelling of it in the original Journal, but it is here given, as the only name
in the list of wounded at Camden that in any way resembles the name as written.

118

THE LONG ROLL

manded us, and Colonel Hawkins could not have imposed the important trust upon a better man, for he is as cool as a cucumber, as brave as a lion, and it is impossible to surprise him or to take him off his guard. Our guide was a negro, apparently of some intelligence, but either through his ignorance or his deep cunning, we became his dupes at last. We were sent out immediately to reconnoiter the woods and the road we were to take.

By this time I had gotten an inkling as to the object of the expedition, and it turned out to be pretty nearly correct. The Brigade was in two divisions: the force from New-Berne was commanded by General Reno in person, and took a different route, though where they landed I do not know. At any rate they stole a march on us, through the duplicity of our guide. The forces from Roanoke were commanded by our Colonel, and it was the intention, it seem, that we should take the advance and meet General Reno or join him from a different direction, and by a rapid march fall upon a body of Georgians and Wild-Cats who were stationed to hold the Locks of the Dismal Swamp Canal. "Bag 'em," if we could, at any rate, dislodge them and destroy the locks and the bridges, thus cutting off communication between Norfolk and the Counties of Camden, Currituck and Pasquotank, and by so doing clear the vicinity for our intended operations in the rear of Norfolk, the then great Confederate stronghold.

After almost three hours of tedious waiting, we heard the order, " Forward March," and then the solid trampling of feet. We were then deployed as skirmishers on either side of the road in the woods, and instructed to always keep within sight of the head of the column. Now, you, who read this, will probably be at home in your snug little parlor feeling all at peace and secure, and if you are a lover of adventure and romance, and on the top of that, have never seen service, you will in all probability think it a fine situation to be in the Advance Guard, and if I judge you correctly, you will " poh-poh " me when I say that it is not. Especially, with the style of warfare with which we are contending. Now, I am a very

119

good soldier, so my comrades say, and I am proud of it, but I lack one great qualification, or more properly may I term it, inclination, and that is I am not favorably inclined to getting killed. I would rather live than die, any day. I don't exactly glory in the idea of being a target for the Southern Chivalry, even though they are poor marksmen, nor do I fancy being tickled with one of those things, I beg a thousand pardons, I mean Bayonets; and for these several reasons, I do not wish the masculine reader, in general, or the feminine reader, in particular, to laugh at me when I say it is not nice to be deployed as skirmisher in the woods at night, when a log looks like a masked battery, and a pile of wood looks like a pile of men; and even in the open field, you are not at any moment sure but that you hear the trampling of hoofs and discern the appearance of a dashing guerrilla band, who could be on top of the poor Advance, have him slashed to pieces and be off again, before he could get any support from the column. But, mind you, I had not been chosen, had I not first volunteered. And, reader, if you should chance to get into a similar position and are constituted like myself, not caring to get killed—not particularly liking it, I mean—just summon Reason to your aid, comfort yourself with the fact that you have but one life to be taken from you, and under whatever circumstances a few moments may place you, make up your mind to defend that as long as you can; for the way I look at it, when a person makes as good a struggle for his life as he knows how and gets worsted, he will not be accused by the Almighty of committing suicide, anyway. What I mean is, that the Good God will make many allowances for a brave man's shortcomings when he dies in a hurry. But I am wide of the track.

The first incident that is worth mentioning transpired after we had marched about two miles from the landing. A Rebel picket ran the gauntlet of our skirmishers, whether intentionally or accidentally, I can not say, but he did it in gallant style. The column was marching up a road between two fields and approaching a dark line of woods in front, and we were deployed on each side of the road, when he shot like a streak of lightning

120

THE LONG ROLL

right before us. His horse was white, which made him plainly discernible for the moment against the dark background. We fired about six shots at him, apparently without effect. For my part I withheld my fire. It is impossible for me to say whether he returned fire or not, but my comrade, Dennis, says he only fired at him because he thought the bold horseman was firing at me. If that was the case, I did not know it.

At daybreak, while our Regiment was stopping a moment to rest, one of our boys accidentally shot himself while fooling with his musket, but he was not dangerously wounded. At eight o'clock, we had made about twelve miles from the landing place, and the order was given to halt for breakfast. We were abreast of a neat, two-story cottage of fair dimensions, and we were glad to take advantage of the nice grass and cool shade. I felt more like having a smoke than anything to eat, and I asked the Lieutenant for permission to light my pipe. This he readily gave, but with the injunction not to trespass on my power by behaving "unlike a gentleman." I hope he would not have thought this necessary, had he known me better. I knocked at the door, and waited, I thought a reasonable time, and then I knocked again, this time in true soldier style with the butt of my musket, and at length the door was opened by a fair representative of a Southerner, with somewhat of a military moustache. so I thought, at the moment his face flashed into mine.

The next moment I was attracted by something else: this was a peep at a pretty leg—well, d——n it, it is out! A skirt, the rustling of woman's dress, the soft closing of a door and turning of a key. All this was in the interval of the opening of the door and my "Good morning, Sir!" but the le—, the skirt and the sound of the key produced a smile that he could not help seeing and knowing the meaning. "With your permission, Sir, I will light my pipe."

To this speech the dignified Southerner apologized for having no matches, and showed me to the kitchen, which was exactly where I wanted to go. At the sight of the gentleman's morning meal, I got "grub-struck," to use the slang of the camp; and

121

instead of smoking, I took to eating nice hot cakes, which I am sure tasted as good to me as they do to Jeff Davis.

"Dinah," said I, while I was devouring hoe cake, "was your master ever in the army?"

"Yes, Massa."

"So! Well, was he an officer?"

"Well, I de 'no', Massa, but de call him Lieutenant."

"Lord love you, Dinah, won't you give me another cake?" and with it in my hand I started out to find Lieutenant Klingsoehr, forgetting all about my smoke. He went to the house immediately to see the Lieutenant and I went back to the kitchen to see Dinah.

"Dinah, I hear the Georgians are up here waiting for us, is that so?"

"Yes, Massa," she said in an earnest tone; "de tole me you-uns would n't dare to cum so far up yer."

"They will find out whether we will or not before night," and I filled myself with cake and milk, and that done, I filled my pipe and had a delicious smoke.

Colonel Hawkins now came up to communicate with the Lieutenant, who told him the Southerner was formerly a Lieutenant in the Rebel Army. Our Colonel no sooner heard it than he rode into the yard and saluted the ex-officer. He recognized him as one of the officers who had been taken at Hatteras and released. "Well, Lieutenant Bell," said he, "you did not expect me up this way so soon, did you?" Bell said he did not expect him quite so soon, and he hoped the Colonel was well, and what they said after that did not concern me, nor need it you.

Fifteen minutes was all the time we were allowed for breakfast, and it passed soon enough, we all found out, and the column was on the road again. We had not marched fifteen minutes before we heard the loud echoing boom of artillery, making the air whistle with the awful moan, and the ground tremble with the reverberation of the explosives.

Our gunboats were probably at work in the river. For about an hour this cannonading was kept up, and it probably

122

gave credit to the rumors which were now flying like wildfire before our column through the country, that the Zouaves were coming. The sound of artillery seemed to give fresh legs to our brave fellows, for we were now pushing on faster than ever, in hopes of reaching our destination sooner.

At this juncture we overtook four " Yogles," as we call them, with two miserable old shotguns among them. To our questions as to where they were bound for, they were fools enough to say they were going to muster. "Here, Punyers, and you, Johnson, take these four men and report them and their intention to Colonel Hawkins," ordered the Lieutenant. After considerable persuasion they were induced to comply with the request, although they did so as if consenting to go to the guillotine. We found the Colonel a little in advance of the Regiment, talking to a couple of the Chivalry, and to his puzzled look of inquiry, I told him, " Lieutenant Klingsoehr reports these four men to you; they were going to muster." He looked at them for a moment and then at us, as if to mark the difference in appearance, and then exclaimed: " My God! do you want to fight us? Do go about your business, for surely you can't fight us." Now, if I had been the Southerners, I would have taken the Colonel at his word; but they were so dumbfounded that they did not know what to do or to say, and while they were in this dilemma, the Colonel changed his mind and sent them to the rear of the column with the others who had been picked up here and there.

Again we pressed on, but now we all began anxiously to inquire how many miles more it was to our destination. The inhabitants told us, nine miles, at one village; and then we would march a mile farther perhaps, and meet some one who would say it was twelve miles. And it did seem to our weary legs that when we had walked twelve miles we were as far from Camden or River Bridge as ever, and at length we got up a very melancholy joke about the length of miles in Dixie. We compared them to the old riddle about the ditch, " the more you cut it the longer it grows," and it did seem as though the farther we walked the greater the distance to go. The guide

123

was remonstrated with and threatened, but he declared that he knew no other way but the one we were traveling. The merciless sun poured down on us continual streams of fire, regardless of our burdens and exposed heads. Our boys began to drop out from sheer exhaustion, and still there was no apparent diminishing in the distance. At last, the Colonel gave the order to halt where we could refresh ourselves with water and cool our hands and faces. He had walked with the men since morning, and he now threw himself down on his cloak, and while he took off his shoes and stockings, vowed that if there ever was a Regiment could march, *his could*. As our Advance was moving up to an appropriate distance, our scout came back and reported a flag in sight, but he could not make out if it was the " Stars and Stripes " or the " Stars and Bars." I was dispatched to report accordingly to the Colonel, who ordered Lieutenant Klingsoehr to make a careful reconnaissance and find out if we had friend or foe before us. Just as I had delivered the order to the Lieutenant, the Colonel came up himself, and we formed around him as an escort, and moved cautiously forward.

Owing to the crooked roads we had taken, Reno's command was ahead of us, while we labored under the delusion that there could be nobody but the enemy in front, for the General had given us the Advance. So this caution on our part was warrantable. We had not gone far when we met Reno's rear guard, with the General among them. Explanations proved that we had marched about ten miles needlessly, all on account of a black scoundrel or fool. I will not repeat either the General's or the Colonel's exact words concerning this guide, for if they by chance should see this page, it might cause them to blush. It sounded for some time as if a bullet would be far too good for him, and a piece of hemp was talked of, but whether the poor fellow was despatched, or just skedaddled, I can not tell, for I have never seen him since, nor heard of him, either.

Colonel Hawkins asked General Reno where the Rebels were, and the General replied, " They are nowhere "; but he found out his mistake before night. We were ordered to halt

THE LONG ROLL

and take it easy while the General pushed the reconnaissance
a little farther with his comparatively fresh men. So we
accordingly stopped and proceeded to take a little refreshment
while General Reno resumed his march, for now we gave up
all idea of having a fight that day. We rested about an hour
when we again fell into line and moved forward at an easy pace.
We had marched thus about a mile when a solemn "Boom-m-m"
followed by a moan and a sharp report rang savagely on our
startled ears. The Advance heard the report in silence, and
the only evidence they gave of their having heard it was by
quickening their pace. A few minutes elapsed when another
report, seemingly louder than the first one, was heard. The
same interval of time, and another ball moaned through the
air. But now we hear something in a different tone. "That's
our metal; we know that ring; Company K and the Marine
Artillery have been challenged to a game of ball and they accept.
The ball is up; they are pitching lively at long range. Well,
we'll be there to take a hand in it."

Here comes General Reno's Aide telling the men to fall in
with their Companies. Here we are in front of the battlefield.
We can see the smoke of the Rebel guns; look! there at the
edge of the woods, there's where their battery is. Look out!
there is one of their messages coming—as if one could look out.
Too low, it falls short. "Clear the road, lads, the Marine
Artillery is bringing another gun into action." Go back, it
will be our turn by and by.

We are now dismissed by Lieutenant Klingsoehr and told to
report ourselves to our respective Companies. Our little band
had grown intimate and now we were about to part, some of
us never to meet again on this side of the grave.

The General had already disposed his Brigade and had
given them their various tasks to perform in order of battle,
and now our Regiment emerges from the hollow into the open
field. We are moving forward into the very teeth of their guns.
"Countermarch by file left!" is the order. What does this mean?
But it is all right. The Colonel smiles at our inquisitive faces
and says, "We will try and euchre them." Very good, if you can.

125

THE LONG ROLL

After countermarching, the Regiment filed to the left and took the outskirts of the woods on the right of the Rebel position, thus menacing their left flank. They were up to our game, however, and while we were slowly pushing our way through the thick woods and thicker underbrush, they amused themselves by pitching solid ball at us. They made a good deal of noise about it, but did n't hurt any one. It showed how warmly they felt for us, for instead of returning the salutations of our battery, they let us have it as thickly as they were able. While we were making very slow progress through the outskirts of the woods, the balls whistled over us as only a cannon ball can, sometimes cutting off tree-tops over our very heads, and with a solid thump or crash as they either embedded themselves in the earth, or came in contact with some stump or tree, near, in fact, all around us.

We were finally ordered to halt while the scouts and officers could reconnoiter a little. We were ordered not to expose ourselves to the fire, by showing the red caps, and the tall underbrush enabled us to comply. No sooner had we disposed of ourselves than the cannonading ceased; even our own guns ceased talking, and there was a calm—that calm, still and impressive, that combatants take when they are drawing breath, summoning all their energies for the death struggle that is to come. Just as the ship's crew prepare in silence, but with resolute hearts to resist the fresh fury of the Storm King, when he pauses to concentrate all his power in a tiger-like dart to crush the human foes who crest his billows, so were we nerving ourselves for the fearful onset which would decide for victory or death: so were we preparing to storm the jaws of Hell, which in silence were opening before us.

Here comes Colonel Kimball on horseback from the field. He has been reconnoitering on his own hook. Quiet; there, he is talking to the Colonel. Hark! the Colonel is turning to speak to us:

" Boys, are you able and willing to make a charge? "

" Yes !" from five hundred voices.

THE LONG ROLL

"Fall in!" ordered Colonel Kimball in his peculiar fighting tone.

"Fall in!" echoed the Captains of Companies.

"Fall in!" re-echoed the Sergeants, and the orders were quickly obeyed.

"Forward March!" was the next command, and we were moving out in the field, in files of four deep, abreast of the enemy's position.

Like a bunch of fire-crackers, the enemy's muskets commenced, by one, twos and threes, to crack till the whole bunch got going on either side. Out of this convincing din, came the order "Trail arms! Battalions into line!" and as the enemy's battery gave us a volley, Colonel Kimball rode up to the head of the line, waved his sword over his head, and with a voice that was heard above the fearful din, gave the order, "Charge Bayonets!"

The reply was a yell that would defy the fiends of Hell, and as we rushed forward, it drowned the noise of both musketry and cannon. A moment and the Rebel guns flashed, and our Regiment was down on "its stomach" like one man, and the shower of grape passed over it. Captain Leahy swung his sword over his head, and with a voice and expression I shall never forget, shouted, "Give 'em the cold steel, Lads!" and with another yell, we were at them again.

It was then as if some superhuman hand, capable of holding bushels of bullets and grape in the palm, itself unseen, was hurling them upon us. So did that storm of leaden and iron hail fall around and pelt us. Every inch of the air seemed thick with whistling messengers of death. It is as impossible for me to describe, as it is for me to conceive, how a person on that field could escape without being hit in a dozen places. Again the Rebel guns belched forth a storm of iron into our teeth, and again the Regiment was down. Up again, and at them more furiously than ever.

If it were possible for an eye-witness to view us now with impassioned eye! What a wonderful, what a terrible and magnificent spectacle would he behold. Amidst this ringing grape,

127

singing bullets, angry " Minie " balls, the roar of cannon, rattle of musketry, yells of combatants, shrieks of the dying, groans of the wounded, all commingling into one horrible din! Fearful! Terrible! Indescribable!

How was it possible that men lived here! What wonderful courage or passion induces men, mortals, to rush into this furnace of Hell, my poor mind can not fathom. A few moments ago, say two moments ago, sixty as brave men as ever handled a musket were enjoying the privilege of drawing breath; now one small cog has caught in the revolving wheel of Time, and they have fallen, some never to move again. And this is War!

Up to this moment, I may say during the whole engagement, I never saw the enemy, although I tasted their lead. This may seem strange, but there is an explanation. When our Regiment charged, the Rebels were in their first position, which they had chosen with admirable forethought, and cunningly fortified. They had placed themselves in a ditch behind a fence and this they set on fire, so while they could see us through the smoke and pour in their fire, we could not see them or know where they were, except as their bullets guided us. From here they poured in that splendid fire, but glory to our Regiment, it did not annihilate us! They, seeing that the Northern " Mudsills " would be apt to use the bayonets if they could not keep them off, fired in retreat, falling back on their batteries in the edge of the woods. So that, when our fellows had exhausted the little vigor there was left in them by charging over a space of three hundred yards, they found the Rebels as far away as ever, and still pouring their murderous volley into our well-thinned ranks.

At this juncture I received a wound in the right wrist by a musket ball, which caused my musket to drop out of my hand. I was much excited at the time and have no distinct recollection of feeling any pain, but I remember the moment I was struck and fancied I could see the ball enter. I could almost swear I heard it sing. Anyway I saw the black spot of blood where it entered the flesh. " Well, if this is the only one I am going to get, I am lucky," was my first thought. I may have said it,

128

Three-Gun Battery

PLATE XXVIII

The Burning of Winton

Earthwork; Built by Sir Walter Raleigh's Colony, Roanoke Island

PLATE XXIX

but of that I am not sure. Somehow or other, it entered my mind that I was of no more use and that I would be safer lying down than standing, and accordingly down I went, for I believe I told you before, that I have no particular liking for getting killed, even when it is necessary, and much less when it is not. While the Regiment was pushing on, my thoughts happened to stumble on the idea that if I had a revolver, I might make another attempt at getting killed, but as I had nothing that I could use with my left hand, I commenced to think about leaving the field, as I had a right to do. But the bullets had by no means ceased to sing over our heads, and I did hate the notion of a bullet in the back. That it might hurt, never entered my mind as it does now. It was only the mortification I would feel in showing the doctor such a wound, that bothered my muddled brain. But by this time, I found out where the bullet had lodged, and as the pain commenced to bother me and the blood flowed rather freely, I concluded to leave the field and find a doctor, even at the risk of the bullet in the back. When I got on my legs I started to run, but I found myself so weak that I soon changed Double-quick to a walk, although the bullets were still plowing up the ground around me and whistling just as close to me through the air. I luckily escaped, however, the painful necessity of showing the doctor a few holes in my back.

I found Doctor Humphreys, but as he was very busy bandaging our fellows as fast as he could, and I knew very well he would be employed for some time, I made up my mind not to trouble him, but to find some of the other surgeons who were not so busy, for the very good reason that most all of the other Regiments were *too tired* to fight. I got to one of the farm hospitals and showed the doctor where the ball was, and asked him if he would be kind enough to extract it, " for our surgeon has his hands full."

" Certainly, in a moment. Sit down. Just in from the field? How goes the battle? "

" Well, Doctor, our fellows are very tired, and I am afraid ——— "

THE LONG ROLL

"Oh! Nonsense, my boy, don't you fear; it'll all turn out right. Here, I can attend to you now."

With a gash and a few good jerks he laid the killer before me on the table and commenced to staunch the blood. While he was doing up my wrist, I lost myself in contemplation of my good luck in getting off so easily with only this. And again, if I had received it one-half of an inch above, my hand might —yes, must—have gone; and one inch below, it would have entered my side and killed me; so here I was between two half-inches which, one way or the other, would have been but the alternative between life crippled, or death. I was aroused from this reverie by a tremendous volley of musketry. "My God, if that is the Rebels, may God help us!" and out I rushed from the hospital. "My God be praised!" and I shed tears of joy, for there was the Sixth New Hampshire Regiment pouring hell after them, and our own Regimental Flag was flying in the Rebel position. The battle was over, and the victory was ours.

Thus did we gloriously commemorate the anniversary of the Battle of Lexington.

When I quit, the Rebels had retreated to the edge of the woods, and our fellows saw that it was nothing but self-murder to try to get an honest shake at the Georgians with the bayonets. Our Colonel had fallen, and also Captain Graham, Captain Hammill and Adjutant Gadsden,* the latter mortally wounded. The lucky ones who were left filed off to the right, and while the Bugle sounded "Rally on the Colors," the first ones who reached the woods entertained the Georgians with a little play of musketry in a bushwhacking style. This was to give the others time to comply with the Bugle, and when the Rebels saw our boys ready to charge them again, they took up their line of march for Norfolk. The splendid volley that frightened me more than a little in the hospital, which proved to be the New Hampshire boys, hurried them off.

---

* Colonel Rush C. Hawkins, wounded left arm.
Captain A. S. Graham, Co. A. Wounded arm and leg. Camden, April 19th. 1862.
Captain William H. Hammill. Co, F. Wounded left arm.
Adjutant Charles A. Gadsden. Killed. Camden.

130

Owing to our inability to pursue, they carried off all their guns, leaving only the dead, twenty of them, showing that the havoc on their side was no less than on ours. They were most shockingly mutilated by our shrapnel, I am told, which was used by Company K and the Marine Artillery, Captain Howard commanding.

I began to hear vague rumors that Colonel Hawkins was badly wounded and that Major Jardine and our Lieutenant-Colonel were killed. If these proved true, how many of the men might I not expect to find dead or dying. At any rate, these rumors were enough to make me feel all anxiety to know the truth, and I started for the hospital. And what a sight met my eyes! Men mutilated in every way were lying about, those who could, standing, others stretched out on blankets, patiently waiting for the doctor, who was busy dressing the worst cases who filled the interior of the miserable apartment. There, among a motley lot of suffering men, lay Adjutant Gadsden, with as serene a countenance as if he were lying in his own tent. I thought he could not be dangerously wounded, and so I spoke to him. "Adjutant, this is rather hard, and your first, too." He had only been in the Regiment a week. "Yes," he answered; "it is my first, and it *is* hard." I have often asked myself if he knew then that he was going to die within the half-hour.

I found that Colonel Kimball was all right and Major Jardine too, and Colonel Hawkins was wounded in the left arm close to the shoulder. He was lying outside on a rubber blanket, looking smilingly at the scene around him, but in his smile there was an unmistakable sign of sympathy. During the fight, he was heard to exclaim, "My poor boys, I won't have fifty of them left." He saw I was wounded and spoke to me about it, and I, of course, explained and showed him the bullet. "Well," said he! "you are a very, very lucky, lucky young man." I admitted that I thought so too, and asked him where his wound was. The report that Colonel Kimball was killed probably sprung from the fact that his horse was completely riddled with grape and killed instantly in the early part of the action, and some one who had seen him fall must have reported his death to us at the lower hospital.

Colonel Kimball was very indignant, though, that he had escaped so easily, for he walked up to Colonel Hawkins and said: "You are a lucky man, Colonel. I'd give a thousand dollars if I had your wound. I am afraid my friends in New York will think me a coward because I never can get hit." And it is a pity that some Rebel would not oblige him by putting a couple of bullets into him just to satisfy his friends in New York.

While standing at the hospital, the thought struck me that I ought to carry a musket back to camp. And as though I were able to do so, I started off to the field where our men were scattered in groups, picking up the dead or carrying the wounded off toward the hospital. I saw Captain Leahy and Lieutenant Flemming conversing, and as I approached them, the Captain accosted me, sternly looking at me through his small, gray, twinkling eyes, "Where have you been, sir?"

I saw in a moment that he suspected me to be a skulker, at which I got a little indignant and answered in his own style, "To the hospital, sir."

This did not throw any lighter shade on his suspicion; for when a Regiment goes into action, those who get a sudden sick turn, generally get off with the excuse of helping the doctor.

"Well, sir, what have you been doing there?"

"Getting my ball cut out, sir," and at the same time I threw aside my coat sleeve and showed the bloody bandage.

He acknowledged his mistake, not in words, but in the complete change of manner.

"You ought to have a sling for that. Haven't you got one?"

"No, sir; but if this sack will serve the purpose, would you be kind enough to fix it around my neck?"

"Certainly, I will," said he, kindly; "but what are you doing out here, man—don't you see it is going to rain?"

I looked up at the sky, and to my astonishment saw that it was threatening a shower.

132

THE LONG ROLL

"I am ashamed to confess that I came out for a musket, for in the confusion I lost mine."

"And what do you want with a musket? When you want one I will give one to you; but meanwhile just you go to the hospital and keep out of the rain, and never mind the musket, unless you want to carry one off the field."

The ridiculousness of my errand now for the first time struck me, and as the rain commenced to fall I started for the hospital. I have related this incident that you may see that I was almost in a "befoozled" state, for whether I was powder-drunk or dizzy from loss of blood or merely excited, I can not tell.

The storm that had been brewing now descended on us in its sublime fury. The lightning flash now took the place of the quick flashings of artillery and musketry. Loud peals of Heaven's artillery shook the air, the woods and the ground, as if trying to show that man's fearful doings could by no means throw Nature into the shade. The thunder shocks broke the frowning clouds of overhanging vapor which now poured down in streams, seemingly desirous of washing the blood from the face of the earth which was crying aloud to the world on high; wiping our sins away, and by tears trying to atone and cleanse the field of its bond of crime.

Our wounded were conveyed to a much better hospital across the field, where everything possible was done for the poor fellows. But alas, for so many, these attentions were of no avail. It was piteous to hear strong men, so lately healthy and able to help themselves, calling "for Heaven's sake" for some one to put an end to their misery. It was awful to stand among men whose souls were departing, with apparently so little attention paid to them; and when I think of it, I wonder how it is possible to be so indifferent to such scenes as this. But no one who has not gone through what we have, can suspect how much a battle hardens the sensitive element in our natures. And what is this that I have described but a mere skirmish compared with other battles that have been fought lately in this unholy struggle. This is but a matter of

133

THE LONG ROLL

tens and hundreds, not worthy of a woodcut in an illustrated paper. What, then, must be the misery where it is hundreds killed and tens of hundreds wounded? What then, when hundreds of thousands are engaged and in proportion have a struggle like ours? But I can not go further, for it sickens my heart to contemplate these horrors, and please allow me to take a lighter strain.

I was standing alongside a corner of the hospital listening to Colonel Howard and Colonel Kimball, who were talking about their different experiences in the battle, and I was much interested in their conversation. It had not entirely ceased raining, and so I had my coat skirt thrown over my arm, which caused a mistake similar to that of Lieutenant Leahy's. Colonel Kimball, seeing nothing the matter with me apparently, thought that I ought to be doing something, and asked me where my Company was and where I belonged. I confessed that I did not know where my company was, and that I presumed I belonged at the hospital for the present at least. The sling now caught his eye, and very much like Captain Leahy he wished to atone for the wrong he had done me. Turning to a drummer standing by, he ordered, " Kill a chicken and give that wounded man something to eat, sir." I told him the trouble would be unnecessary, as I did not feel hungry. I commenced to suffer a little from the swelling in the hand, for inflammation had set in, and as the hand grew larger, the bandage grew tighter. The doctors were all busy, and I dared not touch the bandage for fear of starting the blood again. I found some medical assistant, however, and he tore the bandage looser and I experienced a happy relief from pain.

I wondered what could be the idea of all the feathers that were strewn all over the house, and for some time I could not solve the mystery. On going into a little bedroom, I saw that a cannon ball had gone through the house, smashing through two walls and lodging in a chimney   In passing through the bedroom it took both head and footboard from the bedstead, and plowed the feather bed just where a person would be, thus scattering the feathers all over the house. As soon as I saw
134

this bed, although it was minus feathers, I determined to have a snooze on it, for *I was tired.* Ten minutes after I tumbled onto it, I was fast asleep. From a sweet and refreshing but short sleep, I was aroused by the doctor about eleven o'clock, and told that we must get into an ambulance, for as re-enforcements were coming from Norfolk large enough to smash us, we had orders to leave. I was packed into one of the three ambulances with Captain Graham, Captain Hammill, Lieutenant Bartholomew and Private Hartenfals of Captain Hammill's Company.* Both Captains were wounded in the arms, the Lieutenant in the head, and Hartenfals had both thumbs taken off with one bullet while in the act of firing his piece. There were others, but I don't recollect them, only that there were enough to fill the wagon so brimful that it was an impossibility to stretch one way or the other, like slaves closely packed on a slave-ship.

Ye gods! If I live to be as old as Methuselah I will never forget this night's ride. It rained a slow, dripping, drizzly rain all night long. The darkness could almost be felt, and the roads—God knows how the driver could see them!—were as rough as they are in Minnesota. The wheels would tumble into gullies to the wheel-cobs, and give a lurch that often threatened a soft bed in the mire for us, or some like catastrophe for every moment. God only knows how the poor fellows with broken and shattered bones stood it. Would we ever get back to the landing, was often asked, and it did seem as though the end would never come. But as sure as there is an end coming to all things, so there was for us. Just as day was breaking through the fleeting clouds, we came within sight of the landing-place. But what a species of mud-humans did we look to be now! Some of the fellows had, in the Egyptian darkness, stumbled, rolled and tumbled in the gutters and in mire and clay a dozen times or so, and certainly we were as nearly bedaubed from head to foot as I could ever wish to see anybody. Our wounded were soon stowed snugly away in the little cabin of the " Ocean

---

* Second Lieutenant Thomas L. Bartholomew, Co. B. Wounded, Camden, April 19th. Henry Hartenfals, Co. F. Both thumbs amputated, Camden.

Wave," where we had our wounds dressed by the time we got to Roanoke again.

Our losses were heavy in this expedition. Our Regiment had eleven killed, about fifty wounded, and enough missing to make the total about seventy-five, and add to this the few the four other Regiments lost, making the sum total about one hundred twenty-five. And what had we gained? That is hard telling, although the bridge that it was our object to destroy was destroyed by the enemy to cut themselves off from pursuit, and that was all our gain. But ask us what we did, and I can answer you, even though we will not get one-half the credit for this expedition that we got for our charge on this Island, for the very good reason that at Camden there were no material results. We worked hard enough and lost enough, the reader knows. In a word or two : we made one of the most rapid marches that has ever been made in this war, through severe heat and quantities of dust, and after this march of thirty-four miles (in fourteen hours) we dislodged the best infantry in the Rebel service, besides one Company of artillery and one of cavalry, from their own chosen position. And when we consider our condition, tired and worn out, compared with those who were fresh and well prepared, the achievement is not altogether unworthy of being described. In this plain, unvarnished statement, I have not pretended to give the history of the expedition, but merely to present to the reader the incidents which came under my own eyes, and my own impressions which these incidents produced. It would be foolish for me to ask other members of our Regiment to accept my statements as their own, for I know well that a battle is seen from as many points of view as there are combatants engaged. I am therefore in hopes that this account will be found more interesting as it is than if I attempted to run in opposition to the papers by compiling a history from them.

Let me anticipate in the course of events enough to say that, about three days after our return to the Island, a general order arrived from General Burnside, complimenting all the troops under General Reno's command, and as a testimonial

136

THE LONG ROLL

of his appreciation of our services, and the victory which we gained under such hard circumstances, he ordered that we be permitted to inscribe " Camden " on our banners, with the date, "April 19th," which will be recorded in the history of our country as a day worthy of being remembered. And who knows but that this affair may have stimulated a skedaddling tendency to Norfolk! If I am right, the results of our best efforts were not so little after all.

As soon as we arrived on the Island we were packed off to the hospital, of course. I did not think at first that it would be necessary for me to go to bed at all, but I was mistaken. Doctor Humphreys said that, though my wound was not dangerous, it was serious and must be taken care of. Now what a pity it is that my physiological education has been so much neglected, that I can not describe the exact course that this bullet took; but lamentable as it is, so it is. You must content yourself with a home-made description. It entered the wrist when I was in the act of charging bayonets, and passed through it. In its hurried passage it was kind enough to fracture rather than to mash any bones, so that I had nothing to fear except mortification.

Our officers showed as much kindness of heart as they did bravery on the field. I don't think there was a commissioned officer in the Regiment but visited us, making pressing offers to supply anything we might want. Along toward evening one day, Captain Leahy came in and sat between Cockefier * and myself, chatting for some time about the battle. We were the only two wounded of his Company who were obliged to take to bed. Captain Leahy was pronounced by all to have been ahead of the column in the hottest of the fight, and by every way possible showed himself to be the bravest of the brave, and I told him that "the unanimous opinion in the hospital is that Company I has the bravest Captain in the Regiment." At this he smiled, the first time I have seen him smile from any remark of mine, and said that the boys did better than the officers. This from such a man made me proud,

---

* William Cockefier, Company I. Wounded shoulder. Camden, April 19th.

137

and I told him that I felt glad to know that, even if we had not gained anything, we had not lost any of our laurels.

In a week I was able to get up, and experienced that happy release from confinement that all invalids feel more or less. About this time we first heard that Colonel Hawkins had sent down to New-Berne for a boat to take us to New York, and for the first time we discovered that it was not so bad to be wounded after all. To be allowed the blessed privilege of seeing friends and relatives again, after a year of such an absence from the loved ones at home, is no mean reward for bravery, let me tell you. In fact, I think that a soldier who has been tossed around as we have been, would rather take a furlough than one or two hundred dollars. Imagine then the joy with which we heard the " Eastern Queen " on the evening of the Third of May, as she hove in sight from New-Berne, knowing that she was to bear us to our homes on the morrow. Home— what a magic word that is to a soldier! How many weary two hours I have spent on my lonely beat, thinking of Home. Now I would return, proud and conscious of having done my duty to my country, with victory in my very look. What a joyous moment when I should again embrace my sisters and my brothers. When I should be able to tell them my adventures. When I could promise never to leave home again, and what pleasant moments to compensate for the long two years of toil and danger. Among the beautiful hills of my own home. When my dreams would at last be realized in having some one to care for and to sympathize with me. And though now I can't go to Minnesota, I will see my sister Charlotte in New York and I have a home in Hudson City that is sure in its welcome for me, and I looked forward to the departure of the " Eastern Queen " with as much impatience as any of the others who had parents as well as sisters and sweethearts to welcome them back with open arms.

CHAPTER XI

The Furlough

THE Fourth of May was the anniversary of the muster of our Regiment into the United States Service, and a beautiful day it was. And a pleasant day, too, for us, for in the morning about eight o'clock we were ordered aboard the boat. Our furloughs were made out, and we had them and a small post-office of letters in our pockets, the latter for the friends of our comrades, with instructions to see them all, of course. We were taken aboard the fine little steamer, and only had to wait about an hour for orders from Colonel Hawkins, and then we would be off for home.

He finally came himself to see us off. He told us to be good boys, just as a father would when his children are to be trusted for the first time away from home. He was wounded, carrying a cloak over his bandaged arm, and some one observed that he ought to ask Doctor Humphreys for a furlough. He returned the good-humored sarcasm with a smile, and said he did not remain because he had to but from choice, and after shaking us all by the hand and giving a good word to each, he stepped into his boat. Now, our party was not in condition to cheer him as we would have done had we not been hospital cases, but we had a good substitute, for one of the boys who has a wonderful knack of imitating a rooster hobbled out of the cabin on his crutches and gave the Colonel one of the most lusty crows you can imagine. Loud and long did the crow resound, and we were told that the Colonel remarked to Lieutenant Barnett, "That don't sound as if he were very sick—does it Lieutenant?"

We immediately hove anchor and went toward the Pamlico Sound and anchored in the mouth of the Neuse River that night, and at daybreak we steamed up the River. The scenery is not more remarkable than that of any other stream of this section of the country and it only grew interesting as we approached the defenses of New-Berne. From the hurricane deck of the "Eastern Queen," I saw the breastworks that were taken

139

in such gallant style, causing a general skedaddling from the five or six nice batteries intended to command the river. One of these, a bomb-proof battery of two guns, was very interesting to me. These batteries with the formidable blockade of vessels and more formidable underground blockade of sharpened spikes calculated to sink any vessel that might run against them, formed, I think, a very perfect defense of the pretty little city behind them, which only the confidence that such men as Burnside inspire, could conquer. I do think that Burnside, so far, has done as much in proportion to the men he has commanded, as any General in the field.

We were at New-Berne till the next morning, taking some one hundred sick and wounded aboard who, like ourselves, were lucky enough to get home. Meanwhile, we had a good chance of seeing the place, and a beautiful little city it is, with numerous fine shade trees. Walking up the street, who should we meet but General Reno and General Burnside. We were a squad of us together, and saluted. Turning to Reno, General Burnside remarked, " So these are the boys who are going home, are they? " General Reno nodded, and the old man spoke to us all and inquired about our wounds. He was dressed (or undressed) as usual, with his slouched hat and an old faded vest and was in his shirt-sleeves. All he said about my wound was that he thought it was a " pretty little one to take home."

New-Berne is, or was, a nice little city, very similar in its appearance to Elizabeth City. We had plenty of time to see the place, but I never care much about cities or houses, be they ever so beautiful, and I found after a couple of hours' walk, that I could content myself just as well aboard the boat as in the guarded streets.

The next morning we started again on our journey. We cleared Hatteras Inlet in the afternoon and Cape Hatteras just as the sun was sinking behind that noble sentinel, the Lighthouse. We were favored with beautiful weather, and without anything unusual happening to disturb the monotony, our voyage was ended on the morning of the Ninth of May. How strange it seemed going up the old harbor, and how

140

THE LONG ROLL

familiar everything was, and how long the minutes and the hours after we got in sight of the old city. Oh! New York, I have not much to thank you for, but still I admit this morning I longed for you with strange impatience.

The Adjutant and some medical men came aboard, and after the inspection we ran up to the pier in the North River. There was a large crowd on the dock to receive us, and I soon picked out a boy to carry my knapsack and started for the ferry. But it was all about I could do to get there, for the New Yorkers seemed anxious that I should get home in a befoozled state the first thing. It was in vain I pleaded that I had not yet seen my folks, and that I did not drink. What, a soldier, and not drink! To be a Zouave and not drink, that seemed to startle the New Yorkers. So I found my pockets stuffed with cigars as a substitute, from men I had never seen before, and at last I got on board the ferry-boat, and then I was made the object of the undisguised attack of hundreds of two-gun batteries, which I swear I winced under more than I did before the sharpest artillery force of the enemy. And Heaven only knows how it was that I was not annihilated long before I reached home, but I did finally, and I got more used to these things afterwards. Mrs. Simpson was talking to a neighbor and about me, when I appeared. She saw me before I was within talking distance, but she called out, " Is that you, Charley? "

" Yes, it 's me " Where is Lottie? "

" She is in New York to-day. My Lord, Charley, how black you are! Are you hungry? "

" No, ma'am, not so very."

And then followed questions and answers that I can not attempt to transcribe. I took off my soldier clothes and settled myself down in an old, comfortable rocking-chair, and "Mother" set the table with some strange-looking things, which after considerable rummaging through my brain box, I remembered having used a long time ago. I despatched a Christian meal for the first time in a year, and I felt myself perfectly at home. Let me tell you it was pleasant to exchange charcoal water for

141

THE LONG ROLL

coffee, shingles for bread, home-made bread, and " salt horse " for good tender sirloin with such " heaps " of beautiful gravy.

I said I was not hungry, but my meal was a hearty one just the same, and I then prepared to enjoy the aroma of a good cigar. I was attracted to the front door by the boisterous laughter of children, and if there was not Sammy Simpson with my fez on, thrashing one of his playmates who was indiscreet enough to try how well my Rebel jacket fitted him, thus unexpectedly laying himself open to a thrashing in true " Zou-Zou " style. The jacket was one we had taken in an expedition above Elizabeth City some time before the battle of Camden.

I grew impatient waiting for my sister to come home, for her errands had detained her some time longer than " Mother" anticipated. And when she did come the children spoiled the surprise I had planned to give her, but that was all the same after all.

The next morning I started for New York, determined to get rid of a part of my post-office, and the first place I went was to see Mrs. Hutchings, the aunt of my old chum, Thain.* I took dinner with her at Williamsburgh, and then went up to Sixty-seventh Street near Broadway and delivered Warring's** letter to his mother, in whom I became much interested. She was, of course, glad to see me, as I had been the bed-fellow and friend of her son, and she made me promise to come again, as Mrs. Hutchings did, and I promised. I hunted up my old landlady and settled a small account, and then I waited for Harry Palmer. In the meantime I had to kiss a half-dozen girls of old acquaintance, a very disagreeable duty, which I performed, however, like a heroic soldier, and was most talked to death in the bargain. At last Harry came in, and—" My God, Johnson, is that you? " I assured him it was no one else, and he got reconciled. I had to take supper with him, of course. After getting all the news and promising to see him the next Sunday, I went home tired, and not exactly happy. I had

* Hamilton H. Thain, Company I.
** On a page of writing paper forming the cover of Journal "No. 7," is the name, " William H. Warring," which is presumed to be correct, though it is sometimes in the Journal itself, spelled with an " h."

142

THE LONG ROLL

been all over the city, and had not had much leisure for the errands I was commissioned to execute. New York was not much changed. I was on Broadway, on the Bowery, on the avenues and on the business streets, and all appeared the same, with the one difference noticeable, the presence of many soldiers. With this exception, I would not have known, from the bustle of business and the usual display on Broadway, the number of unmeaning-faced pedestrians saluting so many more dolls in "a-la-mode," or from the eternal outpouring, commingling and separating stream of life, that there was such a calamity harassing our country. New York is New York still, thought I, as I crossed the ferry, not very well satisfied with my first day's experience.

The next day I happened to be in the Sixth Avenue car, and my uniform was, as usual, the object of interest. I have not conceit enough to fancy that I was the attraction: I am quite sure it was the uniform and the sling. I noticed one lady who seemed to wish to speak to me. The car gradually got thinned out as we approached town, and soon there were only two persons in it besides ourselves. She then came over to where I sat, and asked me if I was a member of Hawkins Zouaves and did I come with the last lot of wounded men, to both of which I replied in the affirmative.

"But why is it I have not seen you up at the hospital?" she asked.

"Why, Madam," replied I, smiling, "it must be because I have not been there," and in explanation of this rather rude answer, I added, "I determined to stay at home while I am here, for it is pleasanter for myself and for a sister of mine."

"Granted," replied she; "but if you do not wish to stay with us, you must really come up and see how nicely we have gotten you poor fellows fixed. We want all of your Regiment who need help to come to us for it." She was middle-aged, dressed in half-mourning and, very evidently, a lady. She went on enthusiastically, "Men will have to do the fighting, and all we poor women can do is to take care of them when they are sick and wounded, and that we are willing to do."

143

THE LONG ROLL

"You are very kind, and I will take advantage of your invitation by going to see you at the hospital to-morrow and as an excuse I will go every day to get my wound dressed."

To her earnest, "Do, Sir!" I said, "Good-Morning, Madam!" and left the car.

This will show the feeling for us among the upper classes in New York. It is only one of the very many instances of this kind feeling for our Regiment and for the army generally, which I had the great pleasure to experience while in the city. The hospital is situated on Fifty-first Street and Lexington Avenue, and as far as I know is Mrs. Valentine Mott's own institution. I went the next day and the very first one I met was my lady friend of the car. She must pardon me for the liberty I take in calling her a friend, her manner was such that I can not help myself. She recognized me at once and exclaimed, "I knew I would see you again."

What a contrast to the camp hospitals! Here were all our boys in clean muslin, everything neat, comfortable and home-like, and I fancied their swarthy faces had already gained a lighter shade. Everything that could tempt the taste was alongside of every bed, and as a proof of plenty, I will mention the fact that I never went there but that I was asked to take some oranges or some delicate food. They were really reproached for not eating all the gifts that poured in on them in a continual stream. Books, papers, magazines and choice novels were on tables and chairs, sufficient for a good-sized reading-room; and dominoes, checkers and chess contributed to make the pleasantest home that a soldier can wish for "away from home." But the strangest feature, and of course the most pleasant of this splendid establishment, is the kind and familiar efforts of the ladies to make these patients feel at home, and I know they were successful. What can be more soothing to a poor wounded soldier, who has been so long the patient object of harsh, unsympathetic commands from officers, very often his inferiors, finding himself the object of tender smiles and kindly attentions? Not pity, mind you, for a true soldier hates pity from women, to whom but for the services he has tried to render his country, he

144

Fort Hawkins, Roanoke Island

Fort Reno

PLATE XXX

Ruins of Fort Blanchard, Roanoke Island

Wreck of the " Cumberland "

PLATE XXXI

Currituck   Windmill (Currituck)   Fresh Pond Point
On the Lake   Currituck Canal   Ellen and Mary of Edentrois   Lanier
On the Sound   Burning Salt Works in Princess Anne County, Virginia

PLATE XXXII

Camp Parke   On the Rappahannock

PLATE XXXIII

THE LONG ROLL

might never have the presumption to speak. Ladies who come in their carriages, dressed in rustling silks, with tender, white, tapering fingers which seemed never to have been formed to touch anything other than the keys of the pianoforte, doing little commonplace things here and there for him, trying to find out and to comply with his slightest wish—this is indeed a reward that is worth all the hardships, danger and terror of the battlefield. For there is great satisfaction in knowing that you deserve this from the greatest ladies in the land—great because they are true and good. Mrs. Valentine Mott, the principal lady of the institution, is a pleasant-looking woman, and that she is good need not be asked. Hers is a face that will never grow old. Her character can be partially judged from a little incident I witnessed. I had taken dinner with the boys and had just gotten interested in a game of checkers with Frank Vallade,* who had been wounded in both thighs at Camden. We just about got started when the door opened and in came a young, pretty little woman. I would have said "girl," but she had in her arms a baby about a year old. As soon as she entered, Frank reddened a little, pushed away the board and whispered to me, "She is my wife." I was thunderstruck, but I made haste to get out of the way. Here was Frank a married man and a father, and not yet twenty nor as old-looking as myself. What would we have next in the line of wonders? The conference between them did not last long, for I could see that Frank winced under the grins and glances of his comrades, and as he had kept it a secret from us so far, I judge he was pretty uneasy. Mrs. Mott came in just as Frank's pretty little family had gone, and she asked him if he had seen his wife.

"Yes, Ma'am; I have seen them."

"And, are they gone?"

"Yes, they have just gone."

"Oh, I declare, that is too bad, and I did not see that baby."

Frank looked serious and said, "If I had known, Mrs. Mott, that you wished to see them, I would have detained them certainly."

* Frank Vallade, Co. F. Wounded leg and thigh, Camden, April 19th.

145

THE LONG ROLL

But Mrs. Mott started off complaining that it really was too bad she did not see that baby, "I did want to see it so much," and even when she had reached the other end of the room we could still hear her talking about that "Zouave" baby, at which poor Frank (or *rich* Frank) had to join us in our laugh at the good lady's disappointment.

The next week I spent principally between my own home and Mrs. Mott's *home*, for I was not yet in condition to warrant my being out nights. In the latter part of the week I neglected to go to the hospital for several days, and when I did I found our boys changed from the second to the third floor. I asked how Cockefier was, and they told me that he was much worse and for me to go up and see him. I found him covered with a thin sheet, behind a screen. He was very pale. "Cocky," said I, "how's your arm? Does it pain you much now?"

"No, Charley; it don't pain me any more now—it's off."

Need I tell you how I felt! We were alongside of each other in the hospital at Roanoke, and I used to tremble when they had him under chloroform for fear they would take the arm off, and now, after being allured so long by the hope that it would not be necessary, it had to go at last. I do think, if I lost an arm or a leg, that I would go mad. I never feared death half as much, when going into a battle, as I did losing a limb. That would be a misery I never could reconcile myself to stand; and now poor Cockefier!

As soon as I got home I wrote to Warring, and told him about poor Cocky, and asked him if he would speak to Captain Leahy, for I felt that he was kind as well as brave, and the Company ought to do something nice. The next letter I got from Warring made me happy, for it stated that Captain Leahy had acted on the suggestion and headed the list himself with five dollars, and that he now had a sum of nearly one hundred ready. This was beyond my most sanguine expectation, and I was very glad, for Cockefier is a poor man, and needs money now, God knows. The second Sunday I was in New York he introduced me to a man to whom I shall always feel grateful.

146

THE LONG ROLL

His indefatigable efforts to make my stay in New York pleasant, in which he was assisted by his wife and two daughters, succeeded admirably. John McKensie is a true specimen of a genuine American. He is an ex-member of G engine company, in which he takes great pride as in the fire department generally, and he is also an active member of the order of Free Masons, and in that fraternity he takes equal pride if not more. He always has money, but still is not rich; he lives in comfort if not in luxury. He is near if not over forty years of age, but does not look much over thirty; and to sum it all up, I can find no discount on John McKensie. Such a man I met that Sunday, and it is hard to tell whether I spent my time more agreeably anywhere else than I did that afternoon. I had to stay and take tea with him and promise to come again often. The conversation during a part of the time took in the theaters, and he found out I could appreciate a good play, so he planned with Harry to go up to Wallack's any day I should decide. I think it was Tuesday; and to save me from being out too late, it was arranged that I should sleep with Harry. We went to Wallack's and saw the " Romance of a Poor Young Man " very well played. We went again and again, until I got ashamed of going with my two friends, Harry and Jack, for they would not allow me to pay for anything. So on one occasion I saw Jack down town, after I had known him about two weeks, and told him to make things look a little better, and if he or they had no objections, I would take his daughters to see Miss Richings at Niblo's. I smoothed the matter over with some reasons for the boldness of the proposition on so short an acquaintance; but all he seemed to have against it was that a soldier should not be allowed to spend his money. And now there was something else I had to get over. My Sister would be anxious to know about these proceedings, and it does n't take them long to guess where you have been, when they see the purse. I had taken her to see the enchantress at Niblo's, and she was so shocked at that bit of extravagance that she vowed it would last her for a year, and now mind you, I was about to commit a double folly, and she would be sure

147

to find out whether I told her or not. But I conquered all difficulties and took the Misses McKensie to see the siren, Miss Richings. I had the best seats in the parquet, and was dressed in Zou-Zou rig, of course; Jack had a pair of opera-glasses, and I had great fun looking at those who looked at me, for by this time I had gotten so used to being stared at that I did not mind it at all. One woman on the opposite side of the parquet gazed at me and I gazed at her until, with common consent, we dropped the glasses, and smiled.

The singing was excellent and the play good enough, and it would have been better if the weather had not been so hot. As it was, my guests professed to having enjoyed themselves and how could I help it? But what is the use of following my-self further in New York, for I had one continual round of amusement and pleasure, and I would not have missed it for a hundred dollars. I went to see Alexander in Center Street, my old boss, and there they thought me arisen from the grave. They thought me to be in the end-fire Zouaves, and there was a Charles Johnson killed on picket in that Regiment and that must have been me. I assured them it was not. I saw Miss T——— at Alexander's, and she is more beautiful than ever. I went sailing around Central Park with Lillie Simpson on her birthday, and Lord knows where I was not and what I did not do to pass away the time. To tell the truth, I was not contented at home; for I could not use pen or pencil, as you know, barely being able to scribble short answers to my friend's letters with my left hand. So in spite of myself, I found the hours hanging heavy some of the time. I was most happy at home with "Mother" and Lottie and the children, for though I never was without agreeable attention in New York, yet there is not that feeling that gives so much content as when you are among those whom you love, and if it were possible to love any one in the same way as you do your mother, Mrs. Simpson comes nearer to her than any other woman I ever knew. I sometimes sighed when I thought of Home, and that perhaps I never would see my family again, and it was hard to be so near and not have that pleasure. Eva, Harriet, Augusta and my brothers—the word pleasure is cold—joy is the only adequate word that will come near the feeling I would have in again seeing them all. But then I thought, even if I were there, I would find it hard to leave for the uncertainties of military life, so I consoled myself with the silent prayer that when I did go "home" it would be to stay.

And so did the forty days glide away in peaceful pleasure and domestic quiet, and almost before I was aware of it, the Fourteenth of June was a reality and I reported myself and got my ticket. And then I had to wait nearly two weeks before I could get a steamer. This I found tedious in the extreme, for it meant a trip to the Adjutant-General's office every day, only to be disappointed and told to come the next day. And in the meantime, I had taken leave of friends half a dozen times, and their patience as well as mine was exhausted.

At last, on the Twenty-fifth of June, the Steamer "Cossack" left for New-Berne. We started in a rainstorm, as usual, but still I had the pleasure of seeing my Sister on the dock with Mr. Simpson. I had told her not to come, but she said she could not resist trying to see me again, and I was glad she did not obey my orders. About four o'clock, the "Cossack" shoved off from the pier and cleared Sandy Hook before dark, and now we are off for the seat of war again.

CHAPTER XII

Thursday Eve., Eight o'clock,
June 26th, 1862.

WE started from New York yesterday afternoon and
have had favorable weather. The "Cossack" is
now near Fortress Monroe, where she will land a
Company of Marines.

Nine o'clock.

We are now plowing back again through Chesapeake Bay.
We heard that McClellan had been fighting all day, and that
General Hooker's Division had advanced one mile on to Rich-
mond and gained possession of Federal Hill. I hope it is true!

Friday Morning, June 27th.

Fortunately for us, the sea has not been as high to-day as
when the "Oriental" was wrecked, or we would now be in
the same predicament. We have just been aground, and in
the open ocean, too, about ten miles from land, and thirty
from Cape Henry. And we have to thank Neptune for his
kindness in not providing us with a blow at the time, or we
would be floating around on planks and hay bales instead of
pursuing our course as we are now doing. As it was, every lazy
swell that came along lifted the "Cossack" a little and set
her down again, fairly making every timber in the overloaded
vessel squeak, just as a rocking crate on which a cartman was
practising his strength. But we got off, to the relief of every
one, and now Hatteras Light is in sight. (Night) We passed
Hatteras "Swash," after tugging and rolling a little in the sand,
and we are again at anchor at the mouth of the Neuse River,
and I am going to sleep.

New-Berne, Saturday, June 28th.

We have just passed through New-Berne and left the
"Cossack" for the Steamer "John Farrow," and we were
150

not a moment too soon, either, for we start immediately for Roanoke.

(Night) Again aground in the Sound. This is surely an unlucky trip for pilots, two already being discharged.

Camp Reno, Roanoke Island.
June 29th.

At Roanoke again. We came up to the dock this morning about nine o'clock. The Colonel was there to meet us and he spoke as kindly as usual. When I got up to camp, I was met by a host of friends on every side; in fact, the welcome I received here was only second to that in New York two months ago. The Regiment is on the eve of starting somewhere I am certain, but where I do not know, though I am pretty sure it is to be in the direction of Richmond. I don't know whether I will go with them or not. I can not go in the ranks, that is certain, but I might go on the ambulance and do something. I will propose to go anyway, and be ready for whatever turns up.

Monday Eve., June 30th.

Last Monday evening I was at Wallack's Theater with Jack McKensie and Harry Palmer, and to-night I have also been to the theater. The Zouave Dramatic Club gave an interesting performance and I enjoyed myself to-night as well if not better than I did last Monday, probably for the reason that I did not look for so much talent as there was displayed on the neat little stage in one of the Rebel barracks. A burlesque was well performed and after some very good comic songs and dancing, the entertainment concluded with the farce "Box and Cox." The house was crowded with the aristocracy of Roanoke, escorted generally by members of the Regiment. Colonel Hawkins was present and was received with enthusiastic cheers by the audience. The proceeds of these entertainments go to the wounded of our Regiment.

July 4th, 1862.

What can't our boys get up when they have a mind to? As the song says, "If you had been here to-day, you'd have

151

laughed till you died." So far as I am concerned I do not wish
to have anything better to laugh at on the Fourths of July to
come. In the morning, any one who would go after it, could
have fifteen rounds of blank cartridges to use as he wished.
After the Parade and the reading of the Declaration of Inde-
pendence, two o'clock was fixed for a grand, fantastic burlesque
on the Dress Parade, in which any one who wished to make
himself ridiculous could participate. At two exactly, several
drums and kettles sounded for the Battalion to "Fall in."
The Colors took their position, and the guides were thrown out.
The Colors were one black flag, no quarter, and a white flag,
all quarter, appropriately inscribed. There is no use trying
to describe the rest. You have all been to a masquerade ball,
I suppose, and from that you can fancy something very ridiculous, only I am afraid you can not arrive at anything ridiculous
enough. The artillery was represented by common muskets
tied on wheelbarrows, from which formidable battery, we had
some very good volleys. Sergeant Major was "Colonel"
and had his saddle put on wrong side foremost. The "Child"
of the Regiment was Corporal Farrel of Company B, and he
made the best character of the show. Warring made a very
good Zouave, with a Roanoke medal on his breast, a brass
candlestick with the top knocked off. Corporal Downing of
our Company was a rag-woman and played the part to per-
fection. The Battalion, numbering some two hundred, marched
down to the camp of the Eighty-ninth and to Headquarters,
and gave a magnificent Dress Parade at both places with salutes
from the Batteries. The band accompanied them, but the
martial strains were unfortunate in the harmony, for each man
played his own tune. Colonel Hawkins was not at his quarters
and every one felt a little disappointed. I am going to wind
up the Fourth by going to the theater to-night, this performance
probably being our last, as our Regiment is soon going away.

July 11th.

The Regiment is gone, and I, for the first time, am staying
behind. They went this morning. I had everything ready to

152

go, but the Captain told me I had better stay and take care of his quarters, and I have no doubt that it is best, though I don't like the idea, for I always have been with my Company since we came out, and I would like to take my chances with it whatever it may go through. They are going in the direction of Norfolk, and, if I mistake not, they will have something to say at the taking of Richmond. It is even now rumored that they are going to take Fort Darling, with the rest of Burnside's Division, of course.

Saturday Evening, July 12th.

I received a letter this afternoon from Charlotte. All is well. I have resumed my pencil again these last few days in good earnest, using a little more care than usual, which has resulted, I think, in a material improvement in my pictures. Yesterday morning, I commenced with Fort Defiance, * and it is so much better and more correct than the five or six others I drew and gave away, that I have concluded to keep this for myself. The second picture I finished yesterday, " Fort Bartow " was originally sketched two or three months ago from the " Virginia " while in the Sound, and includes an incident worthy of being preserved : the Rebel Steamer—" Sea Bird," I think it was—waiting under a flag of truce for the body of Captain O. Jennings Wise. Fort Bartow, commonly called the " Nine-Gun Battery," is the strongest fort on the Island and received the principal part of Goldsborough's attention when the Island was taken. My next is a copy of the only print I have seen of the sharp skirmish between the Rebel Tug " Teager " and our " Savannah," which was described in my Journal long ago. This is the first two-page picture I have ever drawn.

This morning I undertook the most delicate piece of penciling I have ever attempted and I succeeded beyond my most sanguine anticipation. This is the copy of Colonel Hawkins' " Carte-de-visite." I think just this much of it, that I intend to

---

* The Sketches have been placed in the narrative as nearly as possible, where the original was made. Some were lost, many were given away, and a few are " unaccounted for."

get the Colonel to put his autograph on it, if he comes back, and God grant he may.

I also drew a large picture of the charge of our Regiment at Camden, partly copied and partly original. I substituted our two-gun battery for the Sixth New Hampshire, which in the published print in the " Illustrated News " occupies the foreground. It is not that I do not want the gallant Sixth to be in the picture, but they were not there when we made the first charge. It was when our flag was in the Rebel position and the Georgians were in retreat, that the Sixth, the only Regiment that did anything there, was where the wood-cut placed them. Now I think you will agree with me that my pencil has been busy since the Regiment went away.

Sunday Evening, July 13th.

I have spent the Sabbath principally with pencil in my hand. I have drawn three pictures to-day, one of Fort Bartow one of our gunboats ascending the Chowan River on the Winton Expedition and the third has a curious history. I commenced it some fifteen months ago, a ruin on Lake Myorson in Norway, and with unusual care, intending to give it to a lady friend, but alas, it has been unfinished all this time, and forgotten until I found it with a lot of drawing paper my Sister Charlotte packed in my knapsack. And now I have touched it up in my best style with clouds and trees, and I will send it to my Sister Eva.

But I am afraid the pencil displaces the pen too much of late. There has been a startling rumor around camp to-day, and the main part of it implies that Company F has been attacked at Plymouth, which city they were guarding, by a body of Rebel cavalry, and been driven off with a loss of three killed and ten wounded. Another rumor is that a Rebel steamer was captured in the Roanoke River. But both lack confirmation.

The fight that was in progress when I was off Fortress Monroe seems to have been a big thing, big so far as the fight is concerned, but not so much for our cause. I have not seen

154

the particulars yet. We hear that McClellan has retreated and I feel badly about it, but I can only hope for the best.

Saturday, July 19th.

Day before yesterday I received a letter from Warring with a batch of information and also one from Captain Leahy. The Regiment is now in Fort Norfolk near the city, on Sewal's Point, and " King Rush " is commander of the post. Captain Leahy thinks we—" they," I mean—will stay there and he tells me I may expect orders to decamp any day. Last year this time, how little did our boys expect to be in Norfolk now, and how much less did we expect to have to take such a curious route to get there. But I am not there yet.

With these two letters came three more, two from New York and the other from Pittsburgh : a note from Mr. Passevant enclosing two letters from my Sisters Harriet and Augusta. Harriet tells me they were delighted with my picture that I sent them some time ago, and Augusta returns the compliment with her ambrotype, which she says does justice to her in everything but her hair. The picture shows me a girl of whom any one should be proud; in fact, as far as looks and build are concerned, our family is not to be equaled—myself excepted, of course. Harriet promises me to go and do likewise in regard to a picture. The letters from Harry Palmer and Jack McKensie are full of news. I have answered all of them except Mr. Passevant's, and that I intend to do to-day.

This is Saturday and we will see what our pencil has been doing since Sunday. " The Burning of Winton," though small and something new, is not bad. I never tried conflagrations before. I have numbered my pictures, for I want the collection to be complete, and I have that excuse for not giving any of them away. Now, turn the leaf. Ha! A moonlight scene, something else I have never tried before. " Burnside's Fleet at Anchor." How do you like it? You don't know? Well I don't either. The Steamer on the right side in the foreground, or forewater, is the " Virginia," and I was on her that night, if you can recollect.

155

THE LONG ROLL

"Three-Gun Battery Captured on Roanoke Island" in front of Colonel Hawkins' quarters. This flagstaff with that pretty flag floating from it, as you will see, serves also as the Colonel's Lookout, for in these cross-trees he can or could command a good view of the Sound. I don't think it makes a bad picture, do you?

Hello! This is something larger than usual, is it not? "Camp Reno, Roanoke Island." Well, that is not so bad. Clouds good. So that is the Regiment on Dress Parade? Well, well, they are too much in the distance to be seen very distinctly. Seems to me that there are too many of them. You are probably right. Well, take it all in all, it is—well, never mind what it is, turn the page.

"Beautiful! beautiful!" Do you think so? I am glad of it, for I think so myself, and your exclamations flatter my vanity, but read the title: "Earth-work built by Sir Walter Raleigh's Colony on Roanoke Island." Well, I declare, I did not think it was anything but a wood scene. Earthwork, did you say? This must be it in the foreground, and not much of a breastwork either. I admit that, Sir, but you must recollect that this has been here some hundreds of years, and in that time the elements have reduced it; but if you will go with me some day, you will discover traces that can not be doubted. How far is it from camp? About a mile Eastwardly. But what object could Sir Walter have in building this work here, I would like to know. For my part I don't think Sir Walter ever had anything to do with the Fort; but if you will refer to the History of the United States, you will find that there was a colony, or a nucleus of one, of fifteen or twenty men left on this Island, of which nothing was ever heard afterward. Not a trace has been discovered, and we have nothing left but conjecture. They were probably butchered by Indians, and that this fort has something to do with them—in fact, that it was thrown up for their defense against the Indians—I have no doubt in my mind. At any rate, we have proofs that it has been the scene of Indian warfare, and as Indians do not throw up earth-works in their line of fighting, we must come to the

156

conclusion that red and white men's blood mingled over this spot in the lonely wood. For I have seen stone and flint arrow-heads that have been found here, and that is sufficient to show that the red men had good enemies to fight before they could annihilate them. As my picture shows, the breast-works are not more than ordinary mounds now, and any one who was not shown the place would probably pass over it a hundred times without discovering anything so unusual as to warrant the thought of a fortification; but it was there, and probably has been the scene of a dark and bloody tragedy. A sudden and terrible surprise; a long, protracted siege, in which the red men suffered as much as the garrison; and at last, worn out with hunger, thirst or bodily fatigue, one by one, careless of life, the white men exposed themselves to the arrows of the unerring marksmen, or perhaps in hopes of savage mercy, only to be deceived and meet the horrible end at the stake or by some other lingering torture. I almost forget that this is all in my mind, but such thoughts came to me while I was drawing the ruins of this interesting relic of the former history of this well-known Island. But, Mr. Journal, we will drop the subject of our pictures, and as I am busy now, meet me to-morrow at the "Barleymow."

July 22nd.

Yesterday I drew my own picture from a "Carte-de-visite" I had taken in New York, and wrote a letter to Mr. Passevant and one to Captain Leahy. To-day I made a sketch of Fort Hawkins, which, unlike all the other forts on the Island, has been built by the Federals. It was commenced shortly after the Island was taken, and furnished employment to about a hundred contrabands almost continually, and it is now nearly completed. It is built in the much-favored half-moon shape, with breastworks to protect it in the rear. It mounts four thirty-two-pound Columbiads, which command the Sound; situated on the Northeast corner of the Island. It is a neat piece of engineering, and reflects credit on the constructors.

(Evening). I must stop a few minutes before going to bed and talk to you about my sketches. I hope, for Friendship's

THE LONG ROLL

sake, you are not tired of the subject, for sketching is something I never tire of doing—and why not bear with me now, when I have nothing else on which I can fix my mind? And, too, my hand is fast getting well, so that I will soon be able to shoulder a musket again, and then you will not be bored with my eternal talk. Now here is as good a picture as I ever attempted, and by far the greatest subject I could wish, finished day before yesterday, and I never spoke of it at all. I fancy it is very jealous, by this time, of its associates who have been more lucky in getting a prompt puff from Mr. Journal. But it is never too late to mend. This tries to represent the " Bivouac of General Burnside's Army—The Night Before the Battle," but no questions have I time to answer, and if you want any explanations you must look up the old copy of the Journal, now safely packed in Hudson City. For I must make haste and tell something about a little expedition I had this afternoon. I had resolved, as long as I had so good a chance, to have Roanoke Island illustrated, and I think I have finished now. So I went out this afternoon to take the two last sketches that were needed to make my collection complete. Fort Reno and Fort Blanchard : I had a good swim at Fort Reno and then went down to Fort Blanchard. I had never seen the latter fort since I have been on the Island, and I was much surprised at the strength and advantages of its position. Five hundred brave men inside ought to be able to hold it against five thousand. Let me explain by the assistance of the sketch. You will see where four heavy guns have been mounted on the right. These guns command the Sound. In front, a boggy marsh, which even Irish bog-trotters could not get over. On the left, the wall faces the interior of the Island, and is protected not only by swamps, but more effectively by a deep dike full of water. What more could a general want, besides courage, to hold this against all the Burnsides in our army ? I will give you a small sketch of Fort Reno. It is the largest Fort on the Island, and mounts twelve guns. It took a small part in the action of the Eighth of February, but did no great execution, firing a shot now and then, making a small show of helping their fleet of gunboats which our ferryboats drove from under its walls. Its original name was Fort Huger. I sketched another———" Fort," I suppose. Why do you interrupt me? Can I sketch nothing but Forts? My pencil has been insulted, but the keenest satisfaction will be to allow the pen to finish. This picture forms a great contrast in its subject, a most beautiful flower I found in the marsh. It was of a kind I had never seen before, and I can not tell its name, but it attracted me by its purest vermilion color. But, Forts, Cannons, Flowers and all beside, I bid you Good-Night!

CHAPTER XIII

MARCHING ORDERS

Friday, July 25th.

A N expedition is starting from here this afternoon, and those of our Regiment who were left are going, with five days' rations in haversacks, and in light marching order. Mr. Journal, you may look out for something besides pictures in a few days, or—nothing at all.

Afternoon.

A half hour after writing the warning above, we were marched to the Parade Ground at the call of the "Assembly," and I found there forty-seven men, two of them commissioned officers, Captain Graham and Captain Prescott, and three non-commissioned, leaving forty-two privates. We marched down to Fort Reno and there met a small schooner, in which we embarked and stood for the gunboat which was ready to receive us, and we are now on our way up the Sound. From all I can learn, we are going up to the Currituck Court-House to stop some drafting that is said to be going on among the inhabitants, under the supervision of the Rebel cavalry.

Saturday Afternoon.

This morning we found ourselves at anchor in the North River opposite the mouth of the new canal (the only name I could find for it), and we went aboard the schooner which was making ready to take us up the canal by having a twelve-pound, mountain howitzer put in her bow. A detachment of marines accompanied us to sail this newly made war-vessel, and as pilot we had a Captain Dowdy, one of General Burnside's spies. In the raging waters of this canal, there was no wind or room for sailing. We had no horses, and in lieu of wind and the useful animal, we had to take our places on the bank and tow the boat. This work was rendered much harder by the quantity of blackberries on the banks which, like "Tantalus in Hades," we were shown but not permitted to touch. In about an hour, we arrived at a bridge where there was a dredg-

160

Great Two-Gun Battery at Fortress Monroe

Frederick City, Maryland

PLATE X

South Mountain Battlefield

The Antietam Bridge

Second Presbyterian Church Hospital, Frederick City, Maryland

PLATE XXXVI

Miller's Farm Hospital

On the Potomac

PLATE XXXVII

ing-machine at work. There had been a two-gun battery commanding this bridge, of which only the breastworks and the flag-pole remained. Relieving the " horses " here, we pushed on again slowly, and soon got into an opening or lake which the canal runs through, though the winds and water have nearly lowered the banks to the canal level. This part of the journey put me much in mind of Gotha Canal in Sweden, though, of course, it is on a much smaller scale. After a stretch of about two miles of this kind of scenery, we came to a cut with high banks on either side, but only for a very short distance, and then we emerged from the square, tiresome canal scenes, and are now skipping joyously along among the islands, through bays, channels and straits, and the numerous windings of Currituck Sound, which, though of low shores, exhibited, from time to time, scenes which will live pleasantly in my memory. In addition to Mr. Dowdy, we have now three pilots following us with their " Cooners," and if they can not take us to the salt-works which we are to destroy, I am afraid some pistols will go off. There is a sloop at anchor up the marsh. She looks suspicious and may be a prize. We are making for her. Bah! she is an old tub not worth having any one on board, though a " Yogle " and his family apparently live here. I have seen Indians cleaner. For such a small craft, she carries a large name, and allow me to add, a queer one, no less than " Mary and Ellen of Edentrois, North Currolina."

The skipper's aid was requested, and he, pleasantly enough, jumped into a nutshell of a boat and came aboard, evidently inclined to make the best of a bad bargain by appearing to relish the joke. But not so his wife, for his departure left her in tears, fearing, I suppose, for his safety among the " Red Devils."

We have had a terrible accident. A few moments ago we hailed a boat in toward shore, but as no attention was paid to our rifle-shots, we gave it the contents of our twelve-pounder. While the Captain of the gun was sighting her, the fuse-cord got entangled and the grape-shot was discharged toward the boat while the fuse-powder went into the eyes of poor Cooper.

161

THE LONG ROLL

Every one likes Cooper, he is always quiet, a good gunner and a good fighter as well, and this unfortunate accident hurts us all. The boat put up a creek and vanished.

Sunday, Ten o'clock.

We got to our destination about nine o'clock last night, on the beach continued from Hatteras, in Princess Anne County, Virginia, not over thirty miles from Cape Henry, where we found a couple of men waiting for us, with two more not waiting for us, whom we made prisoners. One of these was the Mr. Jones who was the chief cause of this Great Naval Armada. We established ourselves in one of the salt-boiling sheds, and by twelve we had a cup of coffee and some crackers, and then slept the sweet sleep that we evidently needed, till roused by the Bugle in the morning. It was too dark last night for us to see the Salt Works, but now we could see five or six tumble-down shanties out on the sandy plain, and these we were ordered to destroy before we could have breakfast. You may imagine our consciences did not labor under much compunction, for we were assisted by that exciting Demon who makes it a pleasure to destroy, and we smashed up a lot of salt-pans and set the shanties into a blaze. It does not take very long to destroy three thousand dollars' worth, you know. That was the estimated value of the property which we left in flames, as, contented with our accomplishment, we re-embarked and sailed away. Well! Well! and now Incendiarism is added to my long line of misdeeds, for I set one of those shanties on fire, myself.

Afternoon.

We did not do enough, it seems, in the destructive line of business in which we are now employed, for about ten o'clock we again landed on this side of the line, at a place known as Fresh Pond Point, where there were two buildings similar to the ones up in Virginia, only differing in this respect: the absence of pans, which the owner swore had been gone over three weeks. But thanks to the animosity of one of our "Yogle" pilots, the hiding-place was revealed and they were found

162

THE LONG ROLL

alongside of the oven three feet under ground, where they had been put not three days ago. And this, much to the fright and chagrin of the owner, who grew pale as the pans were hauled out, and anxiously asked one of our boys what the Captain would do to him now. He was much relieved when he was told that Captain Graham would not blame him for trying to save his property.

About this time, several small pigs and more than several hens and bandy-legged roosters were shot, hung or wrung *by accident*, and were soon in a state most agreeable to the sense of smell, and finally to that of taste—in fact, we made out a pretty good dinner at Fresh Pond Point. We are now on our way again and starting for Currituck Court-House, where we are to pay a visit on some business I know nothing about.

Monday Morning, July 29th.

We arrived at the Court-House about two o'clock and stayed at the dock for over three hours while the Captain was talking to the feminine population of Currituck, and we were industriously, and with a vigor that deserved a better cause, swearing at him, not for talking to the women folk, but for keeping us on the dock. From there we sailed about four o'clock, taking three prisoners with us. About half of our fellows were dispatched by land under Captain Prescott, to meet us down at the bridge at the canal, for what object I do not know, unless to lighten the boat so as to aid us in getting down as quickly as possible. This was rendered difficult now, for the wind had very nearly died out and we had to take to the oars and row all the way. Our schooner was not as large as a vessel, but it was too large as a rowboat, and we found it hard work, and we did not get to the bridge till after one o'clock in the morning, where we found our detachment waiting for us. We had now about two miles more to make to the "Lancer." It was queer how very long those two miles were. We stepped aboard just at six bells (three o'clock), and I lost no time in tumbling to sleep, and it took Murphy's most energetic push to make me understand "Coffee" this morning.

163

THE LONG ROLL

I have just been told that while we were destroying the Salt-Works, ten of the " Lancer's " crew have been some ten miles from here on a private expedition and captured two recruiting officers just on the eve of starting for Richmond with twelve drafted recruits. And now they will go via Roanoke, not exactly the way they planned, but Uncle Sam will pay their transportation. One of them has seen us before, when he was released on parole of honor, and I presume he has some reason for not wishing to see us again just now.

While I am writing, the " Lancer " is trying to turn around and run over the bar at the mouth of the North River, and if she succeeds, we will probably be in Roanoke this afternoon.

Wednesday, July 30th.

Have just finished the several sketches of Currituck scenery which I took while on the last expedition, and I grouped them together on one page, and every one to whom I have shown them says they are good. It certainly makes a pretty effect. Then I sketched a curious little thing, curious to me at least, for I had never seen it until last Sunday while rummaging around Fresh Pond Point. The leaves of this plant, or vegetable, contain a lot of small needles, if I may so term them, and beware of getting them into the pores of your skin, for they are worse than flies. The name, I am told, is " Cactus."

Friday, August 1st.

To-day I have satisfactorily employed myself in drawing a large picture of Lieutenant-Colonel Victor De Monteuil, from " Frank Leslie's " (which has it " Vignier De Monteuil ") ; but though I took the figure from this, I changed the features.

Colonel De Monteuil " was born in France and rose from the ranks in the French Army to Lieutenant of Artillery and served with distinction some years in the service of the present Emperor. Resigning, he came to this country several years ago, and until the Rebellion broke out was engaged in New York as a teacher of the French language and literature. When the D' Epaneuil Zouaves were formed, De Monteuil

164

THE LONG ROLL

became Lieutenant-Colonel and that Regiment was indebted
to him for its discipline." Frank Leslie pays Colonel De Monteuil a poor compliment here, for it was the want of discipline
that separated him from his Regiment.

In the engagement at Roanoke Island, he was in our Regiment as a volunteer, his Regiment being at Annapolis, and as
he was in the act of stepping into our ranks to charge with us,
he was struck down by a musket ball. His last words were,
"Charge, Zouaves! Charge, Mes Enfants!" as it was his
delight to call us. He was quartered, at the request of Colonel
Hawkins, on the "Virginia," the Flagship of the Third Division.
We all respected and admired the gay, good-humored, smiling,
little Frenchman, for we knew he had smelled powder before,
and he seemed to return double-fold our attachment for him,
and his only regret was that his Regiment had not been blessed
with officers who could have made the D'Epaneuil Zouaves
what we were. He was offered a position as Aide on some staff,
but refused and went into action with a German one-thousand-
yard rifle, which he had previously picked out with great care.
The last time I saw this brave man was on the morning of his
death, coming through the swamp, daubed with mud above
his knees, smilingly showing his bedraggled condition to one
of our officers.

We have orders to be ready to leave for Newport News
to join our Regiment, for though there will still be a Camp
Guard here, Murphy and I are two of the fortunate ones who
are to go. So, good-bye, old North Carolina, Hatteras and
Roanoke! The old Dominion of Newport News once more!

CHAPTER XIV

WITH THE NINTH CORPS-D'ARMIE.

Camp Parke, near Fredericksburg, Va.
Monday, August 9th, 1862.

L AST Sunday, the Fourth of August, our detachment broke camp on Roanoke Island, and embarked aboard two schooners, and in tow of a steamer went, probably for the last time, up the Albemarle Sound. For the night we anchored at the mouth of the North River and subsequently passed through the same country, the scenery of which I have noted before as far as Currituck Court-House. From thence we proceeded up the Sound of that name until we entered the Pongo River, which, I think, takes its root, though indirectly, in Lake Drummond. This river certainly is the queerest stream upon which I ever have had the privilege of feasting my eyes. As it empties into the Currituck Sound, it flows through a prairie-like marsh, and as we went further up, the marsh commenced to admit a sprinkling of small, straight pines. Farther on, cedars mingled with the pines, and then cypress mixed their furry branches with the two. Onward, and a thick, impenetrable underbrush bloomed in wonderful beauty under the branches of the cypress, the cedar and the pine. All these and many other kinds occasionally sprinkled into the chaos formed a scene very dismal indeed. The Pongo River is black and narrow, winding and deep. Like a huge serpent it revels in this chaos, curling, coiling, twisting, wreathing and dashing, as it flows through this dark mass, that forms no bank to kiss or overflow, not a spot where one of us could rest a foot without getting up to his neck in mud. Not a cot is built to reflect its shadow in the black ripples; but tall, reedy grass, surmounted by thick underbrush, which again is surmounted by dark, gray, moss-covered trees, looking lonely, dismal and frowning as we pass, and we feel that we have not the slightest desire to make a closer acquaintance. It makes us turn to the puffing of our tireless steam-engine, half fearing that its mighty power may

166

stop and leave us here, and we are thankful that we can not discover any signs of failure in its cough. And we gaze, charmed but still relieved as we pass by the wonderful beauty commingled with the dreariness and despair of the Dismal Swamp. For though this is not the Dismal Swamp that Porte Cayon illustrated in "Harper's" some time ago, it is still dreary enough for my ideal of the sublime and dismal; and if it had not been, the pouring rain that descended on us would have been sufficient to make it so. Come to think, it is the same Swamp, but not the old road that took Cayon through Lake Drummond. Now, I do not know if it rains in the Pongo River country all the time or not; but certain it was, that as soon as we had left it, the rain ceased, and Nature smiled on us now as she had wept and frowned among the recesses of the swamp. After steaming through a few miles of square, up and down scenery of the canal, we came upon a "right smart" village which some one told us was South Mills, and which I would have believed had the Pongo River been the Pasquotank. There were immense forts here, or rather works of every description, holding the Locks which we passed through. They indicated the importance that was formerly felt of the uninterrupted communication between Norfolk and the lower countries we had left. After getting out of the Locks, we were in the Elizabeth River and in civilized country once more, where flourishing fields were seen and cottages and villas ornamented, with everything indicating "Old Virginia." Ah! Virginia! How fair and beautiful thou art! Why, then, nourish treason on your beautiful bosom, when it is fast making a wreck of your beauty, and a desert for thy sons!

It was about six o'clock in the afternoon, when from the rigging of one schooner, the spires of the old city of Norfolk could be seen, and after a few more turns around, a few more bends in the river, we caught sight of the stupendous and melancholy ruins of Portsmouth Navy Yards. The enemy have taken great and praiseworthy pains to scuttle every building in the yard. I wonder that they left the walls standing. The Porte Royal took a couple of turns around the harbor while our band played

THE LONG ROLL

"Yankee Doodle," and then we stood for the James River. We were delighted with the pretty appearance of Norfolk, with her shade-trees, and, passing under the guns of the monster "Minnesota," which has monopolized the old place deserted by the "Merrimack," the wreck of which latter we saw under the ramparts of Crany Island, we were all more than interested.* Then night set in and led by the moon, the stars, the twinkling of the shiplights on the horizon, and the indistinct shore of the James, we made our old post, which we had left nearly a year ago, not expecting to see it again or to take such a curious route to get back to Newport News.

Here a startling piece of news met us. Our Regiment had left there the day before for some point on the Potomac, to re-enforce Pope in Virginia, and so the next morning we started for Fortress Monroe, without the privilege of going ashore. But they could not prevent me from sketching the wreck of the noble "Cumberland," a fit monument to the heroism of our navy. About a year ago, when we were novices in the art of war, these veteran tars, so many of whom are now lying cold in this wreck under the glorious spars, were the first to welcome us with hearty cheers, as we entered and passed alongside of them in the James River.

We were more fortunate at Fortress Monroe, for here we were allowed to go ashore and consequently had a look at things in this Old Point Comfort(able) Fortress. Among many interesting things I saw there were the remnants of the old Sawyer Gun which exploded at Newport News last Summer after we left there for Hatteras. I sketched the enormous two-gun battery composed of the Lincoln and Union Guns.

Toward afternoon, Captain Graham succeeded in getting another larger schooner, to which we were put to work transferring our goods, and by morning we hove anchor and started up Chesapeake Bay. By twilight, we came to the classic waters of the Potomac. The soft, silvery beams of the moon aided our vision and contributed a generous quantity of its silver to the rippling waters and lighted up the many sails that silently

---

* The Sketch-Book with about twenty drawings of this trip was lost.

168

THE LONG ROLL

passed us with a ghost-like paleness, which nearly cheated us into the belief that we were gliding in some spectral, ideal world, where phantom ships chased each other over nameless seas. The next morning found us still moving between the somewhat distant shores of this beautiful stream, and the gentle moonbeams were exchanged for the golden bars of the sun, and oh, how hot it was!

Passing Fort Tobacco and Smith's Point, we soon came in sight of Acquia Creek, our destination, and here we learned that our Regiment was about eighteen or twenty miles South of us on the Richmond and Fredericksburg Railroad. But it was eleven o'clock that night before we had the regimental property aboard the cars ready to start. And the moon this night was fuller and fairer than the night before. I enjoyed this railroad ride in an open car mightily. What sensation is so exhilarating to us humans as swift locomotion, and what makes the common railroad ride so monotonous is that we can not feel this motion in the interior of the car. But this was no common ride. Sitting among a pile of baggage, smashing, slashing, crashing and dashing through hills and over bridges, through ridges and over hollows, at a locomotive speed, is very funny. It always puts me in mind of going to Hell on the back of a screaming Devil. And by moonlight, when everything is light but indistinct, conglomerated into a mass of light and darkness, this fancy looks admirably like a reality.

About one o'clock in the morning of the Ninth of August, the black horse neighed and gradually slackened his headlong speed, and was still. Marching up a hill, we could see by the aid of the moon, tents enough for an army, and all hushed in the peace of repose. We were in Camp Parke, and this was Burnside's army. No longer in transports or in fortified cities, on islands and fortresses on the North Carolina coast. No longer the Burnside Expedition, but the Ninth Corps-d'Armie, doing active service in the open field on the often contested ground of Old Virginia, between the pretty little Secesh towns of Falmouth and Fredericksburg on either side of the Rappahannock. Without much trouble, I found my Company and

169

Number Three Mess, and tumbled alongside of my chum, Warring, and was fast asleep.

August 10th.

What a beautiful country this is! Can it be possible that the miserable places we have gone through make these scenes so surpassingly lovely? This may have some influence on our sense of sight, but still I do think that this country is the prettiest in the world. From this camping ground we occupy, up on the hill, we have a series of most interesting views, and by going down on the left wing of our brigade, we can see the little town, or city, of Fredericksburg, with its three or four steeples rising among the large trees between us in the valley of the Rappahannock. The surrounding hills are dotted with tents, giving an additional interest to the unusually lovely landscape.

We have had quite a little brush in our Division, for yesterday, General Gibbons returned from a reconnaissance down along the wires somewhere. They had three Regiments, some cavalry and one battery, I believe, and had a kind of a running fight with an equal force of the enemy. They tried to cut off General Gibbons twice, but failed, and lost some fourteen men and then gave up the attempt. We lost two or three killed and twice that number wounded, and a little baggage, but of the latter, we captured an equal amount from the enemy.

August 12th.

We have just received the "Herald" with an account of the fight at Culpepper Court-House between Pope and Stonewall Jackson, which transpired last Saturday. I can't say that it is particularly advantageous to our arms, but still it has renewed confidence in our Department, for we all feel that we have a head, which is highly gratifying when we consider that thereby we may be enabled to save our own necks.

August 14th.

Our Regiment has just returned from picket duty around Fredericksburg. Our Company and two others were out about
170

two miles from that city on the road to Bowling Green. Nothing transpired worthy of note. This was the first duty I have done since the Nineteenth of April. Last Tuesday evening, the night before going out on picket, General Reno's Division passed by here on their way to Pope's army, and among them was the Forty-eighth Pennsylvania Regiment which was with us at Hatteras, and with them was Mr. Holman whom you remember I am sure, and that I was glad to see him is equally sure. Our Regiment cheered them lustily as they passed.

Saturday, August 16th.

Company K of our Regiment has just returned from a scout and it was successfully rewarded by the capture of sixteen Rebel officers and their mail and some horses. Warring saw them coming in and he tells me the officers were splendidly uniformed and were returning to their Regiments at Richmond from furloughs. Big thing for Company K.

Sunday, August 17th.

Our Regiment is again on picket to-day on the same road we took previously. We cut a big splurge in Fredericksburg this morning, marching through in full dress, white gloves (how I hate white gloves on a soldier!), etc., etc., etc.

Last night I did up all my drawings and my Journal in a parcel and sent them home for two or three reasons, which you may guess. First, for fear of their being lost in some future skedad—no, not skedaddle—in some future march. Secondly, for fear the Rebels might get hold of them, and thirdly, they would be too heavy to carry. Colonel Hawkins had seen them all, and at his request kept them in his quarters for a whole day that he might have time to examine them at his leisure. I asked him for his autograph under a picture I drew of him on Roanoke Island, and this he granted, of course.

Monday Evening, August 18th.

Returned from picket this morning, having been on duty as sentinel for the first time since April. Countersign " York-

171

town." Received news to-day from New Orleans. They had quite a fight in repulsing Breckenridge at Baton Rouge. Our old General Williams, of whom our Regiment said so many hard things at Hatteras, was killed in this engagement, bravely fighting. God forgive me, if I have ever said anything wrong about him. Peace to his dust. By all accounts, he was a brave man.

Another bit of good news, we read to-day, is that the " Arkansas " is at last gone, blown up. It seems, the " Essex," Captain Porter, son of the Captain Porter of the " Essex," already famous in our history, did the damage. Another Merrimack is gone.

Friday Evening, August 22d.

Out on picket again. We were out about a mile farther on the same road. Warring had the advance picket out by the cavalry, acting as Corporal of the entire guard. We heard heavy cannonading last night and it seems Pope is having a terrible struggle around Richmond, and hard rumors reach us that he is getting the worst of it, for it seems that the Rebel Generals have taken advantage of McClellan's late move, the evacuation of Harrison's Landing, and hurled all their forces on Pope on this side. We can not tell with any degree of certainty, of course, if Pope has gotten any more punishment, but we hear that he has been driven back some distance. I more than half expect that we will be ordered to re-enforce him if he suffers any severe loss.

Saturday Morning, August 23d.

No, we are not wanted by Pope, for though re-enforcements have been pouring out from here in lines of miles long, our Division is still uncalled-for. It was the most wonderful and heart-stirring sight imaginable, last night, to see the brave fellows press on, weary, but without a murmur. Regiment after Regiment passed by, without knapsacks, overcoats or blankets, cheerfully and with no apparent thought for their discomfort. Talk of suffering for your country! If this is not suffering, what is? And I know that they must have seen

172

as much in one week as I have recorded here in sixteen months, for these men, whose Regiments have dwindled down to so few members, have all had narrow escapes from death. Those who have lived to tell of what they have seen and gone through in the Seven Days' Fight have a great history, which I imagine would be well worth recording. Berdan's Sharp-Shooters passed by here last night, and I had the pleasure of seeing "California Joe" of Yorktown notoriety. The pictures do him justice, and with all his fame he is unassuming, quite bashful and shy, shrinking from the fame his deeds have made for him. He wears his hair long in genuine California style, parting it in the middle.

Sunday Evening, August 24th.

The firing we heard last Friday was continued yesterday morning and then the sounds died away in a thundershower. We have only had unsatisfactory accounts of the heavy work. The first reports came in last night and were not calculated to cheer us much, for they were to the effect that Jackson was driving Pope to Hell. This was soon contradicted and now we know nothing better than that Pope is driving Jackson, not to Hell, but toward some of Pope's forces, which he has gotten around on the other side. He has captured some artillery and a few prisoners, and if this report is not contradicted, well and good.

For the first time in this camp, I have had a pass to go outside the lines, and I have enjoyed myself amazingly, viewing this beautiful country. I got a sketch of the camp and a portrait of my friend Frank Hughson. Our Regiment goes on picket again to-morrow.

Tuesday Evening, August 26th.

Had a nice day on picket. Was guarding the house of that rich old Secesh planter, Burnett. Had hardly a wink of sleep, for we had orders to keep awake, probably owing to the fact that some of the enemy's forces were reported to be in motion near us, by a deserter we took in this morning.

Drew a sketch of the Rappahannock yesterday. Have heard strange rumors from the scene of the last fight.

THE LONG ROLL

General McDowell is reported to have been caught signaling the enemy by General Siegel, and shot dead on the spot. If this is true, no wonder that Bull Run was lost. Clear out these men from among us, and we will probably then be able to put an end to this war. This is all the news we have had so far from the late battle.

"Little Mac" was out looking at our Dress Parade last Sunday night, from an old ambulance wagon. Some of our boys claim to have seen him, but I did not. I don't doubt that he was seen, but I think it was a great slight that he did not call on me.

Friday, August 29th.

Wednesday there was considerable excitement in camp. It was reported that Jackson was on his way to this place with twenty-five thousand men, and it caused quite a skedaddling tendency, at least among the sutlers and idlers. We had orders to have everything ready for leaving at a moment's notice. But for all that, we went on picket as usual yesterday morning, and I can do no better than to transcribe a few notes that I took, having nothing else to do.

It seems that Jackson has now possession of both sides of the Rappahannock and is threatening a descent on Fredericksburg, and our position on the other side. General Lee is said to be at Spottsylvania Court-House with twenty-five thousand men, at least our cavalry pickets have just reported to that effect. If this is true, and he should take it into his head to come down on Fredericksburg, we would be nicely caught here. The only thing I can think of for us to do, is to make for the Rappahannock, swim it and then try and make our forces, or if they should have skedaddled, try for the Potomac. But I guess there will not be much danger of such a sudden leave-taking, for we have still a few good batteries that could give them a lively check. Meanwhile, these thundering twenty-five thousand Rebels bother me less than the news from Minnesota. They have had the most shocking time there with the Indians. The awful outrages of Inkpocutah have been completely eclipsed by the very tribe (the Sioux) that disowned

174

and outlawed him some five years ago. At first, I feared for the safety of my Uncle and family, but later news did not confirm the first, that the barbarous fiends had extended their murders and plunders as far down the Minnesota River as Saint Peter, above which my Uncle lives, but down as far as the village or town of New Ulm, about fifty miles above on the borders. The scene of these barbarities seems to be about Fort Ridgely, where they have murdered some sixty families, and sacked and burned as many homes. The terror-stricken inhabitants were flocking from the borders seeking safety in the towns, and every one who could carry a gun was doing so. When the last news left there, Ex-Governor Sibley (now Colonel) had twelve hundred men at Saint Peter marching to the relief of the inmates of Fort Ridgely, who were sending words by scouts that they were being attacked every hour, and only a speedy relief could save them. God grant that Sibley will reach them and that there will be a sore reckoning for these barbarous hell-hounds. I am anxiously waiting for news from that quarter, and when I get it the Journal shall know.

The readers of my Journal will remember that I used to correspond with a certain Sergeant Hodgekins of a Massachusetts Battalion, stationed on the Rip Raps some time ago, whom I liked as a man and a soldier. I just heard to-night that he was dead from wounds received in the Seven Days' Fight. It seems he was left and fell into the hands of the Rebels, in some of those bloody battles, and that is the last of him. War! War! Heartless, remorseless War!

Last night was quiet in spite of Lee's twenty-five thousand and not a shot was fired on our picket. We were released as usual, this morning, by the Fourth Rhode Island.

Saturday Morning, August 30th.

We had quite a lively time yesterday afternoon. While I was engaged in writing, the " Long Roll " commenced rolling in a lively style and my pen was immediately exchanged for the sword. At first everything looked like fight, and it seemed, as the batteries were posted, they indicated an expected descent on Fredericksburg, for we have four batteries on this side of the river commanding the bridges and ready to set the city on fire. The women and children have had notice to leave since yesterday morning. But as the scouts came in, we heard that the cause of alarm was the Rebels retreating from our forces toward the Court-House of this County, after a thrashing, and the pickets thought it was a movement on this place. If all we hear is true, the Rebels above here must have been defeated severely and Siegel and King each had a hand in it. But we can place no dependence on these reports, for they are so contradictory, but we will probably know something in a day or two.

Tuesday, September 2d.

I now write at our new camp on the heights near Acquia Creek. Fredericksburg has been evacuated and Burnside's command has fallen back on this position. When I last wrote, I told of the "Long Roll" and the consequent rumors. I had hardly gotten this Journal packed away in my knapsack, when the "Assembly" called us together and we were told to go and relieve the same Regiment from picket that we did the previous morning. The other Regiments had been out on their arms, supporting the batteries commanding the river, all that night. Nothing occurred on picket in the way of warlike demonstration to trouble us, but the clouds sponged out water enough to make us wet through, say a few quarts apiece. The next morning we marched through Fredericksburg for the last time for some time to come, in weather varying from just rainy to wet. We had no sooner struck our camp when we received orders to march in two hours, and in about four we were ready. In consideration of our being up so many nights lately and of having our clothes so wet, our knapsacks were put in the baggage wagons. The railroad-station and all rubbish were set on fire as we left, and the dark clouds of smoke commingling with the darker clouds of the atmosphere formed a dark scene of unusual interest. After we had been marching some time, one of the bridges or some shop in Fredericksburg exploded with a loud report.

176

THE LONG ROLL

This march to Acquia Creek was a miserable one. We had been up three nights of the last four and were consequently sleepy, and you know it has been raining and the roads are muddy. It is to be hoped you also know what Virginia roads are, but if you do not, I certainly do not wish you to learn by experience. But even under unfavorable circumstances, I was impressed by the wonderful and romantic beauty of this part of the country, and if my kind reader had not read so much of the scenic beauties of the Old Dominion, and if I had more time, I would enlarge upon the subject; but it must suffice this time, to say that we reached Acquia Creek yesterday morning at daylight, in a state of almost complete exhaustion, and got our tents up just in time to escape a good drenching. I hardly stacked my musket before I was off to sleep. From this I was aroused and refreshed by some coffee, and we then proceeded to this camp. And it is beautifully situated on a high hill, or rather a range of bluffs, with its batteries commanding the wooded country toward the rear, overlooking the Potomac, as it glides in silvery beauty below.

Thursday, September 4th.

Yesterday afternoon we struck tents expecting to leave for Washington or Alexandria last night, but we are still here, and waiting for the order to " Fall in." Of course, we had to sleep without tents last night, but we succeeded in making ourselves comfortable, and for my part I was more so than on the night before.

More war news to-day. Another big fight at Bull Run. Have seen the papers of the First. The second Bull Run battle was bloodier than the first by far, and has done more credit to our arms. The second day's events chill this good news, however, for we hear that re-enforcements have compelled Pope to fall back just as it was done a year ago. Pope has been strengthened by Franklin and Sumner, and is now said to be advancing with a strong, consolidated army.

Nothing is heard from Siegel. General Stephens and General Kearney are reported killed. Camp rumor has it that we

177

go to Alexandria from here and from there to the front. I believe this. The fact is something is going wrong with us all the time. They seem to want all the troops they can scare up, at Washington. Wonder where " Mac " is? Heavy cannonading to-day.

Friday Morning, September 5th.

Last night, about dusk, we formed our Regiment and marched down the bluffs and embarked on a fleet of transports, and then I went to sleep. When I awakened and rubbed my sleepy eyes, instead of the fleet in Acquia Creek, I saw a dock, a strange city, a long bridge, and then—the dome of the Capitol of our Country.

We marched through the city to our present camping grounds near Georgetown, which was formerly called Fort Douglass. Washington did not surprise me, neither did it disappoint me. It was exactly such a place as I expected to see.

(Later) I have read yesterday's paper and it presents rather a discouraging row of facts and I must say, with Stephen Blackpool, " Everything is in a muddle." No letters from Minnesota. Nothing but maddening news calculated to fill my mind with keenest anxiety. My home is some three miles from Saint Peter on the Minnesota River, and the papers contain an item of the horrible fact that two women have recently been found within two miles of that town, murdered in cold blood by the red hounds. Of what great crimes has this Nation been guilty, to have to make such terrible atonement? When will this monstrous cup be filled? But, fool that I am, what have I yet suffered, that I dare to ask such questions!

Sunday, September 7th.

A letter from Charlotte to-day, and the only thing she said about Minnesota affairs was that she had a letter from our brother, Gustav. I feel much better, for surely she would have said more, had there been any particular news.

We are now going on some kind of an expedition, but where I do not know. We are not to take our knapsacks and that would argue that we will soon return or it may mean that we are to dispense with knapsacks as do the soldiers on the Peninsula. At any rate I will have to leave this companion of my leisure hours to the mercy of a couple of tents, in my old knapsack, and if I see you again, I am willing to consider myself lucky. But you need not weep at parting, for I promise not to forget you, and I have prepared a little note-book for the especial purpose of jotting down such items of interest as you will want to hear about. And you may rest assured that the Rebels will have something to do, for "Little Mac" is ahead of us, and you know he is our "best." So console yourself in my absence, by thinking of the rich stores we will have laid up to chat about, when we shall meet again.

CHAPTER XV

September 8th.

WE left Washington, or Camp Douglass, yesterday morn-' ing about nine o'clock and proceeded toward Edward's Ferry, which is supposed to be our immediate desti- nation. As soon as we got well started, we were entangled in an endless chain of baggage wagons, and in consequence made rather slow progress, hardly marching seven miles before we bivouacked. The Rebels have crossed the Potomac above Harper's Ferry and now occupy Frederick City, Maryland, and I think we may be going in that direction. If the Rebels don't skedaddle then, some one will get hurt, for McClellan is at the head of us now and he is not the man to make a move for the fun of the thing. There are a great many rumors as to the forces of this expedition and the object, and the most probable seems to me to be that we are advancing to cut the Rebels off from the Potomac and surround them by three columns and from three different directions. I don't think Burnside holds any position other than Commander of his Corps, though it is whispered that he has some higher command. We expect to resume our march to-day, or, at any rate, early in the morning.

September 9th.

At four this morning, we were marching and have fixed camp in a field, to take the road again, however, in an hour. We have gotten our famous " dog-tents " as we call them, and they certainly look more as if intended to shelter the canines than men. They are in pieces about as large as a blanket and one of these is given to each man to carry. When the Regiment halts, it is but the work of a moment to cut a couple of stakes or poles and six pegs, and the tent is up, and buttoned together. They are no trouble to carry and will keep off dews at least and rain if it is not too heavy. And now we can say that we carry our houses on our backs.

180

THE LONG ROLL

September 10th.

We are now with the main army. We hear Jackson is recruiting in Frederick City. But I don't think he will stay there long enough to recruit very many. So far our boys are in good trim and I never knew the fighting spirit to rage so uniformly as it does now. McClellan seems to have put new life into everything, and I hope we will only get a fair shake at the enemy, as I think we can handle them " very easily," as General Phelps used to say.

Thursday, September 11th.

We have executed what our boys call a " masterly movement." We struck tents and marched from here at two o'clock yesterday morning, went three miles and then some one changed his mind, or some one else made a mistake, for we got " Right about face " and came back to our starting place, in a wringing sweat. Some think we are going back to Washington, but that is foolish. I think we branched off on the wrong road and we may have to march back or go across the country. However, we have orders to march again in an hour, and we will know some time.

September 12th.

But I have come to another conclusion since yesterday, that is that we are mighty careful about meeting some one ahead of us. We were not on the wrong road yesterday. We went in the same direction for about fourteen miles, passing the village of Damascus about noon. We occasionally caught a glimpse of the Sugar Loaf Mountains through the trees that line the road. The country is becoming more mountainous and is entrancingly beautiful. This road runs on a modest mountain ridge, and every turn brings to our view the most beautiful and extensive landscapes. Add to this, the picturesque effect of the seemingly endless files of troops in the foreground, and you can imagine the picture.

Our Division pitched in a sloping clover field last night, and we are now eating breakfast of crackers and milk pre-

181

paratory to starting on another tramp. The Rebels are only fourteen miles ahead of us and we expect a fight.

We have heard from Company F of our Regiment, which is stationed at Plymouth, North Carolina. They have had a fight with seven times their number, killing some and taking one Colonel and four other prisoners, losing one killed and several wounded. The Company was led by Sergeant Green, no commissioned officer being present. I hope the main body does as well in proportion as the detachment.

September 13th, Seven A. M.

I write in the city of Frederick, which was evacuated yesterday and immediately occupied by our troops. I did think the Rebels would show fight here, but with the exception of a little cannonading and a cavalry skirmish, there was nothing to speak of. The reception of our troops was extremely enthusiastic and the soldiers who could get out into the city were dragged into the houses and given everything that would fill empty stomachs. Indeed, the cheering of the overjoyed inhabitants exceeded anything I have ever heard, and I was once of the opinion that there was a general row in the streets, so great was the din of commingling shouts. Frederick City is not only loyal but beautiful, as we could see in our first glimpse of its picturesque spires piercing the blue background formed by the Catoctin Mountains, and the white houses nestled lovingly in the valley beneath us. It is a great wonder to me that the Rebels did not blow up the bridge which spans the Monocacy Ridge, for I think that would have delayed us materially. But they may not have had time.

September 14th, Three P. M.

We marched through Frederick yesterday morning, cheered by the masculine and waved at by the feminine population. We were sent out on a road about five miles on the extreme left, to support a Regiment of Lancers who reported a lot of Rebels cornered in an orchard. Our flanking company was sent out and that not being enough, the right platoon of

182

"Ours" was detailed for the purpose, Lieutenant Frank Powell commanding, to start with the Lancers up an abrupt road leading toward the top of the Catoctin Ridge and went about a half a mile to a sort of a ravine or gorge. Here we were attacked, six shots being fired in rapid succession from an invisible foe. The Lancers turned about in a hurry and we were immediately deployed as skirmishers on the right side of the road, and advanced to uncover the enemy. It was mighty hard work, that little skirmish through the timber and then up the steep bluff, thickly wooded, from where we expected, of course, to be fired upon at any moment. But we topped the next ridge, without seeing anything worthy of notice and saw, about a thousand yards ahead of us, was a small party of cavalry. I do not know if the Lieutenant saw them or not, but a shot was fired to the left which attracted our attention and at which the troop disappeared. The shot was fired at a Rebel who had climbed a tree to watch the motions of our Lancers, never suspecting the presence of infantry. He was secured, of course, but the other birds had flown.

A dispatch came just then ordering us to advance on the right side of the road, as the Regiment was deployed and advancing on the left. We started on and went through about a mile of cornfield, finally bursting out into an open field just about abreast of the other boys. And the landscape, as we paused on the open ridge, was indeed magnificent. Beneath us was ten miles of country checkered with fields of grain of various hues, some having already yielded their harvests, thus imparting a stranger brilliancy with the contrast to the rest. Through them all were scattered beautiful groves and the farmers' home-like looking barns and cottages; and the Blue Ridge, in its massive, dark-blue shade, seemingly dividing this spot from the ever-changing landscape of the Heavens.

There were no further events of importance that day, and we marched back to Frederick, where we pitched in the same camp, very tired from our severe day's labor. I might say that I was with two sections who were separated from the Regiment, and the Captain thought we were lost. This was through the foolishness of our Sergeant who commanded us, and it is not worth the paper to relate the particulars.

This morning, our Colonel had us up before daybreak, and though it was with some effort that we bent our stiff joints, at the word "March" we were on our way out of Frederick City, and went two miles up on the turnpike road. From time to time, as we passed up the windings of the road, we could not help but notice the signs of the good fight the Rebels evidently made for every inch of ground, yielding only after severe obstinacy. Coming up on the top of the ridge, the same scene opened before us that I described yesterday, with some differences resulting from the point of view. Here was the same vast plain, but now we had a fair view of the road as it passed through the village of Middletown, glorying in two steeples, from one of which we could see military signals flying. We could see the white puffs of smoke and catch the dull sound of which we all knew the meaning. Troops were scattered about through the plain, more thickly near the village. It was not hard for me to conclude from these observations that Middletown was headquarters, and that beyond the mountains there was to be a game of ball in which we probably would be pitching before night.

And here we are now, in our bivouac near Middletown, watching with anxious eyes the fierce battle now raging up in the mountains, waiting for the word to take a hand therein. The enemy's position is a strong one and the ground seems to be hotly contested. Our boys are hardly in a condition for fight; but if it comes, I am willing to take a hand.

Monday Morning, Six O'clock,
September 15th.

I write on the battlefield of yesterday. It was a glorious day for our Country; costly, blood-purchased, but it was a glorious victory. Poor General Reno is no more. My Journal has been acquainted with him and can be certain of his merit as a General, and not a shadow of a hint can be spoken against

184

Yours sincerely
James D. Loades

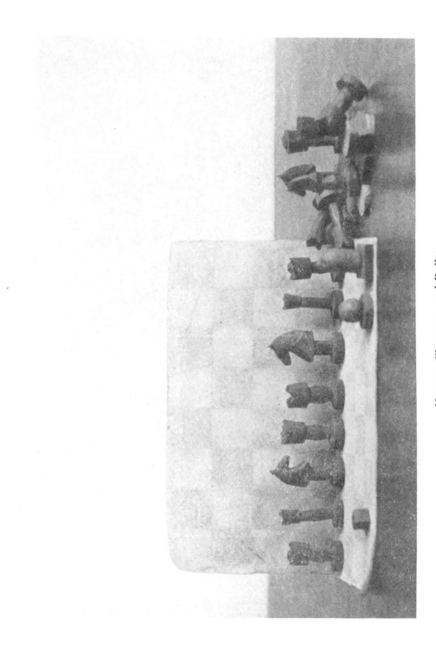

Veteran Chessmen and Bullets

Photograph by J. R. Zweifel

E. A. Kimball

Lt. Col. comanding 9th A. Y. Vol

Fort Nansemond, Suffolk

" Going Home "
From Sketch by Fredrick B. Johnson

his bravery. He fought gallantly and fell late in the day, a
glorious sacrifice to his Country.

About four o'clock yesterday afternoon, the order came
for General Rodman's Division to march immediately for the
scene of fury, and Colonel Kimball tells us this morning that
the order read " Double-quick." This, of course, was impracticable, for our route was through gorge and ravine and over
ridges, up steep bluffs, woods, rocks and fences, and it could
not be " Double-quicked." As we pressed on, up the toilsome
road, we occasionally met ambulances full of wounded, and
squads of prisoners marching to the rear toward the village.
But there were very few shirkers, which bespoke plainly that
the fight, wherever it was, was going well. We could hear no
musketry, though indications told us that we were near enough,
and if it had not been for the loud whizzing of our shells at
regular intervals, I might have thought that the fight was over.
We now came up to the ridge of the plowed field occupied by
the battery we had heard playing, and then we descended a
steep declivity, where we could not see, though we could hear,
the shots of the enemy as they met those of our battery in the
air high above us. Again we went up a steep bluff, and thicker
came the prisoners, strongly guarded by squads and companies.
They were ragged, without anything like shoes on their bleeding
feet, and they looked miserable indeed. I saw one poor fellow
who walked with his head down, mortified that he could not
be allowed to be without the hands of his captor on his shoulder,
to show every one that he had been taken prisoner. I felt keenly
what my own thoughts would be, if walking thus, under a
Rebel's triumphant leer.

Arriving at last at the top of the ridge, we filed to the left
through some woods and had another height to climb, steeper
than any we had yet ascended. Here was the advance position,
and knowing that, when once there, nothing but woods would
be between us and the Rebels, we climbed with high excitement
and commenced forming the brigade along the ridge facing the
woods, as accurately as if preparing for Dress Parade. Our
Regiment formed on the right of the stone wall which had been

the center of the contest during the day, and the One Hundred Third and the Eighty-ninth New York Regiments were forming on the left, allowing the brigade that had been fighting all day, to fall to the rear. This was being done and I was wondering that still no enemy was visible, when a long rattling volley of musketry burst upon us, gradually becoming the irregular firing at will. I was with the guard on the left, by the wall, and the bullets, a whole shower of them, rushed madly over our heads. I could hardly help laughing at the precipitant retreat of the supernumeraries down the hill, when I found out it was them, and not the brigade as I at first feared. Now the fight grew fiercer, and we could see that the Eighty-ninth was doing its work up brilliantly and repelling the sudden attack. A lightning flash and stunning report of artillery near us seemed to frighten both parties of the musketry into silence. This was quickly followed by others in rapid succession and soon the musketry ceased entirely, telling us that the enemy had fled. But they might rally again and Kimball had the right wing of his Regiment out in less time than it takes to tell it, to support the battery, which was evidently the object of the attack. But no Rebels came and gradually there was quiet, with only an occasional interruption of a discharge of grape into the woods.

We were engaged in applauding the gallant Eighty-ninth for its noble conduct, when again the sound of musketry rattled harshly, but more distantly, upon our ears. The sounds proceeded from a hollow on our right and kept up for two hours steadily. The darkness set in long before it ceased, and I was lying on the mountain-top, shivering from the rough wind, vainly trying to go to sleep, with the sound grating in my ears.

The enemy is now in retreat and we are waiting for the word to go forward. Meanwhile let us glance a little over the field. The Rebel dead are scattered about us in every direction, and in yonder wood they tell me the poor fellows are in heaps, and there is every horrible proof that our foes fought for their splendid position here, with a dogged valor well worthy of a better cause. Here on the very spot where we are now, the Rebels were yesterday morning, and up on the face of the precipice,

186

THE LONG ROLL

the Ohioans under Franklin and Reno charged again and again, and with Yankee courage and obstinacy carried the position against almost insurmountable difficulties. My sketch shows a small portion of the field, but I think the most interesting, for it was from the cornfield in the center that the Ohioans finally charged into the enemy posted behind the fence and wall, which is in the foreground. Routing them from this snug little position, they did not stop until they drove them at the point of the bayonet into the woods, and were recalled from their eager pursuit.

It was here, too, that our left was attacked last night, and to the right, in the foreground, a little farther up along the fence, the section of Robinson's Battery was stationed, which, they all swear, would have been taken, if we had not arrived just in time to save it. It seems the Rebels contemplated taking this battery and position at all hazards and so regain the hill, and no troops could be spared from other parts of the field, and our Division was sent for to come up in "Double quick" as I have told you. We were not yet formed, when the charge was made, but the Rebels were disheartened at meeting fresh troops, and soon went back, leaving us in peaceful possession of the field. We have gained a complete victory, taking between three and four thousand prisoners, among whom are some taken and paroled on Roanoke Island. A Doctor Jordan, who attended Captain Wise in his last moments, now lies not many rods from me. A musket ball and a bayonet have pierced his body ⚬ ⚬

And thus ends the Battle of South Mountain.

CHAPTER XVI

THE BATTLE OF ANTIETAM. THE FIRST DAY.

Tuesday Morning, September 16th.

YESTERDAY afternoon we received our orders to forward and commenced to move down the other side of the mountain on a rough and steep road. Here Death reigns in all his most terrible ghastliness. Never have I looked upon a scene so horribly fascinating; such a heart-rending spectacle. On either side of the road were the Rebel dead, literally piled upon one another in twos and threes, their ragged clothes covered with dust and marked with the dark clots of blood from the death wound. The ghastly faces and beamless eyes were upturned to us as though in deadly reproach, as we victors marched along. No moan, even of the faintest, escaped these motionless forms, to sound the solemn requiem for the Death King. I noticed one man, a large, powerfully built soldier, with a huge beard and moustache, and why it is I can not tell, but he haunts my memory above all the rest. I felt, as I passed the lifeless form, how soon I might be lying cold as he was, vacantly staring up, up where I hope his soul has gone! While we were passing these gray piles, each one of us wrapped in his own thoughts, we suddenly heard the dull report of artillery toward the front. But we did not get to our camping ground before eleven o'clock last night. The Rebels tried to shell us out this morning and our ambulances and baggage had to go to the rear. General McClellan just passed our camp, returning from the front where he has been superintending the artillery duel commenced by the Rebels. He was seated on a brown horse and was surrounded by several officers. He turned his eyes toward us once, as we lay on our arms, and then turned to the perusal of a letter. This is the first time I have seen this great man.

On the Battlefield,
Wednesday Afternoon, September 17th.

This day will be a famous one in the history of our country. We are now on our arms trying to console ourselves for the

188

hard work we have had in crossing the Antietam Creek at a ford above here, and then scrambling up the face of an almost perpendicular cliff, to re-enforce the troops already here, who came by way of the bridge which they gallantly stormed and took this morning. We have dispatched a poor apology of a dinner, a few crumbs from this morning's rations of hardtack. As I write, the shells of Company K's Battery are passing with deafening noise over our heads, toward the enemy on our right.

Have just seen the Reverend Mr. Holman of the Forty-eighth Pennsylvania, and had a long talk with him. He showed me a beautiful Secesh sword he captured this morning. It bears the motto " Liberty or Death." The decision was " Death " for that poor man.

I will try to tell something of our adventures since yesterday noon, but the fight is obstinate, and I don't know what moment we will be called for.

It was almost dark when we got our orders yesterday, and moved forward to take our position in line of battle. When we were abreast of our artillery, we halted and were shown the position of the enemy on an opposite range of hills. We could see even their apparently " pigmy " forms in relief against the darkening sky. After about a half an hour we pushed slowly forward for a short distance, cautioned to keep silence, as we were in the immediate front of the enemy. Proceeding thus noiselessly, we reached a corn field, pickets were deployed in front of us, and we were then permitted to sleep. We all knew that the morrow would be signalized by a general struggle, and also that the enemy was within talking distance. Still we slept, hoping that our slumbers might not be disturbed by the coming foe. At the earliest peep of gray dawn, we were awakened, for our officers expected an attack as they always do, and sure enough, we got it. As soon as there was light enough, our pickets discovered the Rebels and there commenced a little battle between them, but such a petty affair was not to disgrace the day. Soon a horseman was seen, and after he disappeared, something struck and kicked up a cloud of dust right by the side of one of our pickets, and this was followed by a terrific noise, indicating as plainly as such things can talk, that a shell had been sent with the compliments of our friends on the other side. And not content with sending one, they sent a whole cloud of them, and a beautiful range they had too. Every one of them exploded just as nicely as they could wish, squarely over our heads, shaking its fragments among us, leaving only a harmless cloud of smoke to roll peacefully away, as if satisfied with its work and glad to return to its proper home in the atmosphere. Things grew savage. There we stood watching these infernal things, afraid to move lest we should get in their way and be the cause of an *accident*. The order came to file back into the woods out of the fire, and some one blundered and would have us up on a ridge where we would be in better range than before. Kimball got mad and said some things and finally told us to get back into the woods out of the fire *any way*. This order was carried out in admirable confusion, and while we were in this pleasant state, the Rebels sent Hell after us in the most approved manner. Corporal McKinley was knocked over with a piece of shell not over three feet from me. Shultz was hit, on the other side of me, and my old friend Dennis got a slight hurt in the leg, right next to my precious self.* We finally got out of range into an open field and into something like shape, and then what do you think we got? No more use for grape and canister, but nothing less than stumps of railroad iron as long as my arm. If this was not adding insult to injury! But we could pay little attention to these unwelcome missiles, and proceeded into a valley by a farm and stacked our arms in a field, while we had breakfast. This was coffee without sugar, but I relished the meal and we were ready then for our orders to take up a new position on a hill. From this place we had a magnificent view of the tremendous contest which is even now raging with unabated fury, on the right arm center, almost immediately below us.

---

* Corporal John McKinley. Wounded at Camden and at Antietam
James Shultz, Company I. Wounded at Antietam.
Edward Dennis, Company I. Wounded at Antietam.

THE LONG ROLL

We could see the smoke of musketry as plainly as we could hear the rattle, and though we knew not then what object there was in such a dogged and spirited contest, for the woods hid the troops from us, it is now clear, for the Rebels defended the bridge stoutly before they left it to the resistless troops of Burnside. We could see from our lofty position too, where the center was pouring in a ceaseless fire toward the Rebels, and our view extended even to the extreme right, as far as five miles. From every hill shot forth puffs of white smoke, which showed, though we could not see a gunner or a gun, that they were occupied by our artillery. Owing to the nature of the ground, we had a much better view of the Rebel position than of our own, and could plainly see their gunners going through the motions. Often we saw clouds of dust from our shells hide their guns, which made us for the moment think that some one piece was annihilated, but a saucy puff would assure us of our mistake, as they sent a reply to our salutation. The vast landscape was completely dotted with pillars of smoke, and the continuous roll of the artillery in the distance, commingling with the loud noise of the nearer guns, and the rattle of small arms beneath, made a noise—not a noise, but a savage, continual thunder, that is not equaled by any sound I have ever heard.

An Aide came to General Rodman, and immediately after we were ordered to "Attention" and sent down the fields toward the creek. The General procured a guide to show him the ford, and after many dubious windings and turnings into the woods, we came to what appeared to be rapids, and into this we plunged. Some Rebel sharpshooters discovered us and did not fail to scatter a few of their bullets from long range, but what little damage was done was mostly from the bubbling waters. Out of the creek, we found the steep cliff before us, and with considerable difficulty scrambled up here, and here we are. God only knows where we will be before the sun goes down.

191

THE LONG ROLL

HARDLY had I put my note-book in my pocket after writing the outline of the preceding notes, when we were again ordered to " Fall in " and we knew our tug-of-war was coming in earnest. Our troops took up a new position under a hill, and from over its top we could hear the whizzing of musket and rifle balls piercing the air. Soon the cannon balls mingled with the sharp play of small arms, and I noticed one of them coming like an india-rubber ball through the air. It struck the top of the hill, boring up a mass of earth, and then bounded high in the air, passing over our heads with a noise I can liken to nothing but the savage yell of some inhuman monster. If it is true that you never see cannon balls except when they are coming toward you, I must have been in a fair way for eternity.

We were all in line and the cannonading as well as the musketry was getting hotter every moment, and I was expecting the order for a general advance, when, to my surprise, our Company was ordered to deploy in front of the Brigade as skirmishers. Captain Leahy was evidently glad of the opportunity, for the hill looked like a pleasant place to him. We were soon advancing up the hill; came to a fence over which we leaped, and it was there, though I did not know it at the time, that poor Murphy met his fate.

From the top of the hill, we could see, at a distance of about six hundred yards, a body of skirmishers playing away behind a stone wall, while on a hill behind them was the main body. Here Captain Leahy ordered us to lie down so as to let the ridge give us all possible shelter, " retain sight of the wall and fire," and so forth. Here I fired my first shot at an enemy I could see. We had not used more than three rounds when Captain Leahy shouted, " There they go, Boys, they are running ! " I will never forget the indescribable thrill that went through my veins. I had been firing silently, and trying to guard myself as much as possible from the showers continually passing with fearful whistles and moans over our heads, but I

192

suddenly did not think that was worth while, and it took too long to load, lying down. We were ordered to advance down in the hollow now, and as the skirmishers had disappeared, we turned our attention to the battery on the hill. We descended into the hollow with an excited shout, and found another body of skirmishers had preceded us there, but they did not deter us from firing. We kept up a continual fire now, exchanging some bits of conversation the while, such as : " What do you belong to ? " " This will be a great day in history." " They fight damned stubbornly." " Getting Hell on the right, though." " There ought to be a charge soon." And the fire seemed to be ten times hotter even than on the hill, for from the batteries the Rebels could see us but too plainly, and if we had not been protected to some extent by the natural embankment, it would have been the worse for us. I had fired about a dozen rounds when I found that some of my cartridges were useless, those in the bottom of the box having become wet while we were crossing the stream. I told Captain Leahy about it, and he said if the Regiment did not come up soon, we would have to return for more ammunition, and if it did, we would join them on the charge. Just as he was speaking, a Regiment came thundering along on a " Double-quick," but we looked in vain for the red caps—they were not our boys. They were met by a perfect shower of shell and grape, but they took possession of the embankment. One poor fellow, who was not able to keep up with the wild speed of his Regiment, came on a little behind, evidently trying to get to his place in the ranks as soon as possible, but his destiny was decided otherwise. A projectile came along with its deafening death-cry, and took him right in his groin, severing his limbs completely from his body. If I could have heard his shriek, it would not have been so horrible, but to see him seize at his limbs, and fall back with a terrible look of agony, without being able to catch a sound from him—*Oh God! May I never be doomed to witness such a sight again!*

From this time I was in a delirium; I was mad. I recollect a stone wall, yes, that part is perfect in my memory. The stone wall where Captain Leahy tried to lead on a whole Brigade, and no one but the Color-man would move, but how we got there, I do not know. I remember I rushed up a hill trying to find where our boys were, but they had passed us while we were skirmishing. I stood for a moment wondering where all the rest of the Company was. The air was filled with a deluge of bullets, grape, canister and shell, and up there to the left, what a picture that was to paint on my memory. Our boys thinned down to a Company, still carrying their Colors, borne triumphantly through Roanoke and Camden. My God! Look! The Colors have fallen! Ah! They are up again! While I was drinking in this scene, I must have reached the wall or fence, for there is where I was sitting, unable to fire my musket, with nothing left in my cartridge box. I did have sense enough to keep my last charge in my musket. I saw the Rebels quite plainly through the smoke and dust of the cornfield, going through the motions of firing and loading, and I had a kind of indistinct notion that they might charge, and in that case, I had one shot ready for them. I will confess to one cowardly thought. Why did I stay here? With no chance to retaliate, why not get out of danger? But even now, when all feeling and common sense seemed to be gone, a rude sense of honor put away the idea quickly and determined me to stay rather than to turn my back to the foe.

Our Major Jardine, who commanded the Eighty-ninth, attracted my attention. He had a Rebel battle-flag in his hand which he had spilled blood to capture. His face was as calm and his manner as cool as though he was going through the ceremony on Parade, while, could the death messengers have left their shadows, as they flitted through the air, they would have clouded the sun. What attracted my attention to him particularly, was an incident which I hear was not the only instance on that bloody day, when the cowardly and miserable trick was practised upon us at the expense of God knows how many men. Displaying the " Stars and Stripes " in front of the line in the heat of battle, to gain the advantage of its protection! As I saw it, the enemy played the trick so

194

cunningly as to deceive for a moment even the cool and practised eye of Major Jardine, for as soon as our flag caught his eye, I suppose he thought some flanking movement had been executed by our forces, and in words clear and ringing so as to be heard loud above the din of battle, he shouted, "For God's sake, don't fire on our own men!" But the words were hardly spoken when he saw his mistake, and in even louder tone, if that were possible, he ordered, "At them, Boys, they are under false colors! Give them Hell!" While noting this, I became pretty much excited, as may be imagined. I was quite alone between the two Regiments and my fez must have caught the attention of the lot in the corn, for I was warned in a polite strain, that I was seen and marked, by the sharp hissing of two "Minie" balls as they came in rather too close proximity to my head, and as if to convince me, that it was an earnest game, the third arrived. Lower than the first, higher than the second, skipping along the ground with an angry noise, it entered my flesh sideways in the left hip, causing a sensation from which I might with reason think my whole side was annihilated. I started up with an involuntary exclamation, which I shudder to think of now, for if the wound had been mortal, I would have died uttering with my last breath a horrible curse. To my joy, I found that I could stand, that is, if in the bewildered state I was then in, I was capable of experiencing either joy or sorrow. At any rate, it was clear that I had been shot and could be of no more use in that day's fight, and in the language of one of our boys when relating his adventures, "Didn't I skedaddle, though, out of that fire!" I would have shown my heels, but I couldn't very well with an ounce of lead in one of my hips. But I cleared the ground pretty well, put it in any expression you please, until I got out of the hottest of that terrific fire. After that desirable feat was accomplished, I took my time and found out that the ball had lodged in the flesh and that nothing very serious had been mashed. It was then, while I was making my way to the rear with the blood streaming down my legs, that one of the most sublime sights that has been witnessed during this war was

195

displayed. The sun was just tipping the wood-tops on its grand, downward course, and the rash and gallant Burnside was exerting his utmost strength, and with almost superhuman effort, resisting the overwhelming force with which the Rebels tried to drive him from his dearly-bought ground, in accordance with the orders from the military genius who ruled this great day. And nobly did his gallant men do their duty. Nobly did they submit to having their ranks torn and decimated with infantry sustained by artillery, while they could only reply with pop-guns. It was in vain that Burnside called for artillery to sustain his infantry, and reply to the enemy's cannon, which seemed to mow his men down with shell, grape and the more terrible spherical case-shot. There was no help for it; for some reason, artillery was not to be had, and *the hill must be held.* The sun, dimmed by an occasional strip of cloud, went down in full, autumn glory, and its last beam saw the hill in Burnside's possession.

And—Afterward.

I reached the hospital some time before the day's strife was over. In fact, by the time I got there, faint from loss of blood and the exertion, I was of the opinion that the Rebels had gained an immense advantage over us; but it may be, that in my bewildered state, the fierceness of the contest seemed greater at a distance, than when I was actually in the hottest of the fire. I certainly experienced the most terrible depression of spirits imaginable, as the battle-heat gradually wore off, leaving me to realize the full force of what I had been through. And the terrible sights and sounds that met me as I approached the hospital did not tend to relieve my mind. There were already over a hundred of our boys alone, lying on straw and cornstalks, with wounds of all imaginable shapes and sizes. Our tireless Doctor Humphreys and his assistants were very busy, I can tell you, bandaging, sewing and cutting human flesh. The sights were terrible, but the sounds were more so, although, as a general thing, our boys made light of their wounds. Some one helped me to a rude bed of straw and relieved me of my accouterments, and my canteen was refilled, but this comfort was denied us, for I had not been here five minutes, when the Rebels turned on a heavy fire from a neighboring height. Our Doctor ordered all those who could crawl, to start out. "Leave everything, Boys, and go for your lives, they are firing at us." In my hurry I forgot my belt and cartridge box, much to my self-reproach afterward. I have not learned just what damage was done by this beautiful piece of work, but I don't see how every one could escape, the way we were scattered about at the time.

In making my way to the rear with the other newly-made cripples, I encountered a couple of our cooks who were bringing up freshly cooked meat to the Company, and of course, I wanted some, for like others newly wounded, I felt savagely hungry. I got two chunks of meat, either one as big as my fist, and the way I pitched into them was a caution. I finished them by the time I got to the farm house, to which we had been sent, Miller's Farm House Hospital, and still I craved for more. Nothing was to be had but apples from the orchard, and I was now in such a state I could not move. But this difficulty was remedied by one of Duryeas' Zouaves, who got me all I wanted, and I had enough at last.

And now I will return to my note-book after this digression in favor of Antietam, myself and you being satisfied, I hope, that I had enough to eat for once. I will commence by giving you the note written on the morning of the Eighteenth, before my wound was looked to or dressed.

Thursday Morning, September 18th.

I have been wounded again. Was struck in the left hip by a musket ball, and I am now lying here on the stoop of a farm house, waiting, with more or less patience, for a doctor to examine and dress the wound. I can feel the ball now below the hip, and I don't think there will be much trouble to get it out. The groans of the poor fellows around me are heart-sickening in the extreme. I reckon the whole number of wounded here is nearly three hundred. My old friend Dennis has gotten it pretty badly in both legs. I would like to know who are killed in our Company. I will probably know to-morrow. Slept a little last night, and was troubled by a dream in which demons, rattlesnakes, Hell, brimstone, cannon-balls and railroad iron, bayonets and pitchforks, powder and smoke were all conglomerated into one shapeless, endless whirl, with me in the midst, though suffering no particular harm. I finally woke up with a severe cramp in my stomach, a likely result of my ravenous eating yesterday.

Friday Morning, September 19th.

After the firing we heard yesterday morning, everything was quiet and the two great powers seemed to be taking a short rest after the extraordinary exertions of the day before. About noon, two or three of our boys were carried up here from the field, being wounded in a skirmish they had this morning " with the retreating enemy." But that they have retreated far is doubtful. We have fought one of the greatest battles of the war. Our killed and wounded is roughly estimated at ten thousand, and our Regiment contributes two hundred seventy-five, as far as we know. This great blood-bath, of which both parties as yet claim to be the victors, will be known as the Battle of Antietam, taking its name from the stream which we crossed, and whose waters received such a liberal contribution of " Life's Red Liquid " from the heroic men of Burnside. Of course, we hear any amount of unlikely stories from the front, but I do not consider them worth repeating. I may except one, however, and that is to the effect that the enemy is retreating, and if that is true, it leaves us the victory.

Shortly after writing my note of the Eighteenth, I requested Doctor Harding, one of Doctor Humphrey's assistants, to look at my wound. I showed him where I felt the ball and his butcher knife was out in a twinkling and I made up my mind to have a jaw-tooth pulled. What was my surprise when the soft-handed little Doctor showed me a good-sized " Minie " ball before I even thought I felt the incision of his sharp-edged tool. One of Professor Anderson's sleight-of-hand tricks would not have surprised me more, or pleased me more, either, for

198

that matter. After this easy operation, the wound was dressed and bandaged, and I felt better, of course.

Saturday, September 20th.

It is now certain that the Rebels are retreating as fast as they can toward the Potomac, which they will now probably be able to recross, owing to our loss of Harper's Ferry. We heard firing this morning, which argues that McClellan is hurrying them up, if nothing more. Lieutenant-Colonel Kimball made a flying visit to us yesterday. He is in glorious humor, shakes hands with every one and says, " Brave Boys, Damned brave Boys." I asked him if he was never going to have the luck to get hit, at which he held out his hand and showed me a bullet and he will have it that it hit him somewhere. No, by all the powers of war, no one could cheat him out of a wound this time. We expect to get sent away soon, as there is certainly no accommodation for us here.

(My next note was written on the Twenty-fifth and I was in no condition to see or to write anything, for I don't think I ever knew what homesickness meant before. The world seemed to be so hopelessly dark and I did long for the influence of Home. Every object in the landscape was tainted with the ravages of war, and around us the eye could not wander without resting on bloody and mutilated forms, some laughing and joking, some praying, some groaning, and some alas, struggling with Death, with the death-rattle in their throats. If I could only get away from all this, to change the bloody and filthy clothes I was compelled to wear for something clean, and what would I not have given for a bed on which I could get one night's sleep ! Our food was poor, and in a few days it became absolutely tantalizing even to look at. I was without a cent of money which would have enabled me to buy something from the neighboring farms to tempt my miserable appetite. Everything conspired against me as if to see how miserable a human being could be made.)

Yesterday, it was one week that we have been lying in this miserable hospital and still there are no signs of getting away.

199

THE LONG ROLL

I don't expect to be sent home, but I do think we have a right to expect the Government to treat us as wounded soldiers deserve to be treated. I should think that we have need of something in the eating line more nourishing than crackers and poor coffee. My breakfast and dinner have been a small piece of pie a friend gave me, for it is absolutely impossible for me to stomach the miserable rations we get here. The talk is that the men receive excellent care in Middletown and Frederick. I do hope they will send us anywhere, so that it is out of this place. Captain Leahy and Corporal Warring have been here to see Dennis and myself. Captain Leahy said he would try to get us both furloughs. I hope he succeeds, but still I would just as soon be sent to Philadelphia or Baltimore as to New York, for reasons you can easily understand. I would have to go into a hospital, even if I was in New York, or spend all the money I have saved since I was there last. Warring gave me the much desired information as to who were killed of our Company. The number is smaller than in any other, owing to our luck in getting that skirmishing to do just before the fight. Levi Collins who was in my mess at Roanoke Island was killed in the skirmish. I remember hearing his death shriek now, but I did not have any suspicion at the time, that it was poor Collins. James Murphy was killed in jumping the fence when we advanced, as I mentioned. Jack Adair, our Color Corporal, was killed at his post about the same time I was shot. These are all who were killed, with about nine who were wounded.*

Frederick City, September 29th.

Yesterday morning, Sunday, a train of ambulances came to Miller's Farm Hospital and took away a hundred of those who could travel. You can easily guess that I was glad to be one of the number. We got started about nine o'clock and took the same road that the army used in their advance from this place, with the exception of not turning out of the road at

---

* Levi Collins, Company I. Killed at Antietam, September 17th, 1862.
Corporal John C. Adair, Company I. Killed at Antietam, September 17th.
James Murphy, Private, Company I. Killed at Antietam.

200

THE LONG ROLL

Thurness Gap in South Mountain, having no Rebels to encounter there. The view from this Pass is grand, including the whole valley to the Catoctin Range, with Middletown in the center of the landscape. But it can not compare with the same view we had from nearly the same elevation and position at the hour of sunset on the Seventeenth, when this magnificent valley, then teeming with a mass of armed men, was covered with that glorious spread of mingling colors of crimson and gold, with the different hues of varying Nature in Autumn, seeking an occasional snatch of admiration from the thousands who were engaged in bloody strife.

How different now is this peaceful valley grown in the short interval of time. And how sad. The thunder-clap of war has now rolled to the distance, leaving Nature slowly to recover from the paralyzation of its recent shock. It were not, perhaps, a smaller contrast, to note the difference in my condition, hopes and prospects now, with two weeks ago. I was then hastening over this same road with thousands and thousands of others. Artillery was shaking this mountain gorge and filling its huge dents with their powerful vibrations. I was full of life and vigor, and yet wondering if my fate might not be to have my bones become a part of the dust of the mountain. I was conscious that our forces would brave many a desperate battle before they would abandon the soil of Maryland, but I placed confidence in McClellan, and was eager to do my best in any contest that was impending, in the hope that we might gain an end to this unnatural and therefore more furious strife. I was fully determined to do my duty to the letter, however hard that might be, that I might be able to acquit myself of reproach in case of disaster, which I prayed would not visit our arms. Now the campaign is ended. I had fondly hoped that I might so term the war. Maryland is free from the tread of Rebel hosts, and the Nation rejoices in a great victory, as it mourns over the countless dead. I am returning with many others, helpless, to the little city of Frederick, seeking tenderness and care. The same city we left long before daylight two weeks ago, with musket in hand, hastening to the scene of action then in progress in the mountains, we will enter to-night, weary, sick and hope-less, praying but for rest and the return of strength.

September 30th.

It was after nine o'clock last night before we entered the city, and after the longest half hour I have ever experienced, we were put into a hospital, formerly a Presbyterian church. I have learned that the Doctor in charge bears the cognomen "Cornish." He is a gentleman 'of the old school apparently, and I have already experienced kindness from him. He wakened me up last night about twelve o'clock from the soundest sleep I have had since I was shot, and washed and dressed the wound. I showed my appreciation of the act, by resuming my interrupted slumbers, with greater vigor than ever.

CHAPTER XVII

October 2d.

I AM still in Frederick City experiencing kind attention from its people. Expect to go to Washington, Baltimore or Philadelphia almost any day, but I don't think I care very much about going.

This morning, in a fit of sentiment, I composed a few verses entitled " Lines to a Lady in Frederick." The object of this " Will-be " famous lyric attracted my attention passing the Church-yard gate, while I was smoking my pipe in a dreamy reverie. I did not know her name, but have since learned that it is " Hattie Wilson." She is very much like a lady with whom I was foolish enough to fall in love, in regular school-boy style, about three years ago, out in the Western wilds, and probably that is the reason I was struck with that peculiar style of feminine loveliness in Miss Wilson which I have always admired.

October 4th.

Abraham Lincoln passed through the city to-day on his return from the review of the army on the upper Potomac. He paid the honor of a visit to a certain General who was wounded at Antietam and is stopping opposite here, and to the crowd which collected around the door and cheered him, he made a speech of his usual brevity. He was then assisted into an unpretentious one-horse buggy by a field officer who accompanied him. They passed the hospital, and I had an excellent view of the features of the President. He looked more worn than when I saw him last, and the heavy load he is obliged to carry, amply accounts for that. My present condition is not overly pleasant, but by far better than is his.

October 9th.

My wound is getting along beautifully, and in about six weeks I will be as well as ever again. I have resigned myself to that long stay in this city. Still no letters from home. They must have been written and are somewhere between here and

THE LONG ROLL

home, and I feel badly not to have them. But I am not quite miserable, for my pencil has been as busy as a bee ever since I got settled. I completed a large and very difficult picture to-day, and am pretty well satisfied with it. It is an attempt at representing an interior view of this hospital. Doctor Cornish thinks it is fine and wants me to make him one. I do not like to undertake it just now, for I am laboring under some difficulties in following the footprints of Art, having nothing better than the pencil with which I write these notes, for both outline and finish. If I could raise the " Spons," even a small amount would remedy the trouble. I could then use a pen and pass away some time by resuming my Journal, which is still in Washington. I am a little afraid that the much valued article will not turn up very soon, if at all. This Journal of mine was the most valuable thing in my knapsack, and I would hate most awfully to lose it. But I suppose I must bear up against the loss of All my valuable Property, with the fortitude of a soldier. I am well contented to stay in this city, and I don't think we could be better off anywhere else. But, look here, I don't want you to think that Miss Wilson, the angel in petticoats, has anything to do with this conviction. My fancy departed from that quarter almost as soon as it arrived. My reconnaissance in that direction, without getting near enough to exchange words, much less to storm the fort, has proven that she is not only proud, though unassuming, but that she is wise enough to keep a corporal's guard of a Governess to look after her. It is easy enough for me to see that she is not the " Gal for me " for I know d – — – Oh—well that she would stick up her nose, and what a pretty nose it is, in holy horror at any one less than a Captain. She would like a Major, smile at a Lieutenant and would adore a Colonel. Accordingly, I will try and content myself with pictures, poverty and memory, and be just as happy as though nothing in the shape of Venus had come nearer to knocking my heart out, than did any of Jackson's famous railroad iron to my silly brains.

204

THE LONG ROLL

October 12th.

One of the poor boys in the hospital went to his "long Home" this morning. His young wife was here and saw him die. They had been married only a week before his enlistment.

Sunday Morning, October 26th.

Two weeks have glided by and we have Sunday morning again. The hospital is being prepared for our usual visitors who generally accompany the minister. I presume the services will be performed by the Reverend Doctor Diehl, who has preached for us on several occasions. He is Pastor of the Dutch Reformed Church here in Frederick. He came in the other day and asked for "Johnson from Minnesota." I was getting my wound dressed, and though I heard him speak, I did not realize that he meant me, but I was the only Johnson in the establishment, and was from Minnesota, so I finally answered. He gave me a letter from Pastor Passevant and told me he would come again in the afternoon and bring me some papers. This he did and I had a nice chat with him. He expressed some surprise at finding me a member of a New York Regiment. I very gladly accepted an invitation to his home, but I am not sure that I can go.

My pencil has made me quite famous. Doctor Cornish is sure to bring every lady visitor who happens in, over here to see my pictures, and I told him the other day that I was quite popular enough. Mrs. Morgan has intimated that she would like something in my line in memory of the Regiment, and Mrs. Wilson, the Mother of the Other Wilson, has sent the same request through three different channels. I have made two copies of the hospital picture and Doctor Cornish sent one to his wife and now he wants me to get up something nice for his little girl, and I don't know what to do for time to spare for writing. I received my Journal some time ago with my knapsack. Our suits came, too, and of course, Hawkins' "Zou-Zous" are now "King Pins" of the town. But I must stop, for the people are beginning to come, and it is time for service.

205

THE LONG ROLL

Convalescent Camp, Virginia,
November 30th.

My nice time in that darling little city of Frederick is over. My drawing, my writing, my chess playing and my reading are all of the past. This Camp is a miserable hole to say the least, and I don't intend to describe it, for my pen might say too much, and I prefer to tell of the last days I spent in Frederick.

Doctor Cornish was ordered to his Regiment about a week before I left. I gave him a little picture for his daughter. He showed me a photograph of Mrs. Cornish and the little girl, and also read me a part of a letter in answer to his with the hospital picture. Mr. Johnson was much honored by Mrs. Cornish's compliments as to its being a very good picture. She said she asked the little girl where " Papa " was and she pointed to him as represented in the foreground. I could not do any better for Mrs. Morgan than to give her a pretty good landscape, a Swiss scene. Mrs. Wilson was duly presented with a portrait of Colonel Hawkins, and a message written on the back of it was intended, of course, eventually to meet the eyes of "Hattie" and the other little curly-headed witch. Sergeant Loades, my chess opponent, got his portrait taken, which I kept with his autograph, and gave him a sketch of the Antietam Bridge, near which he was wounded when helping to take it. And then, when I had finished reading " Luck of Ladysmeade," I was ready to go anywhere they wanted to send me.

On the Twenty-sixth of November, I bade farewell to Frederick and to good times, arriving in Washington about eleven the same night. The following day was Thanksgiving Day, and I spent it in going about the city. I made it my business to see as many of the public buildings as I could. Of these, the Capitol, of course, is the first to attract the attention of a stranger, from its stupendous size and the lofty, and still unfinished, dome which crowns it. I saw Crawford's gigantic statue in bronze, of " Liberty " mounted on a temporary pedestal, on the Capitol grounds, and it is intended to crown the whole mass of beautiful marble beneath, now so near com-

206

pletion. Even now, when ready hands are near, ah, so near, to pull down this structure which has taken years and the best mechanical skill of all nations to build, the workmen are busy with square, rule and chisel, seemingly loath to leave the great work of their hands, while events are crowding fast on time to decide either the destruction of this magnificent pile, or its crowning with greater glory. They are preparing the dome for the reception of " Liberty." When she is there, where Crawford designed her to be, then may she well look around her from the lofty stand, with that pleased and wonderstruck admiration, which the artist's genius has fixed so happily on her face. And You, who revel in these unfinished halls; You, who are the chosen representatives of the mightiest people of the globe; are you conscious that the time you waste is far more precious than jewels or wealth? Remember, that it is in your power to see that this statue is placed to crown this costly mass, and awful will be the consequences forever in your hearts, if, by faction hatred or love of gain, you allow these priceless moments to slip away for naught, leaving this grand pile uncrowned, and its pillars to be crushed by the fiend we now hear in the distance.

Such thoughts as these filled my mind as I stood gazing in a sad reverie from the polished walls of the Capitol, at the busy workmen around the statue in the garden, and it was not without a feeling of pain that I turned to go away, for I knew I might never see this work of art in its destined place. And if I did, would I behold it with that pride which I am wont to feel in our great republican institutions, or with a sense of mortification at the fickleness of the people and our rulers?

I was in Washington two days and then took the boat for Alexandria. Was given quarters in this camp, that is, if a worn-out tent, without a stove, can be called quarters. Fortunately Huss and Brannin were with me, so I did not have to go in a strange mess. Well, what more have I to say? We will have to stay in this hole, till our Colonel or Corps-General sends for us.

THE LONG ROLL

New Year's Eve., 1862.
It is rather a long skip to make, from November Thirtieth to New Year's Eve, but my life has been so uniformly dull that I have not thought it worth while to spoil paper with the narration of any of the sickening events. Whenever I took pen in hand, the splendid marble palaces over the river, which glisten in the sun, would come between my eyes and the paper, and taunt me with their magnificence and invariably cause me to throw away the pen in pure disgust at this miserable place. I should mention, however, that the Camp was moved to the vicinity of Fort Barnard, in a snug valley, which possesses two advantages over the other place, protection from wind and the nearness to fire-wood. I did not deem the event important enough to remember the date. Some very patriotic ladies attempted to give us a kind of a Christmas dinner a week ago, but the result was a failure and it ended in a row. So much for Christmas. Now for New Year's. I do not know whether to laugh or to grumble at my present feelings. That I am not happy, you can well see, but let us make the best of it and hope for a happier New Year's Eve when the year now so near us is old. About dusk, the convalescents commenced firing the old year out, and things looked gay for a little while, until some miserable fools began to use balls. It was fine fun for those who were shooting, but quite different for the three or four men who were hit. The firing has ceased, of course. I have had one luxury for which I am thankful and that is a half-pipeful of tobacco, which I have just finished smoking. As I write, our Mess is engaged in discussing certain points relating to the Antietam fight, and telling their respective adventures on that terrible field.

And for our Country, the new Calendar of Father Time's looks gloomy enough. My earnest prayers are that the Almighty God will look down upon us and change the state of our affairs soon, as He must do if in His goodness He thinks our institutions worth saving from utter ruin. I hope Sixty-three will end in a far happier evening for our whole Country as well as for myself, and that can not be unless this strife is ended in a perfect reunion. With these prayers, do I take leave of this old Year and meet the coming of Sixty-three, almost at our door. I still continue to hope, almost against hope, that all will be well in the end.

CHAPTER XVIII

February 24th.

HOW strange that I should be destined to see the last days of the service in the same place where I served my apprenticeship! After so many curious windings on the sea coast and in the interior of our country, where we have traveled, tramped and fought, to be again at Newport News where we had our first lessons in Camp life, nearly two years ago. Of course, I can not with certainty say that we will be here for the remainder of our time, but I am repeating the assertion of our officers, and though extraordinary events may bring us again within the music of bullets, they think it quite improbable. We are detailed at this Post as Provost-Guard and that is sufficient for the present. I will now go back to where I left you, in the Camp of Distribution, near Alexandria.

On January Twenty-ninth I was surprised to see Sergeant Loades of the Second Maryland, whom you will recollect I left in Frederick City. He was bound for his Regiment, and was stopped as I was, in that miserable abode of miserable beings. I made him spend the evening in my tent, and a long, pleasant chat did we have about old times in Frederick, where, if I had not been a fool, I might have staid till now, and have received as many thanks for it. I can not say that he told me anything worth noting here, of the events in that ever-to-be-remembered city, although what he had to say was interesting enough to me.

Loades and I were together most of the time for the rest of our stay. It was our wish that we might soon get to our Regiments, for to neither of us did Camp Distribution offer any enticements, and we therefore hailed the call for one corps, on the evening of the First of February, with unmixed satisfaction.

I was not disappointed this time, and I went through the endless roll-calls and " waitings " with deserved patience. We got down to Alexandria about eleven in the morning of the
210

THE LONG ROLL

Second, and there had to go through another long roll-call, finally going aboard the Steamer "Portsmouth," which started immediately for Acquia Creek. Though the weather was rather cold, it was clear and fine, and I took pleasure in noting the scenes of interest along the noble Potomac. The last time I made the trip I was sound asleep, and even if I had not been in a state of oblivion, it was too dark for me to have seen much of anything. So that it was all as new to me as if it were my first visit. I noted Fort Washington on the Maryland side, and further down, saw for the first time the wild and neglected banks of the Mount Vernon property. I was in hopes of catching a glimpse of the Washington mansion, but in this I was disappointed, for the neglected state of the grounds shut out every vestige of a building. But still it was no small satisfaction to have even this view of the home of the greatest of chiefs and statesmen that this now unhappy country has ever had. I can not say that the Potomac has any extraordinary attractions in the way of scenery, but it has several good qualities to atone for the fault, the clearness of the water, and the cultivated banks, generally graced by the picturesque mansions of some wealthy, and often, famous men. The sun went down in a magnificent halo of glory, as we reached Acquia Creek, where we landed and marched up to a Soldier's Retreat, where we got a kind of supper and bunks for the night. I went into partnership with a Sergeant of the Twentieth Massachusetts, and as he had three blankets and I had two, we made out to spend a most comfortable night, though the wind was howling in a manner calculated to make us shiver, while we thanked God that we were not without a shelter. By morning the ground was frozen hard as a rock, and with the piercing wind there was a scattering of frozen snow. After breakfast, we were marched aboard the cattle cars, there being no others on this railroad, and were soon rattling away toward Fredericksburg, where, having safely crossed the Potomac Creek Bridge, we arrived about noon. But how changed did I find this region from what it was last Summer! The station was where it used to be, but everything else had suffered a wonderful change. Our

211

old camp ground on the height between the station and the City of Ruins, I found to be the last resting place for a large number of horses; and where the great army was encamped, I could hardly imagine, for where we formerly saw camps, battery buildings and trees, was now a deserted and apparently endless sea of mud.

As soon as we got out of the cars and away from the numberless wagons crowded around the station, we were, much against our wills, given in charge of the Provost Marshal, and then we had more long marches and tedious red-tape to endure. It took until late in the afternoon, when, tired, almost frozen, and much disgusted with the endless and useless ceremonies, we were conducted to our Regiments. I found "Ours" quartered on a side hill directly in the rear of the brick building which was Burnside's headquarters during the Battle of Fredericksburg.

The first man of my acquaintance I met was Corporal Warring, who was not long in extending his hand for a friendly grip which speaks so plainly to the heart. He went with me to quarters which I found more comfortable with the shelter tents, than I had dared to hope. Most of the boys have dug excavations under their tents, and with the assistance of logs, have a kind of house, half underground, and with fire-places, the comfort of which could not be judged by outward appearance. It was my wish to go into a Mess with Warring, but I found that I could not be accommodated, so I put up in a tent with John Work and James Schultz. Having settled this matter to my satisfaction and theirs, I made a few calls. I had a long chat with Lieutenant Flemming, who was in command, Captain Leahy being on furlough, in New York.

"Verily things have changed since Johnny died," was my soliloquy, as I walked through the Company quarters. So many new faces met my eyes wherever I turned, and I found that I did not know one-half my own Company. We have hardly two hundred of our old members left, and still we muster six hundred fifty muskets, so that the majority of the Regiment is composed of recruits. I got into one Mess in my rounds,

212

made up of old members, four of whom were of that gay, old Mess on Roanoke Island, Thain, Keswine, Krohr and Turner. With them were three more, Luckmier, Myers and Watterson. The two first and the three latter ones are picked equals in striking terror to Sutlers and non-combatants. You will not be astonished then, when I tell you that this Mess, joined together as they are by the cohesive power of public plunder, lives well. I had no sooner taken a seat, when they asked me to have something to eat. Expecting a piece of " Salt Horse " or a bit of hard tack, I said " Yes " for politeness, and the shock my system suffered when a pickled " pig's foot " met my wondering and watering eyes, can be imagined but not described. But it was not a circumstance to the way my mouth watered in devouring the precious extremity of the porker. And then, after the pork packing was finished, they offered me a cigar. My pent-up feelings could not longer be controlled, and bursting through the restraint of self-command, I voiced my appreciation with the huskiness of deep emotion. Here was I, from the Capital, where I had not always the luxury of a pipe of tobacco at my disposal, in the wilderness where I expected to starve. Pig's Feet! Cakes! Butter! and then, a Cigar! It quite unmanned me.

Johnny Luckmier has a pretty mouth, and all that mars its loveliness is that it opens like a carpet bag. Johnny Luckmier has also a pretty voice, but it has one fault, hoarseness from continual use, as he only rests it when asleep. Johnny Luckmier occupies the middle of the tent, and is called " The Blockade." It is his duty to keep the boarders in their respective ends of the building; those on the right being " Dumplings " and the rest " Puddings." To keep them apart, it was found necessary to employ Johnny's endless flow of language, and the way he performed his duty was not unlike the thundering of some mighty three-decker in point of noise, though hardly to be compared to it in the musical sense. But enough. If Johnny should ever get hold of this, there would be no help for me. You can imagine what a horrible fate would be mine, for the most terrible of all things is to be talked to death.

213

THE LONG ROLL

To return to myself. I told you that I had not heard from Hudson City for a long time. One of the letters sent to my sister from Convalescent Camp never got to her. I found Warring had a couple of letters for me, and from them I learned that Charlotte and " Mother " had suffered much anxiety on my account. I also received a letter from my Uncle John in Minnesota, telling me of the arrival of a little boy cousin into this wicked world of ours.

The next two days I spent in answering letters and fixing up my tent, and as I was not overly anxious to do duty, I concluded to wait till a musket was handed to me. This was done on the Sixth, when the whole Corps got marching orders. Some thought that Burnside was going to South Carolina and that he would take us with him. Others ordered us to re-enforce Corcoran on the Black Water, and still others were equally confident that a movement on the Peninsula was in progress, and stationed us at Yorktown. But as is always the case, no one knew for a certainty. On one point, however, we were unanimous, for wherever you went, the word was passed, " Anywhere out of the Army of the Potomac."

On the morning of the Seventh, we had Reveille about three o'clock, which was entirely useless, for we did not get aboard the cars till about noon, when for the second time, I left Fredericksburg with my Regiment. I was put on the top of the cars this time, but fortunately it was not cold, so I had a novel ride without suffering any inconvenience worth mentioning.

At the dock we met Captain Leahy, who was rather surprised to see us. He had been home on furlough, and was nice as a mince pie. He recognized me and offered his hand with congratulations. We were put on the Transport "Robert Morris," and another the name of which I did not know, and it was not long after dark, when we started down the Potomac. Had a pretty good sleep and wakened to find the sun smiling on us and our steamer leaving Point Lookout fast behind us. This was the anniversary of the Battle of Roanoke Island.*

---

* February Eighth. And this was to be the day, in the year of our Lord, Eighteen Hundred Ninety-six, when the Zouave was to go to his "last, long sleep."

214

THE LONG ROLL

After a fine sail, darkness closed around us, leaving us still on the gently swelling bosom of the Chesapeake, and the next morning we were at anchor off Fortress Monroe. Warring told me that the boat got aground during the night, but I knew nothing outside of the Land of Dreams.

Was it strange that the all-engrossing subject of speculation should be "our destination?" Norfolk, Yorktown, up the River, down the Coast, where would the rudder guide us, when the "seemingly-never-to-arrive" orders should come? Who could think that our Regiment would for the third time be sent to Newport News? I am willing to wager that no one for a moment entertained the idea as one likely to be put into execution. But here we are.

Wednesday, March 4th.

The other day, while I was walking my post on General Getty's quarters, a member of the Fifty-first Regiment came down to our guard for the purpose of seeing one Freed, who is an enthusiast in the game of Baseball, to make arrangements with him for a challenge from our Regiment. Mind you, to make arrangements for a challenge. It was this man's business to let our club know that the Fifty-first was anxious to play a match, but for some reason, wanted the challenge to come from us. Frank Hughson, President of the Hawkins Zouaves Baseball Club, lost no time in calling the members together and in accordance with their wishes, he wrote and sent the challenge, and immediately proceeded to the necessary selection of a "Nine." And they are now straining every nerve to beat the Fifty-first in this exciting field sport, in the presence of a vast number from both Regiments. Colonel Hawkins has taken a bet offered by Major Jardine that the Fifty-first will beat us. I was out there about a half hour ago, and it looked unfavorable for us, but since, we have gotten our innings and made fourteen runs. Our boys are now in and the game is in the third inning. I guess I will go out and see how things are going.

Just returned from the field. The game is now in the sixth inning and we are six ahead, eighteen to twenty-four. Our side "skunked" the Fifty-first in this inning, and have now the

215

bat. This makes us even on "skunks," as they got one early in the game. Pity it is so cold. It is now two o'clock.

The match is played and Major Jardine lost his bet. How Colonel Hawkins will grin when the Major forks over! I think I see him. But it was a most interesting game. "Skunks" were even, and at the end of the ninth inning the game stood "thirty-one to thirty-four," "Ours" beating by three runs. This is the first victory of the Zouave Club, and is highly gratifying, since the Fifty-first has never looked upon us with any favor since the events of February Eighth. It is likely that this will not be the last game which will be played between these teams, and I hope our "Nine" will not neglect to practise, for this is the first game they have had since we were on Roanoke Island. I forgot to mention that we got the better of our opponents by one home run.

March 5th.

For the past few days I have been much interested in the perusal of one of Bulwer Lytton's strangest of strange stories, "Zanoni." I finished it this morning and I must confess that the text on the title page will express all the understanding I have of this queer, but fascinating tale—"In short, I could make neither head nor tail on 't."

As for any moral that I can pick out of it, there is none. I can not help contrast the marked difference between the angels of Faith, Truth, Fearlessness and Courage and the darker ones of Cowardice, Passion and Despair. Although it may be that I can not comprehend all that this volume unfolds, for it is as mysterious as is any subject treating of alchemic philosophy, I am obliged to the author for engrossing my whole mind in his subject, which few books that I get hold of now, can do.

Sunday, March 8th.

I do not feel very well to-day. Have had a headache and several minor complaints of no importance, though I am made quite miserable by them. But I can not resist the temptation of telling about the second match played yesterday by our second "Nine" and the Fifty-first. This was not as exciting

216

as the first, for it was too one-sided, our boys not giving them a " living show " to win, as you can easily see by looking at the score. There were seventy-seven runs in all, our boys making fifty-eight. If this does not make the Fifty-first sick of our playing, I shall be compelled to think they are afflicted with the terrible mania of " Baseball on the Brain." This disease, which has lately spread its awful, devastating influence, not only through our Regiment, but the whole corps, first originated, I believe, in the brain of poor Freed. How I pity him! He is beside me now, asleep, and I will wager the first silver quarter I see, that his brain is filled with visions of huge bats and balls, bases and home plates, and score books filled to a page with games, glorious games all won by him, poor soul—and poor player, let me add. Now, you may imagine that I am not dealing fairly with him in thus talking behind his back, and I must tell you my object. After the first match was played, he was perfectly insane for nearly two days, and he was so anxious to find out what I had to say in my Journal, that he broke loose from all restraint of good breeding, and read it without leave from me, and very likely he will do so again, and in that case—You understand?

Monday, March 9th.

A Corporal was reduced to the ranks yesterday on Dress Parade, for being inebriated Saturday and missing the usual Parade. So the order read, but that order, I am forced to think, told a falsehood. Had it possessed any regard for truth, it would have stated that the Corporal was reduced to the ranks and fined six dollars, for incompetency—to hold his position— you expect me to say. No, even if that were the case, it would not make the difference. What I would say, if you will not interrupt, " reduced for incompetency to *toady* for his precious position." Let me explain. A man must creep and fawn, be a pattern of a humble dog, or be upheld by some influence superior to a Captain, to hold a position as Corporal or Sergeant in this Company, at least. Thank Heaven, my friend is not built that way, and he stands higher in my estimation than

217

when he wore the glorious stripes. It is to be lamented, of course, that he did not have the Colonel or the Major to keep him in the position, in which case he, like Corporal Davis, could hold Corporalship without the painful necessity of playing dog. But he had no influential friends in the Regiment, so he has been elevated to a High Private, the safest position a man can hold, for he certainly can not be put down any lower than that.

In this precious Company, there are sixteen warders who now hold and always have held undisputed sway over both Captains and Lieutenants, and though Captain Leahy is a man I respect, for he is brave, and that covers many faults, he is no judge of human nature, and he deems that what Sergeant P—— says is gospel, for he can not penetrate his real character. For were it known, P—— is a living representative of the family that wears a Lion's skin. After the Battle of Camden, three Corporals were appointed, promoted for " Bravery on the Battlefield." Bravery on the Battlefield! One was slightly wounded, another was behind a chimney when the fight was on, and the third was not with the expedition at all. They all belonged to the Sixteenth Ward. Were it necessary to proceed further, I could tell you that the precious Corporal who was behind the chimney at Camden, was one of those who kept safely out of the way at Antietam, and was very ready to carry me to the hospital. How sweet he was then! And look at him now! I will not pursue this hateful subject, it makes me feel wicked.

March 14th.

Yesterday, our Regiment got marching orders to leave when the Third Division is gone, and it is embarking as fast as it can. So you see I may yet have some transactions with Powder, Ball and Company, if my time is up in forty days. It is unnecessary to say that this order was very unexpected, and still it is not believed to be in earnest. However, I would not be at all surprised to find myself in Suffolk with Corcoran's Legion, whom it is rumored Lee is attacking with overwhelming force. It appears that Colonel Hawkins is not overly willing to go as Commander of the First Brigade, Third Division,

218

THE LONG ROLL

unless we go as First Regiment of that Brigade, and that is why we are ordered to bring up the rear of the Division. And now Major Jardine is Provost Marshal for the Corps, and he is doing his best to keep us here in spite of the Colonel. Colonel Hawkins is probably doing his very best for us, and I begin to know that I can not with reason expect him to make confidants of us all. One thing is certain, we are going with the Division, for the Fifty-first relieved us from Provost duty this morning.   March 17th.

"Patrick's Day" it is "in the morning." The day of the shamrock and countless broken heads has dawned upon us here at Newport News. I have often wished for the opportunity to ask the noble Saint just why it is necessary to commemorate his birthday by wearing the green sprig and taking the initiatory steps to the breaking of ever so many heads with ever so many wild whoops and capers, only appreciated by the fiery Sons of the Green Isle. But I do not know that I have any more right to ask it than have the Emerald Islanders to respond with the query as to why we waste so much powder and make so much racket on the Fourth of July, and I fear the retort will make me own up to the truth of my case, which is that my pen asked the question not so much for the desired information, as to have something to say. I see there are already some few Shamrocks showing themselves on the red caps of our boys.

But I will take leave of Patrick and talk of something else. Let it be Chess. Some time ago, I designed a set of wooden Chessmen, which Sergeant Pout proposed to cut out for Corporal Gough. They are done and Gough and I have already had a fine game. Sergeant Loades, with whom I used to play in Frederick City, had one game with me and beat me too awfully. But Loades plays a little above the common run, so I was not much mortified. Corporal Gough plays more for amusement and instruction, and I beat him generally.*

---

* A duplicate set of this design was carved by the Zouave and is still in his War Treasure Box, forming a singular contrast to the carved ivory Chessmen of a pleasanter day. And could they but talk, would we not turn with awakened interest to these war-scarred Veterans, who have heard the "Long Roll" and know the pity of it all!

219

THE LONG ROLL

March 19th.

We are still here and as our Division is gone two days since, it seems probable that we will not be disturbed for some time, if at all, before we make the final move for home. We had marching orders the other day, but they were countermanded. Why we should be favored above the other troops here, is hard for me to imagine, but I suspect the Colonel has used his influence as he has always done where our interests were concerned. He has probably shown General Dix the policy of sparing us now, seeing our time is so nearly out, for by so doing, they will undoubtedly secure many volunteers, which they might not get, were they to put us through a course of sprouts, before the Fourth of May.* Meanwhile, the Fifty-first is doing Provost Duty, while we are in our bunks, looking at them.

We pass our days rapidly and pleasantly, at least I do. Warring and I make it a point to exchange visits with Loades every other day. Yesterday Loades expected to be transported to Suffolk, but the order was countermanded half an hour after it was given, and he sent me a note to that effect. Of course, Warring and I must spend the evening with him, for it might be the last one that could be spared. So up we went, and nothing would do, but that we must take supper. We had already eaten what we called supper, and were prepared to resist any attack that might be made on our appetites, but we had no idea that the force arrayed against us would be Beefsteak. We surrendered almost immediately and submitted ourselves to be taken to the kitchen tent. Having disposed of as much as decency and our stomachs—and how they ached—would allow, we went back to quarters, the Adjutant's tent, for be it known Loades is Sergeant-Major now, and Whist was the order of the evening. On a certain previous night, Loades and I were beaten badly at Euchre by Warring and Lieutenant Ball of the Second, and now these two gentlemen were anxious to repeat the process at Whist. Well, they did beat us the first

---

* It is quite consistent with the character of the Zouave that he never, in after life, mentioned any inclination or possibility of re-enlistment. Trouble with the hip wound and a long fight with inflammatory rheumatism incapacitated him for further service.

220

game and the last, but in the interval we won six games through good luck on my part and good playing on my partner's, all in spite of the many and characteristic efforts of our opponents to change the run of luck.

The First Division is decamping to-day for some unknown destination and it is probable that the Second is only waiting for the First. I took a long walk up to the right of the camp, this morning, to see what was going on, and unintentionally I stumbled into the Twenty-ninth Massachusetts in the First Division, formerly stationed on the Rip Raps, who treated us so well nearly two years ago. The recognition of Sergeant Frost and myself was mutual and a long talk of old times was the natural consequence. The Sergeant was sure Lieutenant Riply would be pleased to see me and went to find him. He was the same fine and perfect gentleman, and when I left, my "I will always remember you with pleasure," came from the very bottom of my heart.

To-day is the Nineteenth of March, and it seems the decaying Winter has chosen it to make his "flurry in," as the Whalers would say. Summer in its infancy is struggling for mastery over the old and infirm Winter. Spring commenced this morning, apparently thinking nothing would disturb her projected sprinkling of the earth with the gentle dews. Old King Winter, who can not yet be far away on his journey hence, looked back, and perceiving with jealous wrath the doings of his successor, still so young and feeble, roused up the remainder of his departing strength and hurled back a gust of piercing North Wind, which in accordance with orders from his terrible Master, soon created sad havoc among the tender breezes of Spring, and froze the tears, with which she was trying in her gentle way to awaken slumbering Nature from her long and silent stupor, into hard and biting icicles. Gentle Spring, murmuring something quite inaudibly, retired rather than submit to the fierce insults of this bluff old King. But now, she is melting the icy particles which Old Boreas is hurling down upon us in pure spite, into soft and delicate water, and with the aid of the sun she will reanimate the tender shoots still safe under the surface preparing to spring into life and beauty. Thus, dear Spring, are the means employed against you in wrath and anger, made to serve your own good purpose. But, Pen of mine, I am tired, and we will leave Summer and Winter to quarrel as they please, on the virgin soil of this fair and beautiful country.

March 21st.

But in spite of all her efforts, Spring has been completely hidden beneath a covering of at least six inches of snow. All day yesterday, it snowed and blowed, and as the day progressed the wind grew fiercer, and the keen blasts were felt through any amount of clothing, and the Twentieth of March looked and felt like the Twentieth of January in Minnesota. It is true this is the equinoctial storm, but I had no idea that these consequences of the sun's passage across the line would be felt more here than in my Northern home, and I have come to the conclusion that this freak of the season is something very uncommon for even this strange climate.

March 24th.

Was on guard yesterday, and for once I had the good fortune to be " drawn in " at night and I had a comfortable night's sleep. My old Messmate, Brannen, joined his Regiment yesterday, and I had a long talk with him before I went on guard.

I must tell you something about my doings last Sunday, for certainly that eventful day in my soldier history must not be lost to the world. I was invited by my friend Frank Hughson, who is now forage master of this Post, to come down Sunday and partake of a noon-day meal that he was getting up with the assistance of a Baltimore Sutler. Now I expected something unusual when a Sutler had his hands in the pie, but I was not prepared for the extraordinary Bill of Fare that met my eyes. The recollection of that sumptuous table haunts me even now, and confuses my poor pen. As nearly as I can remember I will give the Menu, though I am afraid that I may be committing murder and will be tried by a Drumhead Court Martial

222

accordingly, if any one in the service should accidentally read this and die in consequence; and I therefore piously beg all soldiers who may read this far, to stop, not so much for their life as to save me from Court Martial. Having all confidence in this philanthropic compliance of a soldier, I commence in earnest and give the

BILL OF FARE

Astor House, Newport News, Virginia
Sunday, March 22d, 1863. Boyer Esq., Proprietor

Stuffed, Roasted Turkey
Fried Onions
Mashed Potatoes
Beef Steak
Apple Dumplings with Brandy Sauce
Stewed Apples
Apple Butter
Biscuits and Butter
Stewed Tomatoes
Stewed Onions
Pork Steak
Wines, not to be mentioned

I suppose that this is not drawn up in a manner calculated to cause the envy of the original Astor House, and it might meet with some contempt, but it is not within my recollection that I have ever had the uncoveted pleasure of dining where it takes volumes to enumerate the uncountable, and in some cases, uneatable, dishes, which the board can not hold.

After dinner was disposed of and the cigars lighted, I sketched a portrait of Frank————of a Michigan Regiment, a friend of Frank Hughson's who was to leave the next day to join his Regiment. I got the general outline fairly well, but the expression was not as good and it disappointed me more than it did him. The fact is, I have hardly touched my pencil since I left Frederick City and am much out of practise. The Sutler went to Baltimore that night, and he promised to bring me some drawing paper and then I will commence again.

A return game of Baseball, just now closed, was played by our first Nine and the Fifty-first. We won by eleven runs, the score standing Twenty-one and Ten. I did not see the game, but the score and those who did see it, will tell you that it was a better one than the first.

Wednesday, March 25th.

Last night I went up to have a game of Chess with Sergeant Loades according to agreement. But in this I was disappointed, for the men were packed deep down in the impenetrable recesses of a monster trunk. But I spent a very pleasant evening, for, finding we could not have an engagement on the checkered field, Loades proposed cards. Euchre was the first order, and with a good run of luck, a Lieutenant and myself gave Loades and the Adjutant a clean sweep. Then my old opponent, Lieutenant Ball, took the Adjutant's place, vowing all kinds of vengeance for my treatment of him the other night. But Euchre did not favor him any better than did Whist on the former occasion, so finally my partner suggested that we try Whist again. Our opponents won handsomely a couple of games, and we left Ball in a partially satisfied frame of mind. I got to bed about twelve o'clock, made Smithy turn over, and was down beside him and in a dreamless sleep.

March 27th.

Sergeant Loades is gone with his Regiment. He went yesterday and managed to come down in advance, so as to have time to take leave of his many friends in this Regiment, of whom I am proud to say I am one. I did all I could to show him my appreciation of that friendship as well as to keep the Regiment in his memory, presenting him with the last Carte-de-visite I had, and also with a jacket and fez. He bade me write and promised to do the same. The drum which we obey, said "Roll-Call" and we left him. This is what makes the life of

224

a soldier so hard. You form acquaintances and they become friends; the order says "March," and you know you may never see them again. And those around you who should to a degree console you for the loss and make the parting less cruel with their sympathy, frequently are of those who, in civil life, you would shun, apparently with no feeling or desire, except of degradation or shame. Loades is a bright exception. He acts from purely patriotic motives, and does not even seem to see the blunders, the ignorance or the incapacity of the leaders of our army, but goes about the duties that he had taken upon himself, as if no mistakes were ever made, and he must see and feel them, too. Now this trait of his character would not be so remarkable, were it not that he is an Englishman, and how seldom do we find an Englishman in our army who does not share in his country's ridicule of our blundering attempts to put down an unjust rebellion. Loades has much before him yet, but he is too noble to complain. I hope that we may sometime meet again, but this I dare not expect, and so I will hope that he will see what he is going to see in a short time and be able to leave this service, physically and mentally as he is now. But I fear for him, for is it not true that the noblest and the best of our men are slain? And who, then, will reap the reward of glory?

CHAPTER XIX

LIEUTENANT-COLONEL EDGAR A. KIMBALL

April 2d.

L AST night, at Roll-Call, Captain Leahy spoke to us about getting up a testimonial of our regard for Lieutenant-Colonel Kimball, in the shape of a medal. The officers propose to give three dollars each and we are expected to give only twenty-five cents. Some one offered fifty cents, but it was not allowed. Every one agreed to it. After Roll-Call, as Kimball was in my mind, I concluded to try to get his autograph under the picture of him I made in Frederick. He was not in, so I left the picture, with my name, with Doctor Harding. This morning he sent for me and I found that he was very much pleased with the picture and uncommonly nice to me, asking me to sit down and to have a cigar. He asked what he should write and I told him all I wanted was his name and title. He was very sorry that he did not know before that I "drew things" or he would have asked me to do a few for his friends. I gave him a fine drawing of a Castle in Spain, and he made me put my name on it and said he would get it framed. Then he asked me where I made the picture of him and I told him the sketch was made on the South Mountain field and it was finished at Frederick City. " Oh, so you were wounded? " And I had to tell him the whole story, and of course Antietam came in for a share of the conversation. Colonel Kimball thinks Antietam ranks all the battles of the war. He read me a letter from Colonel Sturgis who says in reference to our boys in that battle, enough to show that he thinks we are big: " W enever I see a member of your Regiment, dear Colonel, I feel as if compelled to raise my hat." " This, " remarked Kimball with pride, " is from one of our best Generals." After he asked me to draw his picture and one of his dog, I saluted and took my leave.

Camp Hamilton, April 7th.

Received marching orders at Newport News on the Second and we left there on the Third, reaching this camp about three o'clock, very much fatigued. I suffered considerably from my hip wound, and on the last three-mile stretch, it was about all I could do to keep up with the ranks. Camp Hamilton is pleasantly located between the village of Hampton and the old, time-battered fortress on the Point. Its clustering buildings, storehouses, etc., and the many and variously-shaped maritime craft, some grinning with jaws full of teeth, others without the slightest barking apparatus, all make it look more like a second-rate city than a military depot. The village of Hampton gives a melancholy picture of the sad effects of war. It was burned by McGruder a few days before the Hatteras expedition left the fort, but failed in its object of drawing the forewarned Butler out with his then small force, or cautious Phelps from his snug entrenchments we have just left. Not a house but that was ruined, and even the picturesque old church was not suffered to escape the firebrand. The ruins of the church still stand, forming an interesting scene, but oh, how sad!

Fort Nansemond, Suffolk,
April 14th.

On the Tenth of this month I was on guard at Camp Hamilton, dreaming of no other move before the final one for home, and on the evening of the next day, we were in Suffolk, Virginia, in front of the foe again. We started from Camp Hamilton about eight o'clock in the evening, and before daybreak the next morning we were in Norfolk. Here a bit of news reached us that was not overly pleasant. A train of cars had run through a drawbridge on the Suffolk railroad, and instead of going to the front in cars, we were expected to foot it. The steamer left us on the wharf at Portsmouth, and as I was on guard then, I was at the rear during the march through the city. When we were about five miles on our way, Colonel Kimball, the good old man, rode clear back and got wagons to carry our knapsacks, and I can tell you it was a great relief. My old hip was beginning to bother me, and in what condition I would have reached Suffolk, if I had not been permitted to ride occasionally,

I can not say. As it was, I was very nearly played out when we finally got to camp.

And now a sad and melancholy duty awaits this pen of mine. I will write it boldly, however, or my hand might falter. Here is the note. " Sunday, April 12th. Lieutenant-Colonel Kimball was shot dead early this morning, by General Corcoran. It was a useless murder. I have just seen the body and could not control my feelings at all." There is hardly any comment needed to this horrible memorandum, but when I wrote " useless murder,"I might have added" cold-blooded," and "brutal."

Colonel Donohue, of the Tenth New Hampshire, was with him at the time of this sad occurrence, which deprived of life as brave a man as ever wore a sword, and one who had well earned the laurels waiting for him in New York. From Colonel Donohue we get the particulars concerning this terrible tragedy. The Colonel was walking with this friend, about two o'clock in the morning, near General Corcoran's headquarters, when a body of men on horseback came near enough for Colonel Kimball to challenge, with the intention, of course, of finding out who they were, as it was quite dark. They did not heed the challenge as promptly as was desired, and the Colonel again ordered them to halt and to give the countersign, asking the usual question, " Who goes there? " " General Corcoran and staff," was the answer, with a question as to what was the right to challenge, and demanding passage. At these words, which I presume were not couched in the most civil language possible, Colonel Kimball replied in a tone not less calm, that he 'd be damned if they should pass without giving the countersign, and he drew his sword, as officers do when receiving the magic word. At this, General Corcoran fired with so deadly an effect, that the brave old soldier had only time to utter, " Damn you, fire again! " and then came his last breath. General Corcoran, whether possessed of cowardice or coolness, I can not say, galloped off and directed an Aide to see " who the officer was " he had shot.

It is impossible to describe the feeling which this terrible event produced in our Regiment, when it became known, or

228

THE LONG ROLL

rather, when it was believed. It seemed so impossible. The boys raved rather than talked, and many would have gone through the whole legion for the blood of the assassin. But I am proud to say, cooler blood and discipline prevailed, for though strong men who had not shed a tear in many a wicked year, then cried like children, the more reasonable course was adopted, to let affairs take their own way, at least for the present. But as for dropping it from our memory—Ah! General Corcoran may find to his sorrow that it is impossible.

I could not keep my tears back as I looked at the mutilated corpse of the old soldier, and thoughts came of the day long ago on the bleak banks of Hatteras, when I heard of the death of my Father. Colonel Kimball has been our leader ever since this service has thrown us together, for though Hawkins was our Colonel, he has almost always had the charge of a Brigade, leaving the duties of the command with Kimball. From our first charge at Roanoke, Kimball has led us to the last at Fredericksburg, and he has always been in the thickest of the fight, laughing at danger, defying Death. Could he have died by the hand of the foe, as brave De Monteuil did in the arms of victory, even had he been killed on picket, anything, anywhere, but here, to be shot down like a dog, in the dead of night, with not one of his " brave boys," as he fondly called us, near to avenge the deed, the cowardly deed! Oh, it was too hard! I have said enough, perhaps too much, of this melancholy event, but one thing more. Though Colonel Hawkins was the maker of this Regiment, we all know that the " Hero of Tehuantepec " made our fame. I am done. Let the old Hero rest, and may the Ruler of Hosts put the mantle of bravery around him.

229

CHAPTER XX

FORT NANSEMOND

ABOUT ten o'clock on the day of the tragedy, the Regiment was called upon and gotten under arms. Colonel Fairchilds of the Eighty-ninth was to escort us to our position in the entrenchments, but General Getty thought he had better lead us himself, for he knew we liked him for the simple reason that he liked us. As soon as he presented himself, the boys gave three cheers for him, and after that, three as bitter groans for Corcoran as were ever given by five hundred men. I heard that General Getty told Captain Bennett that we were perfectly justified. We were conducted to the front, and after waiting about an hour or so in a field the Generals concluded that the safest place to put us was Fort Nansemond, which is an important Post dividing General Getty's and General Terry's front, being the Northwestern angle of this chain of fortifications and breastworks, which extends eleven miles in an irregular circle. The more I see of this Fort, the more am I convinced of its invincibility, and with twenty thousand men, which it is said we now have, and with more coming every day, we can hold it against fifty thousand. It is a strong, diamond-shaped, earth Fort, mounting ten guns of different range and caliber, with a deep trench of water around it. Colonel Hawkins has command. General Keys ordered us here while both Dix and Hawkins were away, and yesterday he came up evidently to try to blarney the boys. To the Colonel and a crowd of the Hawks, " These boys will fight, won't they, Colonel? "

But the Colonel does n't seem to like the General for upsetting all his plans in ordering us here while he was absent, and so he answered dryly, in his usual basso tone, " I don't know."

" Well, they won't run away, will they? "

" I don't see where in Hell we could run to." And then the General found he had inspected the Fort sufficiently, and left, probably deciding that Fort Nansemond would be as well defended without his observations as with them.

230

THE LONG ROLL

April 15th.

On the afternoon of the Thirteenth, the enemy advanced on General Getty's front, driving in our pickets. The forts within range opened on them heavily and soon drove them back. Captain Morris of Company K had charge of our artillery, and with one discharge dismounted a field-piece, blowing up the casehorn and killing one or two horses. The engagement, if it can be so called, did not last more than a half hour, when the enemy retired. My opinion is they were tempting us to make a sortie, but our general did not see it. Captain Morris' exploit soon reached the General's ear and he is now in command of a battery, his Company acting as artillery men. And he has already had employment suited to his taste. Last night, he was ordered out with some other troops against a battery which has been very annoying to our gunboats, sinking one of them. Morris opened on them with such success that they soon vacated the premises, and in time, too, for they had four of their pieces dismounted. In the action, our Company had one of its own pieces blown to atoms, but with wonderful luck, only one man was slightly wounded, and three horses killed. It may appear that what I write is not true, or that it is at least stretched, but it is the talk of every one, and what every one says, must contain some truth.

Saturday, April 18th.

I am twenty years old to-day. I had hardly mailed a letter home, when two detachments of infantry from the Ninety-ninth and the Thirteenth New York crossed the Nansemond in front of Fort Rosecrans, and advanced against the enemy's rifle-pits and pickets. I was on guard on the parapet of our Fort, and had a good view of the spirited skirmish that commenced as soon as our boys showed themselves above the bank. They behaved admirably in their inferior position and advanced firing at the foe concealed in brush and pits, affording at the same time plain masks for the enemy, in their own upright position. They drove the Rebels into the edge of the woods above, but they then received a severe fire from the

231

picket reserve, and were finally compelled to retreat. This they did in good order, every man firing in retreat, as if on drill. The ground was an even plain, affording no shelter for us, while the Rebels in the edge of the woods could get behind trees and fire without any great danger to themselves. We accomplished nothing that I could see, only I suppose an advanced position for our pickets. Colonel Hawkins, who was watching the fight through a field glass, said there were only three or four killed on our side, but he could not judge the enemy's losses. Two of our men who were anxious to see the fight from a closer position went down to a breastwork to our right, but it proved to be too near, for they each got a bullet for their trouble.

Sunday, April 19th.

We are now sustaining, what in war parlance is termed a siege. Night before last, the Rebels on the front, or rather on our left front, for we have to attend to both, threw up a string of rifle-pits nearer than they have ever ventured before, near enough to be just within reach of our fort, and they have crowed considerably over the matter, and to some purpose, too. Yesterday, while I was sitting under the breastwork, reading, a ball came sailing along, passing between Bell and Berryman and struck Hugh McClocky, a private in our Company, giving him a severe wound in the leg. He had hardly been carried out of sight, when another came from the same direction and struck a man in Company B who was carrying a wheelbarrow of earth for the stockade in the Fort. Here were two of our men wounded within five minutes. About an hour after these two incidents, though I suppose they would be " accidents " in civil life, I was looking over the parapet with a crowd of boys, when a rifle ball struck and buried itself in the parapet about three inches from Bell's face. This is the second narrow escape he has had. Colonel Hawkins received orders to shell the saucy mud-diggers last night, and he tried to unearth them this morning, but instead of complying with our hints to skedaddle, one of them drew a bead on our Colonel, while he was watching the effects of his shots. He did not take the least notice of it,

232

however, but continued to let them have what was coming to them, and when the job was done and he got down from his conspicuous place, I, for one, was very much relieved.

April 20th.

Last night, General Getty executed a nice bit of strategy at the expense of our friends outside, and as Captain Morris and his Company were concerned in it, I have more pleasure in relating all I know about it.

Night before last, under cover of darkness, Getty planted Morris' battery opposite a Fort on the other side of the river and masked it. Last night, when everything was ready, the gunboats and Morris opened a cross fire on the Rebel battery, which was taken by surprise, evidently not thinking they had anything on terra firma to fear. They replied to us very promptly, however, and while the bombardment was going on, two of the gunboats made a pontoon, on which two detachments of infantry crossed, one from the Eighty-ninth, our old comrades-in-arms, and the other from the Eighth, forming the storming party. Under cover of the noise of the cannonade, these veterans marched to the rear of the Fort and surprised it by first throwing in a volley of musketry, and then advancing " Double-quick " with fixed bayonets. The moment the volley was fired, a signal was thrown out to the gunboats and our battery to cease firing. And it is believed that not a man escaped. One hundred fifty men, eleven commissioned officers, and six field-pieces were the fruit of this nice little bit of work. The boys say that the gunners were so occupied with their firing, that some of them did not hear the musketry in the rear, and actually were ordered to cease their fire by our own officers. Everything was gotten over to this side safely but one gun, and that was so badly damaged that it would not pay to bring it. Of course, Captain Morris gets his share of the credit, and it is already whispered that he is to be made Captain of a battery in the regular army.

Meanwhile, Colonel Hawkins makes the climate for our friends in the pits quite warm. Our Artillery Lieutenant, who was put here at our Colonel's request, when Morris went away, has made some beautiful shots this morning. A ten-pound shell of ours exploded right over one of their pits, for they are now quite close, much to our satisfaction. The way missiles have been flying around this morning, though, makes one slightly nervous, if nothing more. Once while walking leisurely in an open space outside the Post, not dreaming of harm, I was saluted with the sharp pin-g-g-n-n of one of the "tarnal" things, as it passed over my head and, coolly enough, dropped on the other side.

April 24th.

We have just been called under arms and sent down to a Post where the guns were booming away like real fun, and of course, we expected nothing less than to see the enemy's column marching on to slaughter, but the fury died away, and even the little dogs on picket, two small pieces of flying artillery, have ceased barking.

Last night I was sound asleep in my shelter tent, when all at once old Flemming had me by the leg. " Who is this? Get up and fall in. Quick!" And I did under the impression that the enemy was trying a midnight sortie. But instead of facing the enemy, we turned our backs to them and marched to camp and were there told to hold ourselves in readiness to march at a moment's notice. And to back up this suspicious order, our cooks were up around their fires, cooking rations for three days. All this smelled like an expedition. As soon as we got to quarters, however, the Say told us we could go to sleep if we wished. And we did sleep till morning, and staid in quarters till to-day, when we were again called out. What effect this has I do not know, but the general impression is that it is a fizzle.

About noon, yesterday, I had the pleasure of hearing a bullet sing over my head and strike a few paces back of me. It came so slowly, however, that if I had gotten hit, it would not have caused much damage, though just at this time it would be extremely inconvenient to carry either the weight or the effect of it.

234

THE LONG ROLL

Sunday Morning, April 26th.

Colonel Hawkins was serenaded last night in fine style, by the band of the One Hundred Third Regiment, formerly under Hawkins' command. The gallant Colonel of the Regiment, Benjamin Ringold, accompanied the band to pay his respects to Colonel Hawkins in person. It was a beautiful night and well fitted to the sweet strains of music borne on its silent wings. Not a cloud dimmed the brightness of the vault above us, lighted by Luna in half her splendor. Not a breath seemed to care to disturb the sleep of Nature, covered with her sparkling mantle of silvery light. Colonel Ringold and his Regiment have endeared themselves to us lately by offering their assistance in case of a row with "Michael's Legion," and as soon as our boys in camp heard the band they knew what was up. I was on guard on the ramparts. The boys were out en masse, and when an opportunity offered, gave three rousing cheers for Colonel Ringold, three for the band and three for the Regiment. Colonel Ringold spoke a few words in his broken English, much of which I could not hear, but he mentioned the " One Hundred and Three Times," which is the nickname we have helped to give the Regiment. I hear that he offered the band to escort us home and wound up by suggesting three cheers for " our dear Colonel Hawkins." Of course they were given and three more for himself, and then the band struck up " The Star Spangled Banner " and the party was over.

May 1st.

On the Twenty-seventh, a party of one hundred fifty of our Regiment were detailed to go outside the Fort to burn brush and stuff that obstructed infantry range. We went and a lively time we had of it, too. There were soon as many fires as men and a gentle wind helped to spread through the loose leaves and other combustibles, and we had a grand spectacle of a prairie fire. In our incendiary expedition, some of us got a little nearer to the enemy's pits than they thought proper, and the first thing we knew, " Whiz-z-z-ph " went a bullet

235

alongside of a fellow of Company D. And I thought it was just time to go somewhere else in another direction, and when another little snorter came singing the same savage song right over my head, my opinion became conclusive. It was not healthy out there, and there were enough fires made anyway, and the officers thought so too, for we were ordered in shortly after.

On the Twenty-eighth, nothing of any moment took place, though the Rebel Sharpshooters took a lively interest in the welfare of our Fort and sent several musket balls into us—I mean, the Fort. I had the gratification of getting a letter from my old chum and best friend, Charles A. Zimmerman. He is in the Sixth Minnesota Volunteers, and has been fighting Indians. He sent me some sketches and I returned him one of our skirmish scenes, of which we are daily witnesses.

Yesterday we were mustered in for two months' pay and we received a proposition from General Dix in the shape of a printed circular requesting us to stay in the service some eight or ten days after our time expires, or in point of fact, as long as the enemy is in front of us. This we read and voted upon. We all thought General Dix was a very nice man, but we could not see it his way, and voted unanimously accordingly. Colonel Hawkins answered the eloquent circular in a well-worded letter which I will not attempt to give here, for I want to get a copy of it. General Dix telegraphed us this morning, and as nearly as I can find out, he is astonished at our want of patriotism, and asks us if we will stay until the Twelfth. Our Colonel took this as an insult, and told him so, and now this political Major-General, out of pure spite, intends to keep our men who joined three months after the Fourth of May, 1861, but who have seen just as much service as we have, till the actual time of their service expires. Colonel Hawkins has gone down to have an understanding with Peck, the General commanding this Fort.

Colonel Hawkins did have an understanding and we now have the order for four hundred fifty men to start from here to-morrow. We were relieved from duty at Fort Nansemond,

236

which General Dix calls the " Post of Honor," yesterday about noon, by the Sixth Massachusetts, and I tell you we were not long in evacuating the premises. I went to the Fort after my shelter tent, and there I hope the last bullet that has threatened to knock me over was fired from the enemy's rifle-pits. I tell you it made me go down low.

Yesterday afternoon, a spirited onslaught was made, feeling the enemy's strength, in front of Fort Rosecrans, by the Ninety-ninth, very similar to that of the Seventeenth, only more destructive to the lives of both sides. I saw only the closing scene. The Ninety-ninth crossed the river with the opening of the ball, simultaneously from four Forts, and advanced in line of skirmishers and made a magnificent dash at the rifle-pits in the face of as deadly a fire as can be given from pits with a steady aim. At this moment General Terry saw a brigade coming at a " Double-quick " to re-enforce the pickets, and ordered the " Retreat " to be sounded, and had the artillery concentrated upon the re-enforcements, which was seen to tear large gaps in their ranks. The brave Ninety-ninth, already having lost one-fourth of their force by the deadly fire, did not, or rather would not, understand the signal to retreat, and advanced until they seemed nearly in the first line of pits, before they saw that the Rebels had been re-enforced so heavily as to render any further advance madness. They were ordered to get back the best they could, as it would be needless danger to go in a body. This part of the fight, I saw. The retreat commenced and the enemy attempted a pursuit, but oh, you ought to have heard our guns! The Ninety-ninth had their colors shot down three times, and the brave fellow who took them off the field was wounded so badly that he could only drag the beautiful emblem behind him. General Terry has found out that there is some one behind those woods out yonder, at the expense of nine lives and enough cruelly wounded to swell the list to fifty. He estimates the enemy's loss at thirty killed, which can be believed, for every one who witnessed the affair from the beginning says our gunning was splendid and caused awful havoc in the ranks. Of course, we were compelled to leave a good many wounded on the field, and at night many went out after them. The Rebels wanted to fire at first, but they were prevented by the officers, who did not object to our taking away our own wounded. One of our Regiment, Bob Lee, went with a Sergeant of the Ninety-ninth, and discovered an enemy who was trying to decoy them on by uttering groans as if wounded, but he was by some means overpowered before he had time to fire. Our boys did not want to fight and told him so, and the Reb, who belonged to the Ninth Georgian, told them they would find some wounded farther down. Old Bob said to him, " You are a damned fine fellow, give me your paw." And they shook hands. The man was attracted by the fez and asked Bob if he belonged to the Hawkins Zouaves and being answered in the affirmative remarked, " I wish my time was as near out as yours."

I am afraid, after all, that the Newport News recruits will be detained. The description lists are being made out now and rations cooked for four hundred fifty men. We start to-morrow for Fortress Monroe.

I have just been over to the camp of the Ninety-ninth with Smith, to have a chat with some of the boys. Talk about sleeping on the battlefield! These men have to eat and sleep and live on the field. I was there only about a half an hour, and in that time I am sure I could have counted fifty balls coming over us or bounding along the ground. Their tents are completely riddled, and every time a man shows himself he is sure to be saluted by a little infernal machine. In leaving the rear of a cook house to go back, we had to go across an open space only ten feet, and we were fired at. Fort Rosecrans shells the enemy almost continually, and as sure as they open a gun, the whole line of Rebel rifle-pits starts in. It puts me in mind of intruding upon a hornets' nest.

In this way, inclusive of the two scraps I have mentioned, the Ninety-ninth has had about a hundred men killed and wounded, without getting any satisfaction. This is soldiering— or if not, what is it? Just as we were leaving, the sad intelligence reached the group where we were talking, that one of the poor fellows who was wounded yesterday was dead. The visit to this camp did not at all make me regret that I am to go home in the morning, if God spares me.

I went up to hear what Colonel Hawkins had to say to us, on this our last night. He was in a peculiar and painful position, for his Regiment was divided into three classes: one on the eve of going home; another, having lived with that expectation and only lately awakened to the disappointment, how bitter we can well imagine; and the third, only having served seven months, not so much pitied, for they did not expect a furlough even and could not be disappointed. Now the Colonel wanted to pacify some of us, but we were all together, and he knows us so well and cares so much for us, and he hardly knew what to say. He told us what he had done, showing his correspondence, and after that he addressed us feelingly, showing plainly his love, his sorrow and his regret. We cheered him, but the cold water of disappointment, or rather the knowledge that some were the victims of malice and spite, dampened even the enthusiasm of the more fortunate. He promised, when he got to New York, to do all in his power to get the recruits home soon and in a body, and in conclusion, told the old Regiment that, in whatever circumstances we might be in after life, we would always find a friend in Colonel Hawkins. The last words were too much for him and he went back into his tent to hide his emotion. Cheers were given, not cold ones either, but more than that, our tears were not suppressed.

We were awakened on the morning of the Third at daybreak, by a volley of musketry ringing in the clear morning air, and had not we given up our arms, I would have anticipated a participation in a fight. But the alarming sounds died away and we were given orders to "strike tents" and for the last time. And then came the sad parting with our companions, whom despotic spite was detaining. It was very hard to part with Smith. How nobly he had done his duty at the post of honor on the Color Guard, need not be told. We were aboard the cars at nine o'clock and soon the engine shrieked out the "all aboard" and with a few spasmodic starts and puffs, we were

239

THE LONG ROLL

rattling off, leaving danger behind, and starting for home. Down below the station, we discovered the One Hundred Third and the Ninety-ninth, with their arms and colors, to give us their farewell cheers. The brave Colonel Ringold was at the head of his Regiment on horseback, his hat on the ground, his horse plunging in affright at the voices in chorus, the steam whistles and the enthusiastic cheers of the men. Little could we then think that, a few hours afterward, many of these men and the fine old Commander would cease to live.

In an hour we were at Norfolk and the Steamer "Kennebec" was waiting for us. We heard there was heavy fighting in progress at Suffolk and that the One Hundred Third was badly cut up in the work of clearing some rifle-pits, but that was all: we did not know the worst. I took advantage of our liberty at Norfolk to see the city and to get a good dinner. We left at four that afternoon and passed Fortress Monroe an hour afterward. We were favored with the most beautiful weather during the passage, and anchored off Sandy Hook night before last. We put in at Pier Number One, North River, and got our arms and started up Broadway. We were escorted by the Twelfth Militia, and the Fire Department turned out, but the rain broke up some of the arrangements. Such crowding, such jamming, such shouting, such drowning noise, and it hardly could have been greater if the weather had been clear. We waded up the great thoroughfare in mud and amid the sea of human beings, some anxious for friends, some only impelled by the curiosity to see the Regiment which has always been a pet of the New York people. We went up Union Square and down the Bowery to Bond Street, turned into Broadway again, and then put for the Sixty-ninth Arsenal, where we were dismissed. It was here that Colonel Hawkins told us that Colonel Ringold had been killed, and asked us to turn out for the funeral.

I found the Bowery and took the cars to the ferry, crossed to Hoboken and was on my way again through the rain. I walked in a hurry, too, got in undiscovered and—was home.

240

THE LONG ROLL

Wednesday, May 12th.

Our Regiment escorted the body of Colonel Ringold to its last resting place in Greenwood.

Saturday, May 31st.

I was mustered out of the United States service Thursday, was paid yesterday, and now my soldiering is done.

Yes, at last, after two years of wandering, hardship, suffering and danger, I am free to act at my will, move as I will and speak what I will. My contract is fulfilled and no longer can any one say " Go! " or " Do! " nor is my time or my life at any one's disposal. No more Roll-Calls, no Inspections, no somber-faced Brigadiers to haunt my vision day and night. No Reveille of the enemy's musketry nor of our own Drum Corps. I can fight my own battles till my work is done. This is a comfort, but the tinge of sadness mingles with the joy. Where are they who should be at the feast with us? Still in front of the foe. Where are they who bought our glory, and worthless does it seem, with their lives? Silent in their graves. And their friends, with no rejoicing in their hearts, as in proud array we marched up the streets of yesterday, could only weep most bitter tears.

Great God: Is not our measure of bitterness quite filled? How many more must mourn for their loved ones? How many souls must depart in agony on the unnatural death-bed of the crimson battlefields? Thy people cry aloud to Thee for deliverance, and O God, grant it before we are destroyed. Thy way is best; then, in Thy mercy, help us to bide Thy time!

SO HERE, THEN, ENDETH "THE LONG ROLL," BEING A JOURNAL OF THE CIVIL WAR AS SET DOWN BY CHARLES F. JOHNSON, SOMETIME OF HAWKINS ZOUAVES, AND MADE INTO A BOOK BY THE ROYCROFTERS, AT THEIR SHOP, WHICH IS IN EAST AURORA, ERIE COUNTY, NEW YORK STATE, MCMXI

This edition of
THE LONG ROLL:
Impressions of a Civil War Soldier
is printed on 60# permalife old white paper by
Hagerstown Bookbinding and Printing, Inc.
and bound by
Hoster Bindery, Inc.
1986